COPING WITH THE LATIN AMERICAN DEBT

COPING WITH THE LATIN AMERICAN DEBT

Edited by ROBERT WESSON

PRAEGER

New York
Westport, Connecticut
London

Library of Congress Cataloging-in-Publication Data

Coping with the Latin American debt / Robert Wesson, editor.
     p.   cm.
    Proceedings of a conference held at the Hoover Institution,
Stanford University, Sept. 17–19, 1987.
    Includes index.
    ISBN 0–275–92996–5 (alk. paper)
    1. Debts, External—Latin America—Congresses. 2. Debt relief—
Latin America—Congresses.   I. Wesson, Robert G.
HJ8514.5.C66   1988
336.3'435'098—dc19   88–2745

Library of Congress Catalog Card Number: 88–2745

ISBN: 0–275–92996–5

First published in 1988

Praeger Publishers, One Madison Avenue, New York, NY 10010
A division of Greenwood Press, Inc.

Printed in the United States of America

The paper used in this book complies with the
Permanent Paper Standard issued by the National
Information Standards Organization (Z39.48–1984).

10 9 8 7 6 5 4 3 2 1

CONTENTS

PREFACE

This volume is the result of a conference held at the Hoover Institution, Stanford University, September 17–19, 1987. Over 30 persons with expertise in the Latin American debt problem attended, including bankers, representatives of international financial agencies, government officials, academics, and Latin American economists.

Conferences (and books) on the Third World debt problem, which is largely Latin American, have been numerous. It was the aim of the Hoover Institution conference to give more emphasis than usual to the Latin American and political side of the problem, while taking into account the role of the financial actors, and to think as far as possible in terms of a solution, or at least an outcome, to the problem. This focus led to illuminating exchanges of information and ideas from different points of view.

Despite their different backgrounds, conferees seemed to be in more agreement than disagreement. However, there was vigorous debate on the merits of a strategy of "muddling through," or proposing incremental adjustments as opposed to a global restructuring of the international lending system, for example through an institution for the assumption of Third World obligations.

There seemed to be little doubt that the process of rescheduling with "involuntary" lending packages is approaching exhaustion, as private banks cannot be expected to provide much more general, or balance-of-payments, support. This type of support is difficult for private banks to continue, as they increasingly acknowledge that Latin American portfolios are worth a great deal less than face value.

In any event, financial assistance cannot solve the problem unless the economic environment is improved. This means accelerated growth in countries belonging to the organization for Economic Cooperation and Development (OECD) and resistance to protectionism. Latin American nations must also reshape their economies for greater efficiency and competitiveness, by reducing budget deficits and encouraging capital return. It is understood, however, that the external debt itself is a major impediment to improvements.

The discussants could not, of course, develop anything resembling a solution; nothing like a painless solution is possible. However, they seemed to approach a clearer understanding of the meaning of the problem and where it may be going.

It is hoped that the present collection of papers, abridged and revised, may assist the reader to this same end. Albert Fishlow gives a sketch of the background; Gary Wynia presents an account of attempts to cope with the protracted crisis, and Charles J.L.T. Kovacs offers some notes on the problem of debt management from an intelligent banker's point of view. There follow more detailed discussions of the largest debtors. Susan Kaufman Purcell treats Mexico mostly from a political point of view and finds reasons to hope that the debt pressures may lead to basic reforms of the system. Clark Reynolds expresses the hope that her approach may lead to serious reconsideration of U.S. policy toward Mexico. Robert E. Looney deals with Mexico from a more economic point of view, and Saúl Trejo gives a Mexican viewpoint and suggestions for dealing with the problem. Riordan Roett discusses Brazil mostly in terms of the greatly neglected aspect of the social consequences of trying to service the debt. Carlos Waisman, like Susan Kaufman Purcell, hopes that the debt problem may be the catalyst for desperately needed political reorganization in Argentina; his conclusions are seconded by Carlos Carballo. Gary Wynia treats briefly the situation of the small states of Central America and the Caribbean, and Howard Wiarda compares the debt strategies of small debtors and large ones. Felix Delgado offers some reflections based on the experience of Costa Rica. James Livingstone deals with the Chilean debt, mostly in the recently rather fashionable terms of conversion of debt into equity holdings. The statement of Peruvian Senator Carlos Enrique Melgar gives the position of the moderate left in regard to the debt, a position that is widespread with minor variations in Latin American democracies. Alfred Watkins takes up a question that should have been discussed in depth long ago, namely, whether sovereign lending is really good business for the banks. Robert Wesson considers the other side of this question, that is, whether it is good for the countries to get loans. Finally, the conclusion tries to integrate the principal ideas developed during the conference discussions, particularly in terms of the outlook if the parties continue to behave, as they have in the past, rationally to protect their own interests within the limits of their respective political systems.

Besides those individuals whose written contributions are included in this volume, a number of discussants added their ideas to the conference. They included: Samuel Amaral, the Instituto Torcuato di Tella of Buenos Aires; Komal Sri-Kumar of Drexel Burnham Lambert; Alejandro Toledo, the Institute of Economic Research in Lima; Miguel Urrutia of the Inter-American Development Bank; Jorge Castañeda, the Universidad Nacional Autónoma de México; Robert Packenham, Stanford University; David Konkel of the Department of State; Bruce Bueno de Mesquita of the Hoover Institution; Francisco Lopes, Macrométrica of Rio de Janeiro; Jacek Kugler, Vanderbilt University; Timothy Ashby of the Heritage Foundation; Carlos Carballo, economic consultant in Buenos Aires; Paul Sigmund, Princeton University; Ronald McKinnon, Stanford University; Richard Bissell of USAID; Guillermo Ortiz of the International Monetary Fund; and Resires Vargas, president of the Association of Panamanian Economists.

COPING WITH THE LATIN AMERICAN DEBT

INTRODUCTION

Robert Wesson

The huge indebtedness of the third world and the consequent widening of the gulf between richer and poorer nations is a phenomenon of world-historical moment, and scholars a century from now will doubtless be puzzled over how it got to be so bad, and how intelligent persons on both the lenders' and the borrowers' sides allowed themselves to be sucked into such a quicksand. Whether they discern naiveté or guile will depend mostly on the prevalent ideology. They will certainly wonder if the rich lenders had ever harbored any real expectation that the poor borrowers could have been made to repay the sums received, given the absence of any enforcement agency and the general feeling of the period that the less developed states should be beneficiaries of aid, not exporters of capital to the more developed states.

Although the problem receives rather little publicity, its magnitude is hardly to be exaggerated. The so-called "developing countries," which were indeed mostly developing at a fairly good pace before the debt problem, owe something over one trillion dollars to the industrialized countries. The sum is far from exact because it is difficult to ascertain which financial arrangements are to be included (for example, are arms credits to be included? concessional loans amounting virtually to gifts? strictly private obligations based on cooperative ventures?), and because authorities for a long time were remarkably unconcerned with keeping accurate accounts. Roughly half of this total is owed by governments to official bodies. A minor but important fraction is government-to-government debt, owed mostly by Third World states to the leading financial powers. Even relatively nonaffluent governments, for example Spain, like to make modest loans to still poorer governments, supposedly mostly in order to extend their influence. Much larger amounts are owed to international agencies—chiefly the International Monetary Fund and the World Bank. Roughly half of the debt owed to nonofficial bodies is held by a couple of dozen big banks in Europe, Japan, and the United States, and secondarily by hundreds of smaller banks that were once eager for a share of the action. Of the bank debt, about a third is held by U.S. banks. Not far from half of the total debt pertains to Latin America.

Of the worldwide debt, over 60 percent is "troubled," that is, payments of it have not always been made punctually according to the contracts. Nearly all of the roughly $400 billion owed by Latin America is, or has been, subject to rescheduling; about half of the loan amounts and a majority of Latin American countries are in default (or would be if the creditors chose to use that ugly term). Complete information is difficult to procure; usually neither creditor nor debtor cares to publicize all the details.

The problem thus centers on Latin America. Several Asian countries, for example the Philippines, Thailand, Malaysia, Pakistan, and Indonesia, have difficulties with debt; but Asian debt is relatively smaller because the banks in the 1970s were less sanguine about Asian than Latin American prospects, and because some of the Asian countries, led by South Korea, have made better use of their money and so have put themselves in a position to meet their commitments. Nearly all African countries are as troubled as the Latin American, or more so, but their debt is much smaller and is owed primarily to governments and international agencies. No one expects many troubled African countries to pay, except insofar as they receive additional infusions. Several East European countries, especially Poland, Hungary, Yugoslavia, and Romania, also overborrowed and have difficulty in meeting payments.

The current debt problem is a historical novelty in terms of the number of countries afflicted, the amounts of money involved, the fact that (contrary to earlier practice) the banks did not merely underwrite loans but held them, and the economic effects on the debtor countries. Bonds were floated for the benefit of Latin American republics, chiefly for infrastructural projects, from the day they gained independence early in the nineteenth century. Sometimes they were defaulted in the context of international trade recessions, but the amounts were generally not large enough to merit much mention, if any at all, in the histories of the countries concerned. A debt problem of a somewhat different nature came in the wake of World War I, when the United States tried to collect on loans extended to allied countries during the war and in the subsequent reconstruction period. Yet the total amount involved, in the range of $11 billion, was small by today's standards, even taking inflation into account; and the debtor countries—chiefly Britain, France, Italy, and

Belgium—never tried so hard to pay that they would cause important damage to their economies. They defaulted at the beginning of the 1930s, although their obligation was to pay 1 percent of their export receipts or much less. This figure contrasts with the 30 percent or more (over 100 percent in some unfortunate cases) that the debtors of today are expected to pay to keep current with their debt service.

The effects are also unprecedented; never before have large numbers of people in many nations suffered severe consequences of attempting to conform to their contracts. The standard of living of hundreds of millions of people has been sharply lowered, along with high unemployment rates, lack of investment, and inflation so severe as to make economic calculation difficult. Both health care and education have suffered, with effects that will last for decades. Overall, Latin America has been set back 10 to 15 years by a depression worse for the region than that of the 1930s. All this has come about merely with the attempt to pay interest; the borrowers have repaid practically nothing of the principal.

The direct importance to the United States is quite high. The situation cannot but represent a threat to political interests, both in terms of having friendly neighbors and ensuring the prosperity and security of democratic institutions. Shortfalls in Third World trade, especially with Latin America, have been a major cause of the U.S. balance-of-payments deficit; it can almost be asserted that if U.S. trade with the Third World had progressed from 1981 to 1987 in the same rhythm as it did from 1970 to 1981, there would be no deficit.

It seems clear that the chief cause of this economic calamity is the foreign debt, which has drained capital out of the region and discouraged new capital to enter in view of the economic, and to some extent political, uncertainties. A secondary cause is the generally low prices of the chief exports of the region, agricultural and mineral commodities. These low prices are to some extent caused by the debt since countries pressed to service debt have to push exports; this causes prices to fall, especially because demand for most products that Latin America offers is inelastic. They ship more goods abroad and get less money for them.

One must ask why countries undertook obligations obviously beyond their ability to pay, or better, why banks permitted them to do so. There is no reason to try to assign blame, but we may note that, since people humanly like to have money in hand, most of the responsibility must rest with those who are able to choose how much to make available. The cause of the trouble, of course, is that in the 1970s it was not very obvious that the debt could not be paid even if the amounts were outrageously high by previous standards of international lending. Inflation was seemingly permanent, and commodity prices kept going up. Mexico should be able easily to handle $100 billion of debt if oil were to go to

$40 per barrel, as seemed likely. Brazilian exports were growing at 20 percent per year or more; a great country with marvelous natural resources deserved a great and growing debt. Then when strains began arising and countries found themselves with problems in making current payments, it was necessary to loan more to tide the debtor countries over what were perceived as difficulties of illiquidity; totals grew ever larger.

In part, mere insouciance was responsible for the problem, as most banks thoughtlessly did what others were doing, often without even an approximate idea how much the borrowing governments owed. It was simply assumed that governments always pay—a rash assumption in view of the fact that nearly all Latin American countries defaulted on bonds in the 1930s. There was no discrimination of governments; banks loaned with equal openhandedness to military dictatorships and to democracies. With interest and fees higher than those obtainable domestically, it was simply good business as long as one didn't look too closely, which hardly anyone did. To the contrary, the policy of lending to governments on faith was generally cheered as an extension of the foreign economic aid programs that were no longer adequate for the needs, or demands, of growing Third World states.

The happy part of the debt story came to an end when the business cycle went from boom to recession and Western governments moved seriously to check inflation; it became harder to meet payment dates, and in 1982, for a number of countries, headed by Mexico, it became impossible. The debt boom became the debt crisis, which has only become worse for the debtor nations from 1982 to date.

In 1982, with the Latin American portfolios of several major banks standing over double their capital, there was genuine fear that default by even a few big debtors could throw the financial situation into bankruptcy. However, as discussed in subsequent papers, the banks and government leaders, with the cooperation of debtor nations, undertook to manage the difficult situation. This process implied learning some very simple things that had not been recognized because they were not needed—that a default is not necessarily a default; that the debtors were eager to remain on good terms with creditors; and that arrangements could be made to keep payments formally in order, even though banks had to put up a good deal of money to enable themselves to be paid. In some ways, debt management after 1982 could be called dishonest, including practices outlawed domestically. However, it worked and the danger of a collapse of the international system was averted. Serious confrontation has thus far been avoided; indeed some complacency has returned from time to time as banks have continually improved their ability to cope with sour loans, and many small banks have liquidated their Latin American holdings.

It is not true, however, that the debtor countries have managed to cope satisfactorily with the problem. To the contrary, resources transferred out have exceeded new loans coming in, and this has been done with painful sacrifices. At best, debtor nations have had to adjust to an end of the bounty of foreign capital being poured into their laps from 1974 to 1981. Whatever they have done has been shadowed by uncertainties dampening hopes for new investment; by capital flight on the part of their own citizens without confidence in the future; and by inflation, almost everywhere high and, in some nations, horrendously rated in four figures.

How this has come about and what it means for the future is the subject of the essays that follow.

1

FROM CRISIS TO PROBLEM: LATIN AMERICAN DEBT 1982–87

Albert Fishlow

Five years have elapsed since that dramatic weekend in August 1982 when the Mexican and developing country debt crisis broke on the world. An assessment of the present situation is not encouraging. While Latin American per capita income is still well below the 1980 level, the ratio of debt to exports is well above 3.5, twice the 1980 ratio. Despite costly adjustment, the balance-of-payments problem threatens continuously.

The principal entry on the positive side of the ledger is the survival of industrialized countries' banking systems. Financial crisis has been averted, but at the expense of creating a longer-term debt and development problem. What was advertised as a brief liquidity crisis with recovery always imminent has turned into the first sustained setback to developing country growth in the postwar period. For Latin America, the decline compares unfavorably with that of the Great Depression of the 1930s.

In this chapter, I identify three sets of reasons why the evolution since 1982 has been so unfavorable. They are: the historically unique dimensions of the surge in developing country debt in the 1970s, the international economic disequilibrium of the 1980s, and the characteristics of public intervention in the aftermath of the debt crisis. I then turn briefly to potential solutions.

UNIQUE DIMENSIONS OF DEBT ACCUMULATION IN THE 1970s

The great increase in debt in the 1970s differs from previous cycles of foreign investment in peripheral countries. Historical capital flows were motivated by longer-term profits, from exploiting natural resources and expanding the market for industrial exports. Investment was financed in large measure by British savings, and there was a reliable long-term private demand for foreign securities at a modest premium over domestic interest rates. While there were recurrent debt crisis before 1945 (Latin American countries first defaulted in the 1820s and frequently thereafter), these events were an integral part of the geographic extension of the international economy. Railroad construction and migration created long cycles. During an upswing, finance was available; after several years, its supply diminished in the face of disappointing immediate returns. Then a balance-of-payments and debt-service problem loomed. Although income growth slowed and service might be temporarily interrupted, recovery through expanded exports of primary commodities and renewed capital flows was regular and predictable.[1]

By contrast, the surge in developing country lending after 1973 was motivated by the need to find immediate and profitable application for a sudden increase in deposits of international banks. The oil crisis resulted in an unprecedented balance-of-payments surplus for oil-producing countries. That wealth was held in short-term form by the oil exporters. Banks somewhat unwittingly converted these dollars into long-term development finance by recycling petrodollars. Middle-income developing countries were attractive borrowers by virtue of their accelerating growth and persistent shortage of capital and foreign exchange. In the midst of successful expansion, many Latin American countries were especially eager to sustain growth in the face of adverse international conditions.[2]

Private market intermediation sustained global demand in the 1970s and averted the international depression that some feared. Oil exporter surpluses were matched by developing country deficits used to sustain imports of oil and manufactures. The arrangements had novel, and potentially costly, features. Banks, and increasingly large numbers of them, were the ultimate holders of the loans and hence were directly vulnerable to developing country performance. Countries took on exchange and interest rate risks as they elaborated ambitious investment projects; they correspondingly reduced their margin of maneuver.

Neither side fully understood the inherently temporary character of the access to credit. The new capital flows did not emerge as a result of a sustained increase in global saving seeking a continuing productive outlet. Banks did not consciously decide to provide longer-term development finance and set aside loan-loss provisions to compensate for the higher risk in sovereign exposure. Profits were initially large, particularly for leading banks and those also participating in developing country domestic markets, and that was enough. Very little thought, and even less concern, was given to the importance of a continuous stream of lending; initially, all of the emphasis was on moving the money out of the industrialized countries' banking systems to those of developing nations.

On the side of the borrowing countries, however, the capital inflow became a regular and increasingly necessary input into the balance of payments. Neither productive capacity nor exports immediately increased to provide the incremental resources to service debt. Even when some projects did produce that result, it was attractive to continue to borrow to take on still more ambitious and slow-maturing investment opportunities. Countries were not prepared to desist from import surpluses while there was financing to permit them. Soon that finance was diverted to other purposes. Borrowing today was necessary to pay the interest on yesterday's loans. Debt dynamics meant that constant inflows transferred progressively less real resources.

Latin American countries, in particular, erred in two respects in following a strategy of reliance on debt finance. First, they opened to the international economy in an asymmetrical way: increases in debt were disproportional to revenues from exports. The unfavorable status of the current account was subordinated to the satisfactory state of the balance of payments as a whole. This was true of oil-exporting Mexico after 1976, which failed to stanch excess imports because cheap loans were readily available; of oil-importing Brazil, which undertook an ambitious program of industrial expansion; and of Argentina and Chile, implementing overvalued exchange rates as an integral part of anti-inflationary strategy. Diverse paths led a number of countries to the same defective exchange-rate policies and excess dependence on continuing capital flows.

In the second place, state enterprises in Latin America rapidly became the preferred vehicle for absorbing external resources. Chile was the principal exception, where large private banks lent dollars, principally to associated enterprises. The public guarantee was attractive to external lenders who had limited information on the risks of lending to private debtors. Public enterprises could directly implement programs of increased investment, particularly in the intermediate goods sectors. In addition, this channel ensured direct control over the foreign exchange proceeds to the national government; projects even became shells to conceal balance-of-payments financing. The problems of the public sector are in no small way a heritage of the public style of Latin American accommodation to capital market access in the 1970s.

Another symptom of the inadequacy of that accommodation was the emergence of large-scale capital flight, a subject much emphasized of late.[3] It is no accident that Venezuela, Mexico, and Argentina were the worst offenders. Oil exporters had less need to borrow; in Argentina, the military government was not pursuing a policy of increased growth and investment. At the same time that the public sector was borrowing foreign exchange, private citizens were acquiring it to send it back abroad. There can hardly be a better index of excess borrowing than a reverse flow of surplus foreign exchange unneeded for imports or reserves. Capital flight goes beyond simply rectifying the capital account. Its irregularity, in response to changing expectations, helps to create and intensify foreign exchange crises. In addition, it saddles the public sector, and ultimately the country, with debt service on assets that yield no domestic return. Borrowing does not then create the means for its own repayment. There is thus a continuing and important shortfall in earnings that must be domestically compensated.

By contrast, historical excess borrowing had its typical counterpart in overbuilding of the infrastructure beyond current demand, a problem soon rectified by the subsequent boom. Lack of compensating earnings was temporary, not permanent. Mistakes might be made in undertaking particular projects, but capital loss was not on the order of the capital flight ranging between 40 to 100 percent of the borrowing undertaken by Mexico, Argentina, and Venezuela.

The capital market seemed to work well enough in recycling vast amounts of petrodollars in the 1970s without official intervention. It seemed so because favorable capital supply conditions and satisfactory trade performance were extrapolated by optimistic countries and banks. Banks lent enough and countries serviced their obligations. The latent dangers of the sudden increase in developing country debt became apparent only when the international economy began to falter with the second oil price shock in 1980 and disinflation in the industrial economies.

INTERNATIONAL ECONOMIC CONDITIONS

Latin American countries have been especially prejudiced by the performance of the international economy in the 1980s. One can differentiate two phases. In the early 1980s, their relatively high levels of indebtedness made them especially susceptible to changes in the terms and amount of lending. While the more open East Asian economies were buffeted by deteriorating trade conditions, both in volume and terms of trade, the Latin American countries were sensitive to increases in interest rates and reductions in capital inflow.

As a result, they had no alternative but to adjust their balance of payments by achieving surpluses on merchandise accounts. Most came on the import side. Imports declined by $40 billion between 1981 and 1983, or by more than 40 percent in volume terms. For relatively closed economies, a larger change in income is needed to produce a given decline in imports because import propensities are small. The Latin American decline in production of 4 percent is actually below what might have been expected; it was as small as it was because domestic supply was relatively successful in substituting for imports. It was easier for the Asian economies to adjust to the second oil shock simply because smaller income adjustments could produce larger trade consequences, quite apart from their longer-standing emphasis upon an export solution made easier by continuing finance.

In the years after 1983, Latin American countries suffered from a continued curtailment of capital flows and also increasingly felt the consequences of the continuing slide in primary commodity prices. Resource richness worked against the region. From 1983 to 1986, Latin American terms of trade declined by almost 15 percent, Asian by 6.5 percent. New commitments to increase exports were frustrated by falling prices. Countries experienced very different patterns. Argentina and Peru were especially hard hit, and Mexico was adversely affected by falling oil prices in 1986.

In the aggregate, had 1986 terms of trade for the region remained at their 1980 level and had 1986 interest rates conformed to a real rate of 3 percent, the 1986 Latin American balance of payments would have registered a net improvement of almost $25 billion. Many independent estimates of the capital flow required by the region to resume a rate of growth of, say, more than 5 percent, are of this order of magnitude. The region would not need capital inflows to grow had the world economy performed more satisfactorily. When it did not, external flows could not cushion the shocks because Latin American countries had borrowed earlier.

The persistent disequilibrium in the U.S. balance of payments contributes to the disadvantage of Latin America. Put in its strongest form, the United States buys manufactured imports from Asian Newly Industrializing Countries (NICs) while siphoning off potential capital flow from Latin American NICs. Japanese and European surpluses are recycled to the United States to sustain higher rates of investment, while capital formation in Latin American countries cannot be financed.

Aggressive export growth is an obvious compensation to these adverse balance-of-payments effects. Furthermore, projections of sustained and rapid export expansion have been repeatedly made by those eager to emphasize an optimistic scenario and the opportunities for better Latin American policy. The actual results have fallen short. Despite more realistic exchange-rate policies, export performance has not been able to carry all of the burden placed upon it; nor are prospects much better. A recent issue of *World Financial Markets* paints a somber picture:

Although the income and price elasticities of demand for manufacturers exports are much higher than for primary commodities, sluggish industrial-country growth and a variety of protectionist trade barriers also confront LDC manufacturers exports. Moreover, countries attempting to diversify into manufacturing must compete for market share with established producers in industrial countries and the NICs, as well as other countries also seeking to diversify their exports.[4]

The Latin American strategy of debt-financed adjustment in the 1970s has thus been doubly penalized by subsequent changes in the world economy. Large debts have proven costly because they built in continuing capital requirements to service them, flows that have not been realized. In addition, the delay in conversion to a more diversified and regular export base has led to more adverse terms of trade and a more difficult market to enter.

THE POLICY CONTEXT

Public intervention in the aftermath of the emergence of the crisis must be judged against this backdrop of the special quality of the debt buildup and the adverse evolution of the international economy.

The first priority in 1982 was to preserve the international financial system, which meant ensuring continuing debt service to the banks. Large-scale default would have more than eroded the capital base of the money center banks. Under International Monetary Fund (IMF) guidance, and with support from central banks, adequate liquidity was provided to sustain interest payments. The Fund imposed new conditions of involuntary lending upon the banks, but at levels lower than their return interest receipts. In so doing, the Fund contributed to a greater coordination among banks as they negotiated with countries. Cartelization had the expected outcome; spreads actually widened and attractive commissions were paid for the privilege of rescheduling principal during this period.

Because capital inflow was limited, the main burden of meeting foreign exchange requirements was left to domestic austerity and import reduction, as we have seen. The IMF programs in Latin America did not, however, work as expected. The large transfers of resources to creditors had an adverse impact on domestic investment and growth potential, and complicated macroeconomic management. Instead of diminishing, domestic disequilibrium and inflation increased as the counterpart of improved external accounts.[5]

For a fleeting moment in 1984, this harsh verdict was in doubt. It seemed, with OECD recovery and a large increase in U.S. imports, that Latin American debtors were about to export their way out of the crisis. This optimistic phase was short-lived. It did not last through 1985. In October, Secretary of the Treasury James Baker conceded at the Seoul, South Korea, meeting of the World Bank and the Fund that not enough had been done to underwrite a return to sustained growth by the largest debtors.

The Baker Plan emphasized the need for domestic policy reform, with an emphasis upon privatization and liberalization; an increase in official lending from the multilateral development banks; and larger flows from the banks, which in 1985, had dwindled to virtually nothing. Its underlying premise was additional debt as a solution to past debt. What had made such an approach feasible was the decline in interest rates and improved trade accounts. Countries could grow into their past debt.

The Baker Plan was never implemented. Countries were reluctant to accept the uncertain new standards of conditionality, and banks were even more reluctant to increase their lending. When pressured to do so in the case of Mexico, the banks succeeded in reaching agreement only after long and protracted negotiations. Official flows remained limited, not least because governments were unable to provide local counterpart resources for projects. In the end, what many had already criticized as an inadequate injection of capital was not attained.

For more than a year, the debt problem remained on hold. The debt regime muddled from one case to another at marginally better terms for the debtor countries. Banks improved their balance sheets by increasing their capital and restricting their lending. Latin American countries showed some improvement in performance, accompanied by bolder policy initiatives such as the Austral and Cruzado Plans. Periodic efforts to induce more systematic solutions had little sympathy. Peru's unilateral limitation of debt service was not followed by other debtors; and the rhetoric of Cartagena, the Group of 24, and others fell upon deaf ears.

This continuity was suddenly broken by two events. The Brazilians decided in February 1987 to cease interest payments on two-thirds of their commercial bank debt. Citicorp opted in May to increase loan-loss reserves significantly, and similar actions on the part of other banks followed. Neither decision has yet had its full impact.

Although the Brazilian attempt to politicize the debt issue has failed, it is a powerful reminder of the inability of world economic growth to solve the debt problem. As long as countries are saddled with extremely large debts and debt service, the situation will remain fragile. The expectation that the moratorium will end is a concession to two realities. One is the limited negotiating power of Brazil by virtue of its very large outstanding interbank deposits and trade credits. The second is the limited likelihood of successful coordination among the debtor countries; individual circumstances are too diverse and the prospects for success too uncertain.

There is another lesson as well. Unilateral reductions in debt service are not as helpful for domestic growth potential as an agreed solution.

The same politics that make external debt the sole culprit frequently contribute to other economic policy inconsistencies, and the sheer uncertainty of a moratorium offsets the advantages of a reduced resource transfer. These characteristics are equally illustrated by mounting Peruvian problems.

Citibank's decision to recognize the impaired quality of developing country loans, now selling at discounts that translate into yields of more than 15 percent, is a first step toward bank candor. Until now the story has always been a positive one; difficulties were temporary and renewed lending was always imminent. Now the objective is to reduce developing country portfolios significantly, with a willingness to accept some cost for cleaning up balance sheets. Stock markets initially applauded the large nominal losses as a first step toward realism.

Banks, however, see the future more in terms of voluntary disposition of loans or their conversion into equity than in terms of debt relief. Despite the considerable publicity, swaps are more a sideshow than a significant inroad toward resolving the debt problem. Their volume is limited to a small proportion of outstanding debt even under relatively optimistic assumptions. Swaps restructure principal, moreover, with limited immediate improvement for the balance of payments. What would be gained over time by reduced interest obligations could be offset by increasing profit remittances and repatriation. Such equity investment is also partially at the expense of real new money that might otherwise have entered. Because debt sells at a discount, swaps offer more favorable implicit exchange rates and hence would be expected to substitute other transactions as well as attract new commitments.

Perhaps above all, the cancellation of external debt requires an equivalent mobilization of domestic resources. In essence, swaps both shorten maturity on long-term debt and provide for redemption in domestic currency rather than foreign exchange. Governments cannot simply print the domestic currency, however, without pumping up inflation. They must secure real resources. Yet that is precisely the problem so many countries already face in meeting interest payments and the reason why debt has had an adverse inflationary impact. Weak public sectors cannot increase saving; that fact, and not merely a shortage of foreign exchange, also constrains performance.

It is not only nationalism but also economics that has made debtors suspicious of swaps. The more they are pressured to establish such programs, the more they see them as opportunities for creditors to use discounted debt as a vehicle for purchasing undervalued domestic assets, with only limited help for their debt-service problems. If banks were content merely to convert new interest payments, and not principal, in this way, the relative gains for debtor countries would dramatically change. Then foreign exchange obligations would be reduced significantly, while the same potential benefits of private initiative in cooperation with foreign ownership would prevail.

Since 1982, the banks' policy focus has been on ways of securing debt repayment at minimum loss rather than on alleviating the adverse consequences of the debt overhang for developing countries and the world economy. Despite greater macroeconomic sophistication, we have not come that far from Warren Harding's response to the Allied countries' debt problem: "They loaned the money, didn't they?" Not surprisingly, that objective of protecting the financial system has been reasonably served. The debt problem is much less severe for the banks than it was five years ago, as they have built up capital and loan-loss reserves and have experienced a positive cash flow. However, it remains no less serious for the debtor countries whose situations, as we have seen, have worsened.

ALTERNATIVE OPTIONS

Those who criticize the policy of muddling through do so because it places a disproportionate burden on debtor country adjustment to compensate for capital market failure and poorer international economic performance. Continuing debt service has taken its toll by preventing debtors from financing needed imports and investments. Economic growth has suffered, foremost in the developing countries but for industrial country exporters as well.

Those who defend the status quo do so on the grounds that no disaster has yet occurred, nor is likely, and that future prospects remain adequate. There is also a feeling, sometimes expressed, that enforced rigorous adjustment will help to convert poorly performing Latin American countries into East Asian clones. The medicine is not sweet tasting but necessary and effective.

This debate has produced more frustration than novelty in recent years. For example, Pedro Pablo Kuczynski, in a recent *Foreign Affairs* article, after arguing that the "the debt containment strategy designed in 1982 has run its course," offers an alternative: "A new strategy is needed for the debt problem. It includes: 1) economic reforms in debtor countries, 2) a new inflow of capital, and 3) if the first two are inadequate, viable formulas for partial and temporary interest deferral."[6] This sounds almost exactly like the Baker Plan advanced two years ago. The article gives no reason to believe that the capital will be provided now, when it was not before, or that banks are any more willing to accede to interest capitalization or other comparable arrangements.

The present policy framework survives less because of its positive accomplishments than because of its capacity to avert disaster. There is danger in extrapolating from it, or in repeating the familiar call for much enlarged flows that will not materialize. Countries and banks are closer to the breaking point, which is what the Brazil and Citibank actions of 1987 signaled.

The hardship view has still failed to turn up a conspicuous success. Minimal capital flows to countries adequate to ensure continuous interest payment have been inadequate to finance needed reform and reallocation of resources. From time to time, one country or another may seem to have made forward strides, but there have also been regular reverses. One important component of Israeli success and Argentine and Brazilian failure in controlling inflation has been the degree of external resources and imports available to back the reforms.

Countries accept worse terms than they need to because the alternative of going it alone and reducing debt service promises no better results. Prospects for an enforceable debtors' cartel are small because the differences among countries make individual solutions more attractive than an uncertain joint alliance. In the absence of a generalized crisis, each country will find it more attractive to accept marginal gains rather than hold out for definitive relief.

On their side, banks see no reason to make large concessions and accept much smaller cash flows. There are no incentives for banks to take a longer view as long as the default prospect is unrealistic. Public policy continues to work in favor of that expectation. Pressures brought upon the banks can be effective in modifying terms marginally, but not in changing the present basic structure. Banks are not persuaded that present concessions will yield improved country performance and higher future profits. Such a linkage is uncertain at best.

The ray of hope in the present impasse is to follow the guidance of the market. Developing country debt has become progressively discounted. Between May 1987 and November 1987, prices in the secondary market have fallen from about 60 to less than 40 for many debtors; even Colombia, the exceptional and heralded Latin American recipient of voluntary lending, received a valuation of 72 to 76 in November, compared with 85 to 88 in May.[7]

There is now a sufficiently wide margin to permit debt relief while offering banks a somewhat higher price and a market yield on a certain security exchanged in its place. Suppose the World Bank were to accept the debt at 60 in exchange for its own long-term bonds yielding 9 percent. Then countries could service the latter and reduce their initial interest obligations proportionally. The incentives for banks to accept the transfer is the higher-than-market price and the certain yield. There is a move along the risk/yield trade-off facing banks; in exchange for risky, high-yield developing country loans, banks can receive a certain equivalent. Banks prefer treasuries to junk bonds, and that is what is being offered.

There appear to be three principal arguments against such a solution. One is that it would send the wrong signals to countries by rewarding the most those nations whose poor policies had deliberately eroded the value of their loans. There is little evidence, however, that countries choose irregular debt service in preference to meeting their obligations. This potential moral hazard problem, moreover, does not appear to be decisive. The degree of debt relief provided by the World Bank and the IMF does not have to be exactly proportional to the market discount; reduced debt service can be determined on the basis of future balance-of-payments needs under appropriate policies. Those debtors needing relief will be subject to conditionality, but now in the context of a much more favorable opportunity for sustainable structural change, rather than relying upon large external flows.

A second objection is that banks would experience crippling losses and eschew further lending. This point is much less valid now than in 1982. Banks have already set aside much larger loan-loss reserves, and they can be used in a gradual fashion while affording an opportunity to build back capital levels. As they are used, moreover, tax offsets will apply. Reduced lending is no great cost when it is not occurring in any event; that is the reason for the problem. If banks were to concentrate on trade credits and leave medium-term lending to other sources, that would be all to the good.

The third criticism is that significant resources would have to be mobilized to effect such a repurchase. The costs should not be exaggerated. In the first place, an exchange of new securities, collateralized on a diversified package of loans and guaranteed, would preclude the need for selling them for cash. What would be required is partial financing and full backing, which is true of the World Bank currently. To purchase $200 billion of debt at a price of 60 with 15 percent capital reserves would mean an initial contribution of $18 billion. That is a one-time cost and hardly in an impossible range, especially with a large Japanese participation. Secondly, any superior solution to muddling through is going to have to produce significant official contributions. The Baker Plan failed precisely because it tried to find a way to promote more lending, but with the private banks' money. It will not work. One can only provide for an effective transition from the capital market mistakes of the 1970s through a larger official presence.

The time is now ripe for such an arrangement in a way that it was not when advocated earlier. Market signals provide new incentives and new pressures. Will countries choose to service highly discounted debt when there is no prospect for future flows? Can banks afford to keep such assets on their books when accounting standards are moving toward market valuation? There is much greater potential political viability in partially charging the banks for their mistakes by using market criteria, than in obtaining increases in multilateral development bank capital, which are only seen to bail them out.

A repurchase arrangement need not, and should not, be total. Banks will benefit from rising market assessments on their retained loans as developing country performance improves. They thus remain involved and have an incentive to continue to provide short-term trade credits essential to recovery. Nor does it resolve the continuing need for future capital flows in which a larger role will necessarily devolve to official capital. Partial repurchase is merely a first phase, one that starts down a path of reduced debt service acceptable to the banks themselves.

The real limits to such a policy option are not the conceptual ones. They are, rather, the combination of lack of political priority and the perceived inability of industrial countries to spend. That is the reason why it was necessary for the banks to do the job of recycling in the 1970s, and why it is so difficult to clear the debris in the 1980s. We do not lack for repeated analyses of how much balance-of-payments help is needed. There is a broad consensus about the need for reform conditioned on new capital inflow, and there is even a new opening based upon the larger loan-loss reserves that more accurately portray bank balance sheet reality. Paradoxically, the very success in containing the explosive potential of the debt crisis continues to favor muddling through rather than a more adequate definition and response to the lingering debt and development problem.

NOTES

1. For a fuller discussion, see Albert Fishlow, "Lessons from the Past: Capital Markets during the Nineteenth Century and the Interwar Period," *International Organization* 39, no. 3 (1985): 383–439.

2. Patterns of Latin American response to the oil shocks are examined in more detail in Albert Fishlow, "Latin American Adjustments to the Oil Shocks of 1973 and 1979," in *Latin American Political Economy*, eds. J. Hartlyn and S. Morley (Boulder, Co: Westview Press, 1986).

3. The subject is treated definitively in a forthcoming volume on capital flight edited by John Williamson and to be published by the Institute for International Economics.

4. *World Financial Markets*, August 1987, p. 11.

5. A National Bureau of Economic Research (NBER) study coordinated by Jeffrey Sachs is about to be published in a series of analytic and country volumes on the macroeconomics of adjustment to the debt.

6. Pedro Pablo Kuczynski, "The Outlook for Latin American Debt," *Foreign Affairs*, Fall (1987): 129, 137.

7. Secondary market prices from Shearson Lehman Bros. are reported in the *Wall Street Journal*, November 16, 1987, p. 29.

2

NEW STRATEGIES FOR AN OLD PROBLEM

Gary W. Wynia

During the past year, one Latin American country after another has suspended interest payments on its foreign debt or threatened to do so. Brazil's February 1987 declaration of a moratorium on $67 billion in medium- and long-term loans was the most spectacular of these incidents, but it was not the first. Ecuador had stopped a few weeks before, and for all intents and purposes, so had Bolivia, Costa Rica, Honduras, Nicaragua, Cuba, and Peru in previous years. Fears that Mexico might do the same prompted the IMF and private creditors to agree to terms beneficial to Mexico midway in 1986, and to look upon Argentina's demands for similar terms early in 1987 with unusual favor.[1]

The high hopes for economic recovery and debt payment that prevailed in 1982 are long gone today. In the words of former Federal Reserve Board Chairman Paul Volcker, "battle fatigue" has set in among debtors and creditors, making mutually acceptable solutions to their problems even more difficult than before.[2] In the most pessimistic public admission yet, in May 1987, John Reed, the chairman and chief executive officer of Citicorp, announced that "We don't see anything in the global economy that will allow these countries to get out of these problems soon."[3]

In this paper, I shall briefly examine a few of the most prominent changes resulting from this situation, focusing primarily on how frustration and disappointment on both sides have altered the process of debt management. Lessons are being learned and transactions shaped as much by innovative methods of bargaining as by market economics.

THE PROBLEM

The debt burdens that have enveloped Latin American nations started with oil price shock in 1973, and the way Latin American countries responded to them by taking advantage of an unprecedented volume of lending by private international banks, facilitated by the deposits of petrodollars in Eurocurrency markets. Enormous borrowing in the late 1970s financed massive consumption and record levels of imports all over the region.

Latin American officials erroneously assumed that a new era of rapid growth had begun. At the end of the decade, however, they were taken aback when recession struck the region, induced primarily by official efforts in industrial nations to drive high inflation from their economies by slowing them down. Panic within indebted Latin American countries incited record capital flight, estimated to be the equivalent of roughly half of what countries such as Argentina, Venezuela, and Mexico had borrowed during the previous ten years. By August 1982, when the Mexicans went to the IMF meetings in Toronto to report that they had gone "bottoms up," the borrowing binge was over and a new era of debt problems had begun.[4]

Creditors and debtors must share the blame for ignoring the risks involved in the unprecedented volume of lending that both welcomed in the late 1970s. International banks assumed incorrectly that a sovereign risk was a small one since governments are not supposed to default. Consequently, they paid far too little attention to the economic policies of debtor countries or to the purposes for which loans were used. Official guarantees proved to be far less reliable than was assumed by profit-seeking bankers. For their part, debtors (either for domestic political reasons or simple wishful thinking) pretended that if private bankers had confidence in them, they were on the right track in their development programs. Moreover, they preferred to ignore the risks they were taking in accumulating obligations to banks that one day would refuse credit when debts stood unpaid. In hardly any country did central authorities keep track of how much their many semiautonomous government corporations were borrowing.[5]

The depth of the crisis that struck the region in 1981 and 1982 was not appreciated at first. International financial institutions, which were accustomed to relying on agencies such as the IMF to carry indebted nations through brief financial crises, gradually discovered that far more was required this time. The size of national debts was unprecedented, and economies that were previously expending the equivalent of 5 to 10 percent of export earnings on debt payments suddenly found themselves paying as much as 50 percent. Moreover, the fact that so many nations ran into payment problems simultaneously was unprecedented.

Gone were the days when the IMF could restore stability by giving assistance and directions to a couple of nations in trouble.[6]

The way in which the cost of recovery should be distributed divided opinion from the start. Old rules did not hold much appeal to debtors, so they demanded that creditors acknowledge their unusual plight and adjust their requirements to accommodate their need to grow economically while paying debts. However, bankers and their home governments resisted, preferring long-established practices of taking one case at a time, using conventional solutions in order to avert any real changes in the process. Since creditors had the upper hand at the outset, debtors unhappily complied.

DEBT MANAGEMENT: THE STARTING POINT

To creditors and debtors alike, the most important question was whether the issue was one of illiquidity or insolvency. If illiquidity, then emergency financing combined with some economic austerity was the appropriate remedy. On the other hand, if insolvency were the problem, more fundamental measures were needed. No country could service the full burden of its debts; only drastic measures aimed at debt elimination by common agreement could bring relief.[7] Naturally, debtors pleaded that they were suffering from insolvency and therefore required major reductions in their debt obligations, while creditors and most economists in the creditor nations stuck with the illiquidity explanation.[8]

Yet even creditors recognized from the outset that the road to recovery through case-by-case renegotiations was filled with uncertainties. The big question was obvious: how long could, or would, debtor countries tolerate a substantial outflow of resources and the concurrent recession caused by economic adjustment programs? In essence, it was a race against time in which recovery had to replace recession in order for debtors to make enough progress to sustain their devotion to programs designed in renegotiations with creditors and the International Monetary Fund.[9]

No one knew how long Latin Americans could live with the pain of harsh adjustment measures aimed at lowering their consumption and ending government paternalism. The Mexicans had not experienced such distress since the 1930s. Though their political system is sturdy and carefully supervised by authorities, there was reason to wonder how tolerant an urban population that had grown accustomed to decades of economic growth would be. Argentina and Brazil were both hit by debt crises simultaneous with their attempts to democratize their polities. Previously they had relied on military governments to impose unpopular austerity measures, but now democrats were assigned the task. Whether newly elected presidents could implement harsh measures with regressive effects on the personal income of the middle and lower classes was questionable. Nevertheless, democratic politics survived the challenge quite well initially. In neither Mexico, Brazil, nor Argentina did domestic political considerations prevent the implementation of tough measures. In various ways, democratic authorities in each nation attempted to cut back consumption, convinced that there was no other choice. Moreover, they were heartened by the belief, propagated by their creditors, that economic recovery in the industrial nations was imminent and that by 1985 or 1986, economic growth would be restored to Latin America. More trade and better prices would follow, generating more income for domestic use after debt payments.

After the crisis struck in 1982, Latin American debt management passed through two stages, neither of which yielded much satisfaction. The first, from 1982 until 1984, involved the involuntary supply of new money by lenders in return for the application of austerity measures by debtors, often accompanied by loans and advisements from the IMF. Bankers loaned more than they wished in order to keep their clients paying, while debtors cut imports to generate more cash for interest payments in exchange for more loans.[10] Initially they did rather well, with imports falling from $98.5 billion in 1981 to just over $57 billion by 1984. However, in 1984, real interest rates were still high. Moreover, the prices paid for commodity exports, which had fallen by 40 percent between 1980 and 1982, rose again only for coffee after 1982. It was a major disappointment to debtors whose economies were worse off in 1984 and whose debt burdens were even larger, though increasing at a slower rate, than they were before 1982.

In the second stage, roughly from 1985 until midway through 1986, several debt restructurings were negotiated, though less new money was forthcoming. Bankers were determined to reduce the relative size of their Latin American accounts and made every effort to resist demands for additional finance. By holding back, they forced IMF officials to become aggressive arbiters who pushed renegotiations in order to sustain the participation of creditors in short-term assistance.

Despite some progress in debt negotiations, 1985 was an unhappy year. Economic growth slowed more than anticipated in the industrial world, and the real export earnings of developing countries stagnated, retarding their economic growth and making debt payment far more burdensome than had been anticipated two years before. The growth rate of world trade fell from almost 9 percent in 1984 to 3 percent in 1985. The weakness in the volume of trade was transmitted to prices, and as often happens, the fall of prices was considerably more pronounced for primary commodities than manufactured goods. Prices were also depressed by unusually ample supplies of agricultural commodities, and when the year was over, the terms of trade of developing countries had deteriorated by 2 percent.[11]

Around the middle of 1986 a third phase began, one that is still unfolding. Latin American governments have become more aggressive, experimenting with new tactics that are only now beginning to extract innovative responses from their creditors and revisions in the debt management process.

Signs of truculence were there all along. What the region's leaders lacked was not the desire to change the rules but the clout needed to do it. In 1984 they began expressing their discontent, usually in the form of manifestos that became more demanding as time passed. The first was issued in January 1984 as the "Quito Declaration and Plan of Action," asking for the creation of a mechanism for limiting interest payments to amounts that would not throttle economic growth, namely, that foreign exchange earnings not be committed to debt repayment beyond reasonable percentages. In June 1984, Argentine Economy Minister Bernardo Grinspun repeated the plea in a letter to Jacques de Larosiere, managing director of IMF. A month later, 11 Latin American debtor nations met in Cartagena to announce the Cartagena Consensus, which made two requests of creditors: that they give permission to postpone some interest payments until economic growth and income from trade improved substantially, and that all debtors be allowed to limit interest payments to "a percentage of export earnings that is reasonable and compatible with the maintenance of appropriate levels of domestic productive activity."[12]

They issued another statement on September 9, 1984 from Mar del Plata, Argentina, this time asking for a direct dialogue with creditor governments and insisting that banks could not understand the political and social implications of the problem. It was a deliberate attempt to politicize bargaining by involving foreign governments in what, until then, had been primarily a dispute between private international banks and Latin American governments. The U.S. and European governments ignored the request, determined to avoid assuming major responsibilities for public financing or mediation. Undeterred, the debtor nations met again in February 1985 in Santo Domingo to reemphasize their demand for dialogues among governments and to warn that "if this dialogue is not accepted there will be a serious risk not only of financial and economic but also of social and political instability throughout the region."[13] Yet once more their pleas fell on deaf ears.

Discredited by failure to achieve anything concrete, the Latin American effort soon took on the guise of ineffectual rhetoric by frustrated leaders. However, in their own minds the Latin Americans were quite serious. As they saw it, theirs was not a liquidity problem as their creditors insisted, but one of solvency that could not be relieved with more austerity and new loans. Only comprehensive restructuring of the debt for long periods of time offered any hope of real recovery. Such "bank bailouts" were anathema to creditors and the U.S. government, who argued that such schemes were not only too costly to bankers, but also opened a Pandora's box of difficullt issues, such as how much loss banks should absorb and how much foreign governments should do to relieve creditors and bankers of their burdens. Moreover, it risked giving relief to debtor nations who did not really need it, allowing them to become "free riders" on the grand bailout train. Every scheme that debtors suggested was filled with similar uncertainties, giving bankers plenty of ammunition for exposing their "impracticality."[14]

The debtors suffered as well from the ability of creditors to sustain a rather effective cartel of their own. In constant communication with one another, bankers were able to prevent radical changes in either the terms of existing loans or those set for the new ones. They preferred to bargain with individual countries and to deal with one loan package at a time, thwarting debtors' efforts to change the process by bargaining jointly. To a large extent, they were successful in exploiting the weak financial position of their clients and differences among them, making their alliances ineffectual.[15]

It was not the first time that indebted nations, their creditors, and international agencies such as the IMF had dealt with debt problems; but the enormity of the task after 1982 was unprecedented. Far more banks were engaged in the process of extending credit to Latin America, thanks to the consortia created by major international banks with dozens of smaller ones in each major loan agreement. In addition, much more money was involved, making creditors and debtors more vulnerable to each others' behavior. It gradually became obvious to everyone but the most conservative bankers that changes in old ways of handling those matters were essential.

THE LATIN AMERICAN PERSPECTIVE: UNFULFILLED EXPECTATIONS

Initially, Latin Americans had little choice but to bargain on the terms set by their creditors and the International Monetary Fund, since a failure to do so invited too much economic risk in the short run. The bargaining process started as a very simple choice between cooperation and default. The latter option, it seemed, carried very high costs, since defaulting invited foreign banks' denial of short-term credits, putting a nation's trade on a cash only or barter basis. Most imports must be paid for immediately, and without ample reserves, the loss of short-term credit could prove disastrous. Talk about "going it alone" was cheap, but unless export receipts could generate a positive balance, defaulting could deprive factories of materials and employees of their jobs. That is why formal defaults by the larger nations seemed out of the question, regardless of their nationalism.[16]

Latin Americans never denied that the battle with their debt crisis had to be waged at home. Structural changes in their economies were essential to recovery, starting with drastic reductions in public sector deficits. Accordingly, some effort has been made to reduce the growth of public expenditures and to privatize public enterprises. The debt crisis served for a time as a political pretext for unpopular reforms long advocated by moderate and conservative economists within Latin America. Presidents who at other times might have favored more nationalist, statist solutions, such as de la Madrid of Mexico and Alfonsín of Argentina, this time chose structural reform. One after another, they executed programs intended to secure the financing they needed to get through what most hoped was a temporary misfortune. The whole idea, they told their nations, was to cut back now in order to grow later. How long recovery would take was seldom stated, but the implication was that within a few years inflation would be cut and growth resumed.

A monetarist crusade it was not, however. The economists who made policy in the indebted nations after 1982 were interventionist in outlook from the start, most of them "structuralists" with Keynesian tools of economic management in their arsenals. Their task, as they saw it, was to engineer recovery using any combination of instruments appropriate under the circumstances. While they granted much of the case made by their creditors about the domestic causes of their predicament, they were quite pragmatic about their methods, mixing fiscal and monetary austerity, import restrictions, price and wage controls, and subsidies to exporters. They refused to pull all of their decisions out of the same ideological basket, as the monetarists had attempted to do in Argentina, Chile, and Uruguay in the late 1970s.[17]

Despite some initial progress with fiscal reform and combating inflation, disappointments grew quickly after 1984 throughout Latin America. Failure to develop any kind of effective regional bargaining position added to their discontent. Both the creditors and the Reagan administration refused to consider regional solutions, going only as far as the Baker Plan, which advocated additional loan packages for countries that agreed to accelerate the privatization of their public sectors and to become more hospitable to foreign investment. Yet new loans only meant more debt.

What really upset the Latin Americans was the discovery that they were worse off economically than they were four years before. Officials who had been asking their people to trust them as they engineered painful recoveries had very little to show for their efforts. They had cut

Table 2.1

	% change in per capita GDP (1981–1986)	Growth in Export Volume Since 1980	Growth in Export Revenues Since 1980
ARGENTINA	-15.5	30%	-13%
BRAZIL	4.0	50%	22%
CHILE	- 6.2	38%	-12%
ECUADOR	- 3.3	49%	-19%
MEXICO	-10.4	57%	-12%
PERU	-10.1	95%	-36%
VENEZUELA	-21.9	93%	-53%

Source: Data provided by Alfred Watkins, Staff Member of the Joint Economic Committee, Congress of the United States.

imports and public spending and raised exports, but more exports did not generate more income. Between 1980 and 1986, Argentina increased its export volume by 30 percent, Mexico by 57 percent, and Venezuela by 93 percent; but their income from exports fell by 13, 12, and 53 percent, respectively. (See Table 2.1.) The major exception was Brazil, whose export volume grew by 50 percent and revenues by 22 percent.[18] The terms of trade had worked against them, the prices of their exports having fallen and their imports risen, and there was no indication that they would improve any time soon. The results are shown in Table 2.2.

It was easy for Latin Americans to conclude that the deck was stacked against them. Whether it actually was or not mattered less than the perception of victimization. They had watched as commodity prices fell to their lowest level in decades (with the exception of coffee). Reducing their imports had improved trade balances substantially since 1982, but their gains were far less than anticipated since exports, which increased considerably in volume, nevertheless earned insufficient income to allow the simultaneous repayment of debt and the financing of necessary economic growth. Moreover, they continued to face barriers to trade with Europe and North America at a time when creditors in both continents were insisting that they export far more in order to pay a reasonable interest on their debts. In addition, real interest rates, though somewhat lower than they had been previously, remained high for the debtor.

Capital flight added to their woes. Although it is difficult to measure,

Table 2.2

	Cumulative Growth of External Debt (1981-86)	Cumulative Growth of Export Revenues (1982-86)	Ratio of Interest Payments to Exports 1986
ARGENTINA	41.3%	- 7.9%	51.8
BRAZIL	27.3%	21.9%	37.7
CHILE	32.9%	10.8%	39.2
ECUADOR	29.3%	13.0%	32.2
MEXICO	33.5%	-35.9%	40.0
PERU	49.0%	-27.3%	27.3
VENEZUELA	7.2%	-46.0%	

Source: Data provided by Alfred Watkins, Staff Member of the Joint Economic Committee, Congress of the United States.

substantial amounts of dollars fled indebted economies at a time when capital was desperately needed. According to one estimate, between 1983 and 1985, $6.6 billion left Brazil (33 percent of what it borrowed during that period), $16.2 billion left Mexico (180 percent), and $5.5 billion left Venezuela (100 percent).[19] A great deal of this represents money invested abroad by people who have little or no faith in the management of their own economies, but much of it consists of billions of dollars sent abroad by corrupt officials and wealthy individuals who want to guarantee their economic future. There is no single culprit or cause, but as long as they believe that conditions beyond their control are preventing economic recovery, Latin American authorities are going to feel sorry for themselves, blaming others for their failure to recover.

Latin Americans felt trapped. Indebtedness required austerity measures intended to improve their capacity for long-term growth. However, austerity, accompanied by very slow recovery in the world economy, stood in the way of growth. Cutting inflation, increasing exports, and reducing imports were supposed to restore price stability and renew investor confidence; instead, they perpetuated recession and dampened the enthusiasm of investors. After making debt payments, too little remained to pay for necessary imports. In short, they could not pay debts and grow simultaneously.

None of those problems helped efforts to reconstruct political institutions. One of the great ironies of the 1980s is the coincidence of the debt crisis with the restoration of democratic governments in nations that were governed during the previous decade by military regimes whose members thought that they were uniquely qualified to restore stability and growth to inflation-ridden economies. With the exception of Brazil before 1973, they did not keep their promises, so it was only a matter of time before they had to depart. In Argentina, Uruguay, and Brazil, they retreated to their bases in the midst of economic crisis, leaving it to politicians to restore growth, pay debts, and institute democratic politics.

Not surprisingly, the new civilian leaders complained to their creditors about the threat that austerity posed to their insecure democracies. Yet bankers claimed that politics were none of their business, and governments in Europe and the United States, while expressing concern about democracy's fate, did not want to let political factors influence their reliance on the private sector to handle debt collection. Moreover, as is their habit, most foreign economists denied the utility of adding political variables to their already complex economic equations, often arguing that by their survival democratic presidents were denying the validity of their claims of unusual duress. The result was ever-increasing cynicism in creditor nations about democracy's imminent collapse in Latin America. Despite increasing public discontent with economic stagnation all over the region, the gap between leaders of the fragile democracies and those with whom they dealt abroad remained very wide.

As 1985 ended, officials in debtor countries became more restive, unhappy with the lack of progress and the continued high cost of debt service. They met again in December, in Montevideo, Uruguay, where they warned that industrialized countries would have to change their economic policies, increase trade, and lower interest rates if they wanted Latin Americans to cooperate further. It was not so much a threat as a prediction of what would happen if conditions did not improve. They proposed an emergency plan that went far beyond the Baker proposal, asking commercial banks to boost their lending to the region by $12 billion, accompanied by a sharp increase in lending by the World Bank and the Inter-American Development Bank. Actually it was a rather mild proposal, one that accepted the principle of more finance rather than default. At the same time, however, they threatened "alternative measures" if their plan was not adopted, though without spelling out what action they would take. Moderate economists were still in charge in most economics ministries, but even they were beginning to tire of uninterrupted setbacks.[20]

In February 1986, Mexican president Miguel de la Madrid and Venezuelan president Jaime Lusinchi called another "emergency" meeting of the Cartagena group to emphasize their dissatisfaction with the status quo and to demand "significant changes in existing [loan] agreements, especially with regard to interest rates."[21] In other words, if lower rates cannot be obtained by a debtor country through negotiations with banks, unilateral action by any debtor would not only be justified, but also would be supported by the other ten members of the Cartagena Consensus.

This was a major change in attitude among debtors. Rather than presenting a common front as they had previously done to no avail, they now endorsed individual nations taking independent action, assured that the others were behind them. Still, the statement's wording was quite temperate at the insistence of de la Madrid and took on the character of a warning of what would inevitably happen if better terms were not offered. In other words, the message was clear: "If you do not cut interest rates Mr. Banker, some of us will have no choice but to stop payment." As it turned out, it was also an accurate prediction of what would occur over the next 12 months, though at the time bankers thought otherwise.

GUERRILLAS OR OPPORTUNISTS?

There are two hypotheses about what happened next. According to one theory, the Cartagena countries masterminded a well-coordinated "guerrilla war" guided by a strategy that called for a concerted effort to threaten default in order to force concessions from creditors.[22] What they could not do with declarations or by acting separately, they could now do by attacking their creditors where they were the most vulnerable and rushing to take advantage of the consequent panic among them. The theory seems supported by the fact that several nations have gone on the attack, and some have benefited from more aggressive tactics. There is no evidence, however, that any plot was hatched and implemented so proficiently.

A more plausible explanation accepts Latin Americans for what they are: relatively weak vis-à-vis creditors, but still clever opportunists who only recently accumulated enough confidence to become more aggressive. They did not suddenly discover new tactics, but made familiar ones more effective after five years of trial and error.

It may be recalled that Latin American nations have followed something of a relay-race strategy ever since 1982 in their dealings with creditors. Though neither planned nor carefully coordinated, that strategy fostered a style of bargaining that is now firmly entrenched. First Mexico in 1982, then Brazil in 1983, Argentina in 1984, Peru in 1985, Mexico in 1986, and finally Brazil and Ecuador in 1987 discovered that they were in a state of crisis, unable to continue debt payments on terms set in previous negotiations with their creditors. The fact that the major crises arose in only one nation at a time facilitated their resolution and pre-vented serious damage to creditors. One by one, each Latin American government negotiated the best short-term solution that it could, little by little setting precedents for future settlements by winning an inno-vation or two that others could later imitate. Slightly better terms, larger-than-normal renegotiated settlements, etc., were incrementally added to the assortment of tools available to negotiators. This was most obvious when Mexico demanded and received from the IMF in mid–1986 the right to peg payments to export earnings if the price of oil fell below $11.00. Mexico enjoys a special relationship with the United States, mak-ing it unlikely that anyone will imitate its achievement exactly, but that has not prevented Argentines from going after a similar settlement.

The debtors also discovered an ability to get away with a kind of "defacto defaulting" in 1985 and 1986. It became apparent to them that if creditors and creditor governments would not reduce the financial hemorrhage, relieving some of the debt burden, they could relieve it simply by reducing interest payments.[23] More and more, they began slowing their payments and demanding better terms for rescheduling existing debts. That strategy was also part of an attempt to buy some time in the hope that the opportunity for better terms would arise as creditors began to acknowledge that little progress had been achieved by their conventional solutions.

INNOVATION AT THE EDGES

Simultaneously, the debtors have begun to experiment with several minor changes in the way that old debts are managed, aided by creative financial entrepreneurs in New York, London, and Tokyo, who are devising a variety of new ways to make a little money from the Latin American debt. It would be a mistake, however, to regard such ventures as anything but marginal to the debt-reduction operation. One need only add up the dollars involved to discover that no more than about 10 percent of current debt obligations will be affected by these latest efforts.[24]

Some innovations are truly novel and others have been around for years. While the optimistic want to see them as highly promising, most refuse to become too enthusiastic about what seem little more than bandaids. The fact remains that some changes have been put into effect: Ecuador's creditors have agreed to make loans based on the country's future oil revenue; Argentina's creditors have proposed a new financial instrument, called an "exit bond," which will permit smaller banks to withdraw from future debt talks; and nearly everyone is involved in debt-for-equity swaps. None of those changes create anything resem-bling a long-term solution, however.

Debt-for-equity swaps wiped out $5 billion of a total third world debt of nearly $800 billion in 1986. In a typical swap, a multinational corporation buys at a discount all or part of a bank's holdings of obligations of a particular country. The corporation presents the paper to the country's central bank, which redeems it for local currency in an amount roughly equal to the debt's original face value. Within the past year, Mexico received 178 requests from foreign companies to convert $1.49 billion in government debts into pesos for local investments, with 41 percent of the requests coming from U.S. firms. Some critics fear that swaps will be inflationary by tempting officials to print local currency to redeem debt. Central banks may also sell bonds to sustain more control over their money supply, but replacing the foreign debt with domestic borrowing may create even greater problems. To avert such problems, the Mexicans have announced that they will limit debt trades to $100 million monthly, and treasury officials have admitted that "swaps are not the panacea that will solve our indebtedness problem."[25] Swaps also risk provoking domestic protest because they increase foreign ownership. That is the reason why Argentina recently included in its debt package a provision limiting swaps to companies willing to invest one dollar for every dollar received in the swap.

PROSPECTS

There is no secret about what it will take for debts to be handled satisfactorily if no fundamental changes are made in Latin American relations with creditors. As IMF economist Eduardo Wiesner put it: "While it is not possible to predict what will be the final outcome, it could be said that the answer will largely depend on what happens to the world economic recovery and to the export earnings of indebted countries."[26] The Inter-American Development Bank suggested that several conditions had to be met for recovery to occur: (1) imports, which have been reduced all over Latin America, must grow only slowly, no more than 3 percent annually during the rest of the decade; (2) economic growth in the industrial countries must average 3 percent in real terms for the rest of the decade; (3) industrial countries must not increase protectionism; (4) dollar interest rates must decline gradually in nominal terms by about 3 percent from present levels; (5) inflationary shocks to the world economy must be avoided; and (6) new bank lending to Latin America must grow by about 7 percent a year—the same rate of increase as in 1983.[27]

Few of these conditions are being met. According to the World Bank's preliminary analysis of Latin America's economic performance in 1986, per capita output failed to increase significantly for the sixth consecutive year for the region as a whole, despite recovery in some countries; it remains about 8 percent below the 1980 level. Worse yet, per capita income is now estimated to be about 30 percent below what it was in 1980 because of the 20 percent cumulative deterioration in the region's external terms of trade which has taken place during the last six years concomitant with the rise in interest payments abroad.

Externally the region has been hurt by the continued weakness of commodity prices in 1986, caused by slower growth in the industrialized nations and by agricultural regimes in developed countries that continue to reduce the market access of Latin American countries. The region's merchandise trade balance fell by 45 percent as a consequence of a 15 percent decline in export earnings and a slight recovery in the level of imports, causing a substantial increase ($10 billion) in the current deficit of the external accounts. Moreover, the external terms of trade for the region fell by 9 percent, and declines in world interest rates were not large enough to compensate for the deterioration of the region's merchandise trade balance.

Moreover, the interest-coverage ratio, (that is, the portion of interest payments on external debt that is covered by the surplus on merchandise trade) fell from 89 percent in 1984 to 80 percent in 1985, and then to 46 percent in 1986. The debt-to-exports ratio increased from 3.2 in 1984 to 3.4 in 1985, then to 4.0 in 1986. The only good news was that the ratio of interest service payments to exports of goods and services remained constant at 35 percent, as a consequence of declining world interest rates.[28]

Combining lessons learned from unsuccessful debtor cartels, unsatisfactory bargaining with creditors, and working with the IMF, debtors had little choice but to experiment with more aggressive haggling. Still, it seems that most of them will have to be content with benefiting from each other's bargaining successes rather than undertaking drastic steps such as the one that Brazil was forced to take in 1987. The specific character of each nation's relationships with its creditors and the differing costs of default and other drastic measures prevent their imitating one another in every detail. Yet benefit they can, as several did in the wake of Brazil's action.

Argentines and Venezuelans, for example, in close communication with the Brazilians both before and after their moratorium in February 1987, immediately pushed harder in their own renegotiations, promising to continue payment if better terms were given. Meanwhile, the United States Treasury, anxious to clear the table so that all attention could be focused on reaching a mutually satisfactory solution to the Brazilian problem, put pressure on the IMF and private banks to settle with Argentina and Venezuela, which most creditors did with unusual speed. Nothing was really solved by this action, of course, since record debts still remain to be paid, but by taking advantage of one another's efforts,

Latin Americans have found ways to gain a little more breathing room. When compared with their objectives, such accomplishments are meager, but the fact that they have forced creditors to bend a little is a significant break in what had been a rather paralyzed manner of doing business.

CREDITORS RESPOND

By 1987 the impossibility of immediate Latin American recoveries had become undeniable. This fact of life was the best leverage that Latin Americans had. It also helped that, by 1987, some creditors were becoming less vulnerable in their accounts than they had been when the crisis had started five years earlier.

On May 19, 1987, Citicorp chairman John S. Reed announced that he had just added $3 billion to the bank's foreign and domestic loan-loss reserves. His statement was an admission that many of Citicorp's debts might go sour, and it was also an attempt to strengthen the bank's position in its dealings with its debtors. Moreover, by creating large reserves Reed made it easier to remarket his debt. A secondary market is possible where the debt can be bought and sold, securitized, and swapped. Remarketing, in turn, adds substantial flexibility for handling future debt crises.

Citicorp's bold initiative broke two of the bankers' most fundamental rules. Banks were not supposed to act unilaterally, but Reed did, ending five years of collusion with the other U.S. banks. He put pressure on them to bolster their own reserves, something that financially weaker institutions such as Manufacturers Hanover and the Bank of America found it much harder to do. Consequently, even if Citicorp gained some leverage over the third world nations that owe it $15 billion, Reed launched a new relationship between creditors and debtors that may help the latter in their dealings with the weaker banks.[29]

Second, and most important, Reed conceded publicly that Latin America's debt was not a liquidity problem after all. By admitting the impossibility of collecting all of it, he allowed that something like solvency was involved. "Muddling through" has failed, and the time has come to try something else, as the Latin Americans had argued for the past half-decade.

While it might seem that Citibank is preparing to concede losses as debtors have demanded, its actions may be intended to do just the opposite. Having taken its lumps, Citicorp wanted to put itself into a better position for handling future debt renegotiations without being intimidated by threats of default. To its customers in Latin America, Citicorp is saying that it is not afraid of their postponing paying interest for awhile. Citicorp prepared to absorb such costs and stick with its demands for conformity to its own plans. Moreover, it may no longer feel compelled to make new loans in order to keep interest payments on the old ones flowing. As one commentator summarized the situation in May 1987: "New lending to debtor countries will probably fall, debt reschedulings will become more painful, calls for a governmental solution to the debt problem will grow even louder, and a divided banking community will become even more fragmented."[30]

Not long after the Citicorp's announcement, debtors responded by demanding additional changes in the terms of the bargain. In an appeal to officials of industrialized countries who attended a meeting in Venice, Italy in June 1987, Presidents José Sarney of Brazil, Raul Alfonsín of Argentina, and Julio Mario Sanguinetti of Uruguay asked for measures that would lower interest rates in their debts permanently. It was the growing consensus among Latin American economists that interest rates on old debts ought to be fixed at 2 or 3 percent over the long term. In its agreement with its creditors early in 1987, Argentina had reduced its interest rates only slightly, but Alfonsín insisted that they be dropped even farther in order to allow Latin American countries, which had paid a total of $130 billion in interest in the past five years, a better chance at economic recovery.[31]

It may be left to the American, European, and Japanese governments and international agencies to step in and ensure that something constructive is done. As the *New York Times* editorialized after the Citibank move:

The most realistic resolution is for governments to bear most of the risks. Some of the money might come directly from government-guaranteed private loans. But the most promising channels are the multilateral lending agencies, the World Bank and its regional bank counterparts in Asia, Africa, and Latin America. They can best access the capacity of borrowers to use capital productively. They are also better equipped than individual governments to nudge borrowers into unpopular economic reforms. Lending nations have as much to gain as borrowers: A hefty portion of every dollar and franc and yen sent to developing countries comes back as demand for industrial exports. . . . [32]

Those steps are more easily said than done, of course. However, a new era in debt management has definitely begun, and for the first time, there is no certainty about who will write its rules nor what they will say.

CONCLUSION

It was not long ago that one read the following hot off the presses:

The problem of international debt is likely to recede as international economic recovery proceeds, and it remains appropriate to manage the problem as one of illiquidity, not insolvency, and on a case-by-case basis. In 1983 major debtors experienced much faster external adjustment than anticipated, and the emerging external performances of Mexico and Brazil are particularly impressive. Overall external adjustment is ahead of schedule, not behind schedule. Moreover, internal recovery is beginning to occur.[33]

The fundamental relationship between creditors and debtors has changed during the past half-decade. After five years of misplaced hopes and bitter disappointments, a new realism is setting in. Debtors comprehend that there is no easy way out for them, and creditors have finally admitted that they will never collect all that they have loaned to Latin America.

By accepting the possibility of loan loss, Citibank and others have conceded that old solutions will no longer work and that banks can absorb more loss than they once thought possible. Such changes in attitudes offer opportunities for more constructive solutions, though they do not ensure them. Instead of forcing one-sided solutions some accommodation is now essential.

Moreover, it is imperative that the adverse political consequences of outdated solutions be given far more attention. New democracies have done remarkably well in the region under the most adverse economic circumstances, but that does not mean that they will continue to do so. Strains are already apparent in Brazil and Peru. As economist Martin Feldstein warned recently: "Unless there is a satisfactory rate of economic growth, the political pressures for unilateral debt repudiation will be uncontainable. The political stability of Latin America and its continued allegiance to the newly established processes of democracy could also collapse if its economies fail to achieve satisfactory growth."[34]

Feldstein might have had Argentina in mind when he wrote this. Early in 1987, a victory was anticipated for Raul Alfonsín, the popular president at that time, and his Radical party in the congressional and gubernatorial elections held in September 1987; the year ended with defeat of the Radicals by the Peronist party. The Peronists had made the pain suffered from Alfonsín's Austral program their campaign issue, and it worked remarkably well. What in a normal democracy would have been nothing more than an incumbent's loss in off-year election was far more serious in Argentina, where any escalation of conflict between the government and its opponents threatened to make the nation ungovernable once again. To avert political disorder, Alfonsín resorted to the well-known tactic of blaming the IMF for his people's woes, promising after the September election to take a tougher stand against the Fund and private banks. Soon thereafter, however, he resorted once more to price and wage controls, desperate to restore confidence in his economic leadership.

Debts alone do not cause democracies to fail, nor is it the responsibility of creditors to ensure their political success. But if debts are to be paid and the Latin American economies to grow once more, the region's politics cannot be dismissed as irrelevant. Dedication to democracy is frail throughout the region. One need only look back a decade or two to recall how quickly the middle classes in these countries turned to the armed forces when social protest rose and order was broken. They should be expected to do so again under similar conditions.

With creditors refusing to facilitate recovery, North American and European governments must do more to promote economic growth in the region with trade and other means. Growth is good not only for democracy, but also for Latin America's trading partners, since a hefty portion of every dollar sent to developing countries returns as demand for industrial exports. Self-interest alone demands a better effort.

NOTES

1. Since mid–1986 Costa Rica has paid only about $3–5 million a month in interest, well short of the $12 million due; Bolivia has not paid interest on its $600 million public sector debt since 1983; Cuba stopped paying interest on its $3.5 billion debt to private banks in capitalist countries during the summer of 1986. See *The Economist,* March 14, 1987, p. 76.

2. *Washington Post,* March 16, 1987, p. 18.

3. *New York Times,* May 20, 1987, p. 1.

4. See Alfred Watkins, *Till Debt Do Us Part* (Washington, D.C.: Roosevelt Center for American Policy Studies, 1986) (hereafter cited as *Till Debt*). Refer to chapter 3 for an excellent summary of the financial events leading up to August 1982.

5. Watkins, *Till Debt,* p. 193.

6. Several books and articles have been written about the events of 1981 and 1982. In addition to the works cited elsewhere in these notes, also see: Brian Kettal and George A. Magnus, *The International Debt Game* (Cambridge, Mass.: Ballanger Publishing Co., 1986); Morris Miller, *Coping Is Not Enough* (Homewood, Ill.: Dow Jones-Irwin, 1986); Chris C. Carvounis, *The Debt Dilemma of Developing Nations* (Westport, Conn.: Quorum Books, 1984).

7. William Cline, *International Debt: System Risk and Policy Response* (Cambridge, Mass.: MIT Press, 1984), p. 34 (hereafter cited as *International Debt*).

8. As William Cline concluded in 1984: " . . . the debt problem so far remains one if illiquidity and that accordingly the basic strategy of dealing with the problem through international measures to provide special liquidity is the right approach." Cline, *International Debt,* p. 34.

9. Marko Milivojevic, *The Debt Rescheduling Process* (New York: St. Martin's Press, 1985), pp. 105–106 (hereafter cited as *Debt Rescheduling*).

10. For analysis of the rescheduling effort during this first stage see Milivojevic, *Debt Rescheduling.*

11. International Monetary Fund, *World Economic Outlook 1986,* pp. 1–3.

12. Watkins, *Till Debt*, p. 47.

13. Watkins, *Till Debt*, pp. 47–48.

14. Jonathan Hakim, "Latin America's Financial Crisis: Causes and Cures," in *Latin America and the World Recession*, ed. Esperanza Duran (Cambridge: Cambridge University Press, 1985), p. 27 (hereafter cited as "Latin America's Financial Crisis").

15. On the bankers' success with "divide and conquer" tactics see: *New York Times*, May 21, 1987, p. 31; *Wall Street Journal*, May 22, 1987, p. 24.

16. Hakim, "Latin America's Financial Crisis," p. 32.

17. In his address to the Latin American Studies Association meetings held in October 1986, economist Albert Hirschman noted the switch in roles between North American economic policy makers, who had previously been quite pragmatic but were now rather dogmatic, and Latin American policy makers, who have acted in the opposite manner. He also warned that the latter were likely to give up their unusual flexibility very soon if no gains were made toward ending their debt crises.

18. Unpublished data supplied by Alfred J. Watkins, U.S. Congress, Joint Economic Committee, Washington, D.C.

19. *Washington Post*, March 26, 1986; *Wall Street Journal*, April 8, 1986.

20. *Washington Post*, January 19, 1986.

21. *Washington Post*, March 9, 1986.

22. The term is attributed to Armen Koyuyoumdjian, a leading bank specialist on Latin America. See: *Latin American Weekly Report*, March 5, 1987, p. 7.

23. Watkins, *Till Debt*, p. 57.

24. For an excellent listing of these techniques see: *New York Times*, May 5, 1987, p. 33.

25. *Washington Post*, June 15, 1987, p. 21.

26. Eduardo Wiesner, "Domestic and External Power of the Latin American Debt Crisis," *Finance and Development* (IMF-IRAB), March 1985, pp. 24–26.

27. Hakim, "Latin America's Financial Crisis," pp. 30–31.

28. The date in the previous three paragraphs is taken from: IBRD, "Annual Report—Latin America & The Caribbean," unpublished report (Washington, D.C.: IBRD, 1987).

29. *New York Times*, May 21, 1987, p. 31.

30. *New York Times*, May 21, 1987, p. 1; also see *Wall Street Journal*, May 21, 1987, p. 10.

31. *New York Times*, May 29, 1987, p. 5.

32. *New York Times*, May 25, 1987, p. 14.

33. Cline, *International Debt*, pp. 199–200.

34. *The Economist*, June 27, 1987, p. 22.

3

RESCHEDULING: A BANKER'S VIEW

Charles J.L.T. Kovacs

The debt rescheduling problem has been with us now for over five years. Although the numbers vary depending on one's definitions, the problem centers on approximately 40 countries and $600 billion. Commercial banks are owed over $330 billion. Latin American countries account for roughly two-thirds of the entire debt and nearly 80 percent of the debt owed to commercial banks.

Most of the debt, and virtually all of the debt owed to banks, was incurred in the aftermath of the first and second "oil shocks" in the 1970s. At that time, commercial banks functioned to recycle the enormous petrodollar surpluses of the oil-exporting countries.[1] This was a major change because until then, most non-OCED countries had only very limited access to commercial long-term credit. Such credit as they enjoyed was obtained chiefly through the bond markets for general purpose borrowing, although a number of Second and Third World countries were able to borrow from banks for specific purposes, usually in packages tied to export credit agency loans. By and large, commercial bank exposure to the poorer countries was limited to short-term (that is, less than one year) trade transactions.

The expanded role of the banks was encouraged by the OECD governments. It was made possible by the rapidly growing Eurodollar markets, and it was deemed to be justified by the expected short-term nature of the problem, as well as by the general increase in commodity prices that was benefiting many Third World countries. Beyond that, many banks adhered to the conventional wisdom that the coming decades would belong to the developing nations, which would expand and prosper.

The petrodollar recycling was not limited to developing countries. Indeed, at first, the largest borrowers were industrial countries, which had to borrow to meet their quadrupled oil bills. Japan, for example, borrowed $6 billion for balance-of-payments purposes in 1974 alone.[2] In the subsequent years, these countries adjusted and eliminated their imbalances. They succeeded so well, in fact, that today hardly any of their governments borrow from banks.

As will be seen, the results in the non-OECD countries were considerably more mixed. Although most of the loans through 1981 were contracted by today's rescheduling countries, other developing nations such as South Korea, Taiwan, Thailand, and Malaysia were also large borrowers. In addition, virtually all of the East European countries incurred very substantial debts.

Bank lending to the Second and Third World grew from a small base to well over $300 billion by the end of 1982. Table 3.1 shows figures for most of the relatively poor countries where commercial banks had exposure in excess of $1 billion at the end of 1982. These data provide an interesting indicator of bank lending in the preceding years.

The debt owed to the most commercial banks was held by more than 500 banks from dozens of countries. Most of the banks were from the industrialized nations, but by 1980, banks from Arab countries and from several developing nations were also actively involved in syndicated credits, mostly as participants but often in more prominent roles.[3] Although U.S. banks led the rescheduling efforts in the mid–1970s, their market share began to decline after 1978; by 1982, in most countries, they held only around one-third of the outstanding bank debt. The Europeans usually held over 35 percent, the Japanese between 12 and 15 percent, while the rest was divided among the Canadian, Arab, and developing countries' banks.[4]

The dollar amounts of debt, however, were very large everywhere in relation to bank capital. Consequently, in 1982, when Mexico's failure to pay maturing installments was followed by many other nations, this problem could have easily become a global financial crisis. That eventuality was averted through long, arduous, and extensive negotiations between the banks and the debtor countries. These negotiations were of critical importance and without historical precedent. The international financial community played its pivotal role in a highly professional manner, which remains widely unappreciated to this day.

In the course of the process, both sides made major concessions. The banks rescheduled (that is, extended) the tenor of their loans, reduced their spreads, and by the end of 1985, committed over $33 billion in new money. The debtor countries, in turn, eschewed radical confrontational policies and, with the assistance and overview of the IMF, sought to reduce their fiscal deficits, fight inflation, and improve their balance of

Table 3.1

Country	Total Debt (in $B)	Owed to Banks	Owed to US Banks
Korea	37.2	22.1	12.4
Indonesia	27.7	10.1	2.7
India	26.3	2.0	1.4
Philippines*	24.7	16.1	5.5
Singapore	13.6	7.2	2.0
Malaysia	12.3	7.3	1.7
Thailand	12.2	6.3	2.0
Taiwan	11.7	6.2	4.9
Portugal	26.5	9.2	2.2
Poland*#	26.0	9.0	1.1
Turkey	18.7	3.8	1.4
Yugoslavia*	18.3	7.6	2.2
East Germany	13.0	7.7	0.9
Romania*#	9.9	4.0	0.2
Greece	9.7	5.7	2.7
Hungary	7.7	6.3	0.9
Egypt	23.7	5.6	1.2
South Africa*	22.6	12.0	3.6
Algeria	18.2	5.2	1.2
Nigeria*	15.8	6.4	1.7
Morocco*	11.3	3.3	0.7
Ivory Coast*	6.5	2.7	0.6
Tunisia	4.6	1.1	0.2
Mexico*	91.1	67.3	24.3
Brazil*	85.7	66.5	22.0
Argentina*	43.6	30.3	8.6
Venezuela*	37.6	30.8	11.2
Chile*	18.0	13.8	5.9
Peru*	11.5	5.3	2.4
Colombia	10.3	6.6	3.7
Ecuador*	6.6	4.5	2.1
Uruguay*	4.2	2.0	0.9
Costa Rica*	3.8	1.5	0.5
Bolivia*	3.7	1.5	0.4
GLOBAL TOTAL	714.3	379.8	135.4 (3)

* Indicates country which rescheduled its debts after 1982. Turkey was a rescheduling country before 1982 but has since regained market access.

Banks' exposure to this country is estimated from various sources.

payments. The degree to which changes were made and the results varied greatly from country to country and from year to year, but meanwhile public sector interest payments were maintained. Both sides gained the time and experience that ultimately enabled them to turn a crisis into an evidently manageable problem.

On the down side, however, the policies followed by the rescheduling countries were at the cost of considerable hardship for their people, often for the groups politically the least powerful, albeit sometimes the most numerous. By 1985, it was becoming increasingly evident that the rescheduling countries could not or would not continue to sustain the political cost of austerity coupled with the continuing net outflows of funds to foreign lenders. The banks, however, could not resume voluntary lending because most of the fundamental problems that had caused the initial crisis were still present.

This dilemma was addressed by Secretary of the Treasury James Baker at the 1985 IMF meeting. His framework for a solution, the Program for Sustained Growth, recognized that the status quo in the rescheduling countries was becoming untenable. As an alternative, Secretary Baker proposed that the rescheduling countries resume growth, not simply by borrowing still more money, but through extensive structural reform to attract investment and to cure the long-standing distortions in their economies that have had an adverse impact on most of them. In turn, the commercial and multilateral banks would support this process with substantial new loans over a three-year period.

The initiative was welcomed positively by virtually all segments of the international financial community. However, because the initiative was (and remains) a framework and not a plan, it took time to clarify its implications and to develop a common understanding of its components. Since the debt problem involved several multilateral institutions, hundreds of banks, and dozens of lending and borrowing countries, this delay was understandable but unfortunate. In the month following the Seoul, South Korea, meeting of the IMF and World Bank, there was a definite lull in financing activity, causing a loss in momentum. This might have been avoided had the initiative been crisper and more detailed, or if the banks had been able to digest it and coordinate their responses faster. As it was, beginning with October 1985, the debt problem was affected by two major developments: the widespread recognition of the size and scope of the flight capital problem, and the rapid decrease in the price of oil.

While there is some, mainly technical, disagreement about the flight capital numbers, they are undoubtedly in excess of $100 billion. Indeed, it is not too much of an exaggeration to suggest that without capital flight, we would not have a serious debt problem today. The emergence of the capital flight issue also created a still unresolved dilemma for bankers; is it consistent with their fiduciary responsibilities to make new loans to rescheduling countries that are unable or unwilling to attract their own citizens' money? More importantly, perhaps, the vast sums that left the rescheduling countries have underlined both the need for structural reform and Secretary Baker's prescience in insisting on those reforms as a prerequisite for new money.

The falling oil prices, meanwhile, turned Mexico from 1984's success story into 1986's premier problem. It was resolved only through a great deal of pressure by the creditor country governments on their banks. The size of the package was larger than the banks had thought would be necessary, and the terms of the loans bordered on the concessionary. Opinions on this point vary, but not by much. Consequently, it took nearly nine months to get the Mexican package signed and implemented and even then, only at the cost of considerable goodwill.

In the aftermath of the Mexican agreement, many rescheduling countries tried to get terms similar to Mexico's, while the banks were determined not to see that situation become a precedent. In the subsequent round of negotiations with Chile, Venezuela, Argentina, and the Philippines, both sides made some concessions. Neither side attained their maximal objectives, which led to a continuation of the *modus vivendi*; yet once again, events pushed the problem into a new phase.

In February 1987, Brazil stopped servicing most of its bank debt. Although this by itself was not unprecedented, the suddenness of the move, as well as the subsequent freezing of trade and interbank lines, was unprecedented. Also unlike conditions in the past, the interest payments were not resumed within 90 days, which obliged U.S. banks to stop accruing income on almost all of their Brazilian portfolio.

Since May 1987, many U.S., British, and Canadian banks have announced major additions to their provisions for doubtful loans, mostly against their exposure to rescheduling countries. The increased provisions do not mean that a part of the rescheduling debt is either written off or forgiven; they simply provide the lenders with greater flexibility to respond to subsequent developments, whether they are negative or positive.

WHERE DO WE GO FROM HERE?

Although the rescheduling countries will undoubtedly require more money, capital by itself will not be the answer. These countries have already received great amounts of money; the years following the oil shocks of 1974 and 1975 saw an unprecedented transfer of resources from the First World's private sector to the Third World. This was widely applauded at the time, often by the same people who now accuse bankers of having thrown too much money at the rescheduling countries. The fact of the matter is that many countries (mainly in Asia and some in Europe) have used the money borrowed well, while most of the ones now rescheduling their debts did not, certainly not well enough to withstand the post–1981 economic developments (which many other developing countries rode out successfully).

For the future, it seems essential that the rescheduling countries analyze and, as much as possible, emulate the successful developing nations. Most of these are in Asia, but Turkey, Portugal, and perhaps Hungary, might also serve as useful examples. Although these countries have all taken different paths to development, they have all adopted an outward-looking and more or less market-oriented stance. Instead of complaining about the vagaries of fortune, they have successfully sought to exploit and master change.

Having said this, however, one must not underestimate the difficulties and complexities inherent in structural reform programs. The required measures, such as greater scope for the private sector, some personal and economic liberty, reasonably levied and collected taxes, sensible fiscal and monetary policies, relatively free capital markets, etc., in many rescheduling countries fly in the face of centuries of tradition. For these states, genuine structural reform will require major changes in their philosophical, economic, political, and social orientation. This will be traumatic for some and delicate for all. The process will not always be successful, if only because change often makes for instability, and it will certainly take time. The debt problem will be with us for many years even if all goes well.

However, if everything is to go well, it will take more than money from the lenders and structural reforms by the debtors. The governments of the First World must play their part, for reasons of both national interest and global responsibility.

In addition to the usual prescriptions for more foreign aid, export cover, support for multilateral institutions (and these are important), it is essential that the rescheduling countries' exports have full access to the markets of the First World. This is vital, because the countries that have developed successfully could not have done so without exports. Exporting was important both as an engine for economic growth and as a stimulus for adopting the foreign (that is, new) ideas, which eventually resulted in political modernization. Unfortunately, today we are seeing too many signs of a resurgent protectionism on both sides of the Atlantic. If these evolve into a trend, the rescheduling countries will be obliged to turn even more inward. If they do so, over time the subsequent debt crisis will seem to be only one of the secondary consequences of a new global alignment.

Creditor country governments should also do more to recognize the vital role played by their banks in maintaining the stability of the rescheduling countries. Doing so was very much a matter of self-interest for the banks at the beginning of the problem in 1982, but it is becoming progressively less recognized. Even before this year's headlines, many banks (especially European ones) had already written down or provided against their exposure to rescheduling countries; still others had decided to do nothing more voluntarily with them. If this trend continues, in the coming years there will be few players left and the governments of the First World will have to deal with a major foreign policy crisis, instead of a "mere" banking problem. To avert that possibility, they should be doing a great deal more for their banks through relevant and useful regulatory and tax policies. So far, there has been very little action on this score.

Instead, in the United States at least, we recently have seen a number of proposals from congressional and academic circles to solve the debt problem through varying degrees of debt forgiveness and/or interest rates below the lenders' cost of funds. These ideas seem to be motivated by the following: (1) a desire to somehow punish the banks for having lent to the rescheduling countries; (2) a desire to help the rescheduling countries on eleemosynary grounds; and (3) the fact that domestic concerns are most often expressed as a desire to improve the U.S. balance of trade through increased exports to Latin America. In this context, interest payments by the rescheduling countries are seen as a barrier to greater imports, and it is assumed that if they would pay less interest to the banks, they would import more American industrial and agricultural goods.

As a banker, I find it somewhat difficult to address the first element of this line of thinking. No doubt, with the benefit of hindsight, bankers now wish that they had identified today's "problem countries" earlier. On the other hand, given that almost all sizeable banks in the wealthier countries became lenders, it may be also argued that the present situation is as much the result of unforeseeable external variables as of faulty analysis. In point of fact, banks made the right decisions vis-à-vis almost all of the Asian and two-thirds of the European countries. Today, actions against the banks may make some people feel good—money lenders have never been popular anywhere—but as a solution to the debt problem this is a non sequitur. It is, however, an emotional component of a political equation and, as such, it should not be underestimated.

In regard to the other two elements, however, the proposed remedies will be almost certainly counterproductive; they will worsen the plight of those they are intended to help. Specifically, lending at a rate that is below the banks' cost of funds, over an extended period of time, is simply incompatible with providing new money. The cash-flow effects for the rescheduling countries, which will pay less interest instead of borrowing more money to pay a market interest rate, may be the same; but the lower-than-market rates could cost them their still extensive, short-term trade lines. That, in turn, will have a very negative effect on their cash flow and would, of course, also oblige them to reduce their imports from the lending countries. Perhaps, a few countries could operate on a "cash" basis, but this is unlikely to be a viable option for most.

Forgiving some principal would have symbolic impact but, again, would do little for the rescheduling countries' cash flow. As the rescheduling states have made virtually no principal payments, any principal forgiven will save them only the cost of interest on the forgiven portion. In the context of most of the proposals floated so far, this would not amount to much. It would however, compromise both their continued access to trade credits, as well as any future access to long-term loans from the banks for a very long time.[5]

In effect, this would be a reversion to the status quo before 1971, when today's rescheduling countries could look only to the multilateral development banks and to the export credit agencies for their term credit requirements. These institutions do not, and probably will not, have the resources to meet these needs. The leaders of the heavily indebted middle-income countries understand this reality, which has been one of the strongest underpinnings of the current rescheduling process.

In addition, both of the contingencies just described would have a chilling effect on banks' willingness to lend to countries not now rescheduling, but having some vulnerability to adverse economic or political developments. That effect, in turn, could force them into illiquidity, with again negative effects on their people and their ability to import from the developed countries.

Another factor to consider is that if banks lend at below-market rates and/or forgive (and charge off) debt, their capital base will be reduced. Since in many countries, including the United States, the amount a bank may lend depends on the size of its capital, a lower capital base inhibits banks' ability to grow and to lend more. Pressures on capital will also increase the banks' risk aversion and thus reduce their inclination to lend to the more vulnerable domestic market segments, such as heavy industry, agriculture, etc. If, in the worst of all worlds, the banks are somehow obliged to take hits, reduce their rates on existing debt, and lend new money at below-market rates, then, depending on the numbers, lending to the rescheduling countries could require a reduction in exposure to existing customers elsewhere.

In view of these points, it should be clear that converting the outstanding rescheduling debt into a transfer payment (whether at once or over time) from the First to the Third World will not be in anyone's true interest.

Today, the debt problem is at a crossroads. In June 1987, many banks signaled through the Institute of International Finance that they cannot continue to serve as lenders of last resort to the rescheduling countries. They also indicated, however, that they are willing to remain engaged in the Third World if: (1) they can at least begin to revert to their traditional role of financing trade and productive investment; (2) they are taken more seriously by the Bretton Woods institutions and their own governments; and (3) if there is evidence that the highly indebted middle-income countries are adopting policies that are clearly aimed at restoring business confidence and a viable international financial position.[6]

In the absence of some or all of these conditions, more and more banks are now beginning to conclude that recognizing losses is preferable to throwing good money after bad loans.[7] It remains to be seen whether this attitude will survive the next round of rescheduling negotiations, but it is a major change from the approach of the earlier years.

Clearly, there are no instant cures here and there are many pitfalls. However, recent history demonstrates that countries can regain market access, and the fundamentals of many of today's debtor countries are actually better than those of Asia's success stories. Financial engineering centered around debt-equity conversions and securitization has immense possibilities, provided these vehicles are welcomed by the debtor countries. In this context, the increased provisions of banks could serve as an enormous reservoir of capital for productive investments.

We will very soon find out whether the problem takes a turn for the better or the worse. The choice is almost entirely up to the debtors because the banks have virtually no concessions left to make if they are to remain engaged on a meaningful scale with the rescheduling countries. Consequently, we must hope that the borrowers, the multilateral development banks, and the creditor governments will try to build on the successes of the present process and thus enable the banks to continue to play a constructive role.

NOTES

1. G. P. Szego, "The Role of International Banking in the 'Oil Surplus' Admustment Process," *Journal of Banking and Finance* 7, no. 4 (December 1983), p. 512. The surpluses were very large. The annual oil export income of oil-producing states increased from $35 billion in 1972 to $112 billion in 1974. These were enormous numbers in the context of that period.

2. H. Peter Gray, *International Trade, Investment, and Payments* (Boston: Houghton Mifflin Company, 1979), p. 626.

3. "Syndicated Loan Rankings," *Euromoney*, February 1981, p. 42.

4. Irving S. Friedman, *The World Debt Dilemma: Managing Country Rise* (Washington, D.C.: Council for International Banking Studies; Philadelphia: Robert Morris Associates, 1983), p. 19.

5. Chairman of the Federal Reserve Paul A. Volcker to Senator Bill Bradley, November 5, 1986. Also see: David C. Mulford, "The International Debt Situation: Toward Stronger Growth, Trade, and Financial Stability" (Washington, D.C.: U.S. Treasury press release, 1987). There are a number of other public pronouncements by bankers and senior government officials to support this view.

6. Institute of International Finance, Inc., "Restoring Market Access—New Directions in Bank Lending" (Washington, D.C.: Institute of International Finance, Inc., 1987), p. 2.

7. "Thump, A Debtors' Triumph It Is Not," *The Economist*, May 23, 1987.

4

MEXICO: PRESSURES FOR RESTRUCTURING

Susan Kaufman Purcell

Not long ago, Mexico's economy was regarded as one of Latin America's greatest success stories. Throughout the 1950s and 1960s, it grew an average of 6 to 8 percent annually, one of the highest rates in the world during that period. The growth was not only in agriculture, extractive industries, and services, as was true of many developing countries; Mexico became one of a small group of Third World nations with a relatively large manufacturing sector.

The Mexican peso was one of the most stable currencies in the world. The exchange rate established by the 1954 devaluation remained in force until the 1976 devaluation. Inflation, which today averages about 130 percent, was virtually nonexistent during the 1950s and 1960s. Confidence in the economy and in the peso was reinforced by the absence of exchange controls and the free convertibility of pesos into dollars. In response to these conditions, foreign investment in the Mexican economy grew rapidly, with most major multinational corporations establishing subsidiaries in Mexico during this period.

This stable and growing economy helped keep Mexico one of the most politically stable countries of the hemisphere. Unlike other Latin American countries, which are characterized by repeated and often violent alternations between civilian and military governments, Mexico enjoyed continuous civilian rule under a dominant political party. High levels of economic growth also enabled Mexico to avoid the conflicts that otherwise would have been generated by the growing gap between the rich and poor. As long as everyone experienced an absolute improvement in standard of living, the government did not have to risk making politically difficult decisions to redistribute wealth from the "haves" to the "have nots." Economic growth also made it possible to accept delays in the gratification of desires; people had confidence in the future and believed that their turn would eventually come.

Signs of trouble, however, began to surface as early as the late 1960s. Initially, economic growth had been intimately linked to a highly protectionist economic development model. "Import-substitution industrialization" aimed for the creation of a domestic industrial economy by protecting or isolating weak or new Mexican producers from international competition by means of high tariffs, import duties, government subsidies, and similar policies. The assumption was that once Mexican industry was developed to the point where it could successfully withstand foreign competition, these barriers could and would be removed.

Mexico never reached that stage. Both the government and the private sector became so accustomed to cooperating in their "alliance for profits" that neither was able to wean itself from the relationship. The government liked being able to depend on business leaders following its lead and accepting its priorities, which were often political rather than economic. For its part, the private sector enjoyed a protected and captive domestic market and consequent large profits.

The arrangement worked well enough for some years, but by the late 1960s, it was beginning to take its toll on agriculture, which until then had been a principal source of foreign exchange. As a result of having to rely increasingly on domestic inputs that were expensive and inferior to imported ones, agricultural exports became uncompetitive in the external market. At the same time, government policies to control domestic food prices for political reasons discouraged expansion of production. As the population continued to grow, consumption rose, reducing the amount of foodstuffs available for export. It became necessary either to generate more resources to satisfy the demands of the population, or to control or decrease such demands without undermining the peace of the ruling party.

By 1970, however, even the continued stability of the Mexican political system was in doubt. In 1968, a student demonstration in favor of a more open and democratic political system had ended in the so-called Tlatelolco Massacre, during which the Mexican army opened fire on thousands of Mexican demonstrators, killing at least several hundred, mainly youths. This incident greatly undermined the already weakened legitimacy of Mexico's "revolutionary" political system, raising questions about whether the tried and true ways of maintaining political peace were still effective.

The president elected in 1970, Luís Echeverría Alvarez, had been the minister of government during the Tlatelolco Massacre, a position that gave him some responsibility for the killings. In an effort to increase his own support, as well as that for the political system in general, he

skipped an entire political generation, appointing to office young technocrats who either had close ties to the student movement or strongly
sympathized with its goals. Their solution for the economic and political
problem involved vastly increasing government spending, both to spur
economic growth and to ensure that the fruits of the anticipated prosperity would benefit disadvantaged groups. "Stabilizing development,"
the economic strategy in force until then, had emphasized growth over
equity. The assumption had been that resources would automatically
trickle down to the poor. However, by 1970, with economic growth
slowing and the population increasing, the poor were faced with the
prospect of a declining, rather than improving, standard of living. The
Echeverría administration therefore opted for a strategy of "shared development." Henceforth, the state would emphasize equity as well as
growth by implementing policies that would channel a greater share of
economic gains to Mexico's lower classes.

It was a good solution except that it committed the government to
spending resources it did not have. The obvious solution, to increase
taxes on the rich, who contributed a relatively small portion of their
wealth to the government, failed. Not only the rich, but just about
anyone with something to lose, including government officials, opposed
tax reform. The administration then resorted to domestic and foreign
borrowing and inflationary spending.

In order to restore the "revolutionary" legitimacy of the political order
and offset increasing private sector resistance to government policies,
Echeverría encouraged greater militancy by trade unions and attacked
foreign investors and domestic businessmen for exploiting the country.
As conflict increased and confidence in the administration's policies
evaporated, capital flight began. The government was forced to devalue
the Mexican peso twice.

Echeverría's growing frustration led him to expropriate vast tracts of
private agricultural land in the final weeks of his administration and to
give them to landless peasants. This action triggered rumors of a military
coup for the first time in recent Mexican history. The president's attempt
to spend his way into growth and equity had clearly failed by 1976,
when José López Portillo succeeded him.

The new president had a conciliatory approach and seemed to promise
a return to normalcy. Yet his administration coincided with a period of
skyrocketing international oil prices and the discovery in Mexico of vast
petroleum reserves. This allowed President López Portillo to continue
the failed policies of his immediate predecessor. Unlike Echeverría, however, López Portillo had access to huge oil reserves.

The vast oil reserves led López Portillo to adopt a more grandiose
plan. He decided to use Mexico's oil to borrow additional capital in order
to transform Mexico from a developing to an industrialized country

during his six-year term. At the time, the strategy made some sense. Everyone expected petroleum prices to continue to rise well into the 1980s. The international ennvironment seemed favorable in other ways as well. High rates of inflation abroad meant that debts could be repaid in the future with greatly inflated dollars. In addition, low interest rates, combined with inflation, meant that the funds could be borrowed at negative interest rates. Finally, commercial bankers were lining up to lend Mexico money in an attempt to reinvest billions of petrodollars that Arab governments had placed on deposit.

For a few years, all went well. Huge new investments were made in roads, ports, and industries such as oil and steel. The economy boomed, hundreds of thousands of new jobs were created, and there was unprecedented spending in education and health. Unfortunately, the increase in available resources also translated into an astronomical increase in waste and corruption.

In 1981, however, the international context changed dramatically. Oil prices began to decline, in response to the economic recession that hit the United States and other industrialized nations. The efforts by oil-consuming nations to reduce their consumption of petroleum also began to produce results. The Mexican president, believing that the decline in oil prices was temporary, refused to adjust Mexican oil prices downward in conformity with the new market price. Instead, he decided to replace the country's lost oil revenues with foreign borrowing.

Imports continued to surge in response to the government's refusal to devalue the peso. At the same time, the growing belief that a major devaluation was unavoidable and probably imminent produced billions of dollars in capital flight. This situation forced the government increasingly into short-term borrowing at ever-higher interest rates. Unlike earlier loans, this new borrowing had no productive rationale but was used to plug the growing gap between government income and expenditures.

Such borrowing could not continue indefinitely. By August 1982, Mexico could not obtain enough loans to service the existing debt and ran out of money. With his term drawing to a close and his dreams in ruins, López Portillo made a desperate attempt to stem capital flight and refurbish his historical image by nationalizing the Mexican banking system. His action did neither. Like his immediate predecessor, he left it to his newly elected successor, Miguel de la Madrid, to find a solution to the increasing disintegration of Mexico's economic and political systems.

President de la Madrid's initial approach to the problem did not differ greatly in its goal from that of his two immediate predecessors. Like them, he set about trying to close the yawning gap between government income and expenditures. Unlike them, however, de la Madrid could not depend on foreign loans to bridge the gap, since private commercial banks were ill-disposed to lend money to Mexico, other than to help the nation service its approximately $85 billion debt. Nor could de la Madrid depend on oil reserves. Petroleum prices plummeted, from approximately $40 a barrel when he first took office to $10 a barrel in 1986.

De la Madrid was compelled to implement a program of economic austerity. He first purged the government of the big spenders who had occupied key positions under previous administrations and promoted young technocrats who supported the need to reduce government spending. Their initial target was government imports, which had surged during the oil boom years. De la Madrid also announced plans to reduce government expenditures by decreasing the number on the state payroll, selling off or closing costly state-owned enterprises, and reducing government subsidies to all groups. These policies allowed Mexico to begin rebuilding its reserves, as well as to attract fresh infusions of capital from the International Monetary Fund. The improvement in its economic situation then allowed Mexico to begin slowly opening its economy once again to foreign trade.

The gradual improvement in Mexico's economic situation during the first years of his administration encouraged President de la Madrid to experiment with some political reforms as well. The immediate problem was how to restore confidence in the PRI and, by extension, rebuild the legitimacy of the political system as a whole. Corruption and the antidemocratic nature of Mexico's one-party dominant political system had been the focus of repeated and growing criticism, particularly by the middle class. The answer was an anticorruption campaign and a democratic opening.

The government, however, grossly underestimated the political risks of both policies. Corruption was so pervasive throughout the political system that a genuine effort to eradicate it could divide and weaken Mexico's political class. The combination of a sick economy and a divided political elite could ultimately undermine the stability of the entire political system. However, after promising to rid the system of corruption, President de la Madrid had to take some steps in this area, including the arrest of the former head of Petróleos Mexicanos (PEMEX), Jorge Díaz Serrano.

On the electoral front, the president's support for free and fair elections backfired. The administration had apparently believed that its responsible handling of the economy in the aftermath of the August 1982 crisis and the signs of some improvement in Mexico's economic situation would translate into continued support for the PRI. Instead, the main opposition party, the Partido de Acción Nacional (PAN), won 12 important mayoralty contests in cities along Mexico's northern border during the 1983 elections. Badly burned, the government decided to terminate the brief experiment until the economy improved enough to increase support for the PRI at the polls.

Increasingly, however, the government saw its options narrowing. By 1984, the population was living through its third year of economic austerity. Per capita income continued to decline and unemployment to increase, as nearly one million persons entered the labor force each year. Long an important power base of the PRI-dominated political system, organized labor was hard hit by the combination of inflation, growing unemployment, and government policies that tried to keep wage increases below the inflation rate.

The administration also was concerned by the increasing alienation from the PRI of the middle class. Until the onset of Mexico's economic problems, the great beneficiary of the Mexican Revolution had been the middle class, but it lost the most in relative terms after August 1982. For this, it blamed the PRI and particularly, the administrations of Presidents Echeverría and López Portillo. Middle-class discontent was centered mainly in urban areas, especially Mexico City and in the prosperous northern states along the border with the United States. The north had long been a PAN stronghold. Unless something could be done to improve the economic prospects of the middle class, there was some danger that it might become permanently lost to the PRI.

Urban areas in general had become a source of worry for Mexico's political leaders. Although Mexico had become an overwhelmingly urban country with a sizable middle class by the time de la Madrid took power, the PRI's best organization constituents remained as they had been since its founding in 1928, the peasantry and organized labor. Little thought or effort had been given to incorporating the growing urban massive cities into the PRI.

The increasing political costs led the government to relax its austerity program in 1984. However, the relief generated by the loosening of the government's tight rein on the economy proved temporary. Inflation rapidly increased and the economy did not revive. A more drastic solution to Mexico's problems seemed in order.

Repudiation of Mexico's debt from the beginning had seemed to be an attractive way out of its dilemma, at least for the more left-wing groups within the ruling coalition. This was a potentially risky course that could increase, rather than solve, Mexico's difficulties, particularly if Mexico were to act without the support of other major debtors. Neither Brazil nor Argentina was prepared to take drastic action in 1984. Nor, for that matter, was President de la Madrid.

Until 1985, the president's top advisors still generally believed that the country's economic health could be restored by reducing government expenditures. By 1985, however, they concluded that Mexico could no longer hope to prosper by isolating itself from the international economic environment and focusing almost exclusively on producing for a captive domestic market. Instead, the Mexican economy would have to become more export oriented. To do this, it would have to become more productive and efficient if its products were to compete successfully on the open market.

Even before 1985, the government had taken a number of steps that led in the direction of greater efficiency and economic openness. Import licenses had been gradually removed, tariffs had been reduced, foreign investment had been made to feel more welcome, and a number of state enterprises had been sold to the private sector or closed down. However, these had been ad hoc decisions rather than part of a carefully thought out change in development strategy. Once the decision was made to change course in 1985, the de la Madrid administration stepped up its efforts in all these areas.

Mexico's decision to enter into the General Agreement on Tariffs and Trade (GATT) in 1986 symbolized its new commitment to a more open economy. Its more realistic exchange rate policy was another indication. Even when oil prices plummeted to $10 a barrel in 1986, giving Mexico an excuse to depart from its difficult readjustment process, the de la Madrid administration held its course. Its decision paid off, as Mexico began to steadily increase its nontraditional exports and wean itself from dependence on petroleum exports.

In the political sphere, a similar evolution in thinking took place. As the de la Madrid administration began to realize that an economic restructuring was needed, it also became evident that a more profound effort at political reform was also necessary.

It is true that many of the immediate political problems could be solved by a resumption of economic growth and the restoration of a sense of optimism regarding Mexico's economic future. In the meantime, there were ways of offsetting the supposedly temporary loss of political support. At worst, these included blatant electoral fraud, as in a number of gubernatorial elections during 1985 and 1986 in important northern states. At best, they involved selecting more qualified candidates, with stronger bases of local support, to run on the PRI ticket.

Yet none of these ad hoc changes dealt with the more difficult issue of political liberalization. The administration argued that democratization had become an important issue only because of the economic crisis and would recede once economic growth was restored. By 1985 or so, it also came to realize that some degree of democratization was necessary in and of itself, if the political system were to retain support and regain legitimacy among Mexico's urban citizens.

The 1983 debacle, when the administration had suddenly allowed completely free elections in the north that resulted in an unprecedented sweep of PAN victories, had taught the government an important lesson. It was not feasible to move from a relatively closed to a completely open electoral process overnight. Instead, it was necessary to carefully lay the groundwork for a gradual transition to a more democratic system. Toward this end, the administration took steps to decentralize political power.

For example, the resources available to the states were approximately doubled. The PRI also instituted intraparty primaries at the local level, a first step toward increasing public participation in the selection of candidates for public office.

The de la Madrid administration has not chosen to liberalize the political system because it wishes to hand over the presidency to an opposition party. Its underlying assumption is that reforms will strengthen the PRI and enable it to retain control. The PRI's failure to respond to long-standing demands for greater democracy had begun to erode its support among key groups. By responding to demands for greater popular participation in the selection of party leaders and elected officials, the PRI hopes to win the loyalties of new generations of Mexicans.

It is far from certain that the economic and political reforms being implemented by President de la Madrid will be continued by his successor. Even if the candidate is personally committed to carrying through the reform process, there are many groups and individuals within Mexico with a vested interest in the traditional economic and political system. Their ability to turn back the political and economic clock will grow if the steps that the administration is taking to revive the economy do not restore faith in the country's economic future. In addition, since external events can have a great impact on Mexico's economy, to an important extent the success or failure of the administration's economic strategy depends on developments over which it has little or no control.

Economic liberalization mainly benefits Mexico's most efficient or export-oriented industries. Included in this category are the mining and petroleum industries; most privately owned agricultural enterprises, particularly those in northern Mexico; and the textile industry. Subsidiaries of large multinational corporations generally, but not always, fit this characterization better than do smaller, wholly Mexican-owned, firms. Some sectors of the communications industry also have major markets abroad, while banks and other industries in the service sector are intimately linked to the international economy.

Businessmen, workers, and government officials involved in these industries will benefit from a continuation of President de la Madrid's efforts to further liberalize the economy. The coalition in favor of economic liberalization, which is still far from consolidated, therefore cuts across class lines and usually across regional ones as well. Those who oppose a continuation of the reforms begun by President de la Madrid, in contrast, are most tied to industries oriented toward the domestic market or toward those parts of the government that have little to do with foreign trade or investment. This coalition, which also is multiclass, is fighting to stem the rapid deterioration in its power and importance since President de la Madrid took office.

Within the PRI, there is a similar split, although it is not wholly correlated with economic interests. Some of the division is based on ideology. On one side are those who support economic and political reforms such as those begun by President de la Madrid. On the other are those who believe that Mexico needs strong state involvement in the economy to maintain the dominance of the PRI and to ensure social justice. They distrust private enterprise and "the magic of the market." They want the political system to remain strongly centralized in Mexico City. They tend to favor politicians over technocrats and believe that populism still has a place in modern Mexico. They are also highly nationalistic, which means anti-American, at least in their rhetoric.

Recently, members of this latter group have organized themselves into the so-called "corriente democrática" or democratic current, headed by Porfirio Múnoz Ledo and Cuahtémoc Cardenas. They are highly critical of the continuation of undemocratic practices within the PRI, particularly the selection by the incumbent president of his successor. They are demanding, instead, that the PRI choose the party's presidential candidate in an internal primary.

Despite its name, the corriente democrática is not more democratic than those who oppose it. Instead, the two groups favor different kinds of democratization. The corriente wants internal competition within the PRI to select de la Madrid's successor because it opposes the administration's economic policies and believes that they have generated substantial opposition. The corriente, which groups together old "Echeverristas" as well as officials from the López Portillo administration, would like to return to the populist, statist, more social justice-oriented and big-spending policies of the pre-de la Madrid period; it believes most party members, many of whom have been displaced by the technocrats, feel the same.

Those who are against the corriente are not necessarily opposed to greater internal democracy, but do not want the process to begin at the presidential level. If de la Madrid's successor is chosen by the party rather than by the outgoing president, one of the corriente's leaders could be named, leading to the reversal of many of de la Madrid's reforms. In addition, a sudden change in the process of choosing Mexico's next president could prove conflictual and destabilizing, particularly during a period of severe economic hardship.

Instead of democratizing the presidential selection process, therefore, opponents of the corriente would prefer to begin the experiment with greater party democracy at the lowest levels of the political system and work their way upward. To accede to the corriente's demands at this time, they believe, would not only condemn Mexico to a lower standard of living, but could also ultimately undermine or destroy the PRI as well.

The importance and impact of the corriente democrática, or a similar group that may develop, will be directly dependent on the success or failure of de la Madrid's economic restructuring efforts. If the attempt to liberalize the Mexican economy starts producing steady, although not necessarily spectacular, growth; if nontraditional exports continue to find international markets; if capital flight ends, and new investment capital begins to enter Mexico, then confidence in Mexico's economic future will begin to be restored. This will reduce the potential for political conflict, as once again Mexicans would focus on eventually obtaining a piece of an expanding pie instead of competing with each other for a share of a shrinking one.

The future performance of the Mexican economy depends to a large degree on how well President de la Madrid and his advisors perform during the final year of this *sexenio*. Traditionally, it is a period of tempting opportunities to engage in demagogic and irresponsible behavior in order to secure one's place in history and build a popular support for the PRI in the upcoming presidential election. To date, there is little evidence that President de la Madrid will mimic the unfortunate behavior of his two predecessors. His personality seems more stable and the economic and political situation of Mexico is under considerable greater control than was the case during the two earlier *sexenios*.

In fact, everything indicates that de la Madrid would like to go down in history as the president who began a successful transition toward a productive economic system and a more democratic political system. He therefore has nothing to gain by radically changing his behavior. Instead, he needs to use his final year in office to try and solve the economy's more intractable problems, such as triple digit inflation.

Whether external developments cooperate with his plans is another matter. The Mexican economy is still very dependent on oil, although less so than a few years ago. What Mexico needs is a stable oil price, so that the resources available to it will be predictable. A precipitous drop in oil prices, such as that which occurred in 1986, would strengthen pressures to depart from austerity measures. A spectacular increase in the price of oil, which seems unlikely, would also be unfortunate, since it would create pressures to abandon the restructuring of the economy and slip once again into an easy and dangerous overdependence on oil.

Mexico's economic revival also depends on the behavior of the international economy in general and on the U.S. economy in particular. Efforts to open the economy will be frustrated if the United States becomes more protectionist. The United States' willingness to cooperate with Mexico in seeking ways to constructively manage the debt can also be important. Mexico's economic revival will also be affected by the health of the U.S. economy. If there is growth north of the border, the chances for growth south of the border improve considerably.

Mexico has accomplished a great deal since the onset of the debt crisis in August 1982. Much remains to be done. If Mexico's next president is committed to continuing the economic and political restructuring begun by President de la Madrid, and if external developments are helpful, the debt crisis may turn out to have been the catalyst that enabled Mexico to make the difficult transition necessary for it to prosper during the remaining decades of the century.

5

THE MEXICAN CRISIS: A COMMENT

Clark Reynolds

The point made by Dr. Purcell that Mexico's debt crisis may become its salvation by forcing the imposition of long-overdue economic and political reforms is half true. It is rather like the comment that an obese person may be "saved" by a massive heart attack. The danger is that even though the attack might call attention to long-neglected health measures, the sudden imposition of diet and exercise could be fatal if applied without consideration of the underlying conditions that brought about the crisis in the first place.

Since 1982, the Mexican government has been imposing major adjustment measures on the economy, while attempting to maintain uninterrupted debt service, even during the oil price collapse of 1986. The results have been mixed. On the positive side there was a major reversal in the balance of payments from deficit to surplus, a slow recovery of private sector confidence, and a dramatic cut in the nonfinancial fiscal deficit. On the other hand, per capita output has stagnated, real wages have plummeted, and inflation continues to grow. Many fear that unless a long-overdue recovery of private investment takes place the cure could be worse than the illness. Yet the combination of tight credit markets and excess capacity of existing (import-substituting) enterprises discourages investment in more productive activities.

Part of the problem is attributable to the earlier success of the import-substituting industrialization strategy. Until the late 1960s, the Mexican model provided more than two decades of growth with political as well as economic stability. That stability was no accident, since the economic strategy was part of a broader social pact favoring private investors in import-substituting industries, while giving a share of the proceeds of those industries to the official unions and creating hope for a steady rise in output and employment to the population. There was a cost to the strategy, however. Support for the new industries drew on the gains from growth in the production of raw materials, primary products, and domestic goods, thus exacerbating the diminishing returns to investment in these sectors. The fiscal burden for the infrastructure of supporting rapid population growth and urbanization could not be met by tax policies under the old model, causing increased fiscal and trade deficits, inflation, and foreign borrowing. The debt was a symptom, rather than a cause, of the shortcomings of the old model.

Dr. Purcell does not make clear why the government was so reluctant to give up an economic program that had clear shortcomings. Echeverría's program of shared development was inhibited by his unwillingness to alter a time-proven model, because it would have meant introducing reforms in both the economic and political process for results that remained uncertain. Indeed, many of his advisors were pressing for just the opposite approach, involving increased state intervention in the economy and central planning. Instead of moving clearly in either direction, the president expanded the share of the state in a what remained a private mixed-enterprise economy, without fiscal reform and with considerable rhetoric against the property-owning class. As a result, private investment languished, which was compensated for by rising state expenditures financed by increased fiscal deficits and foreign borrowing.

By 1976, the incoming administration of López Portillo attempted belt-tightening and policy reforms, including undervaluation of the exchange rate and a reduction in the fiscal deficit. The announcement of new oil discoveries helped to reverse private sector expectations and to expand the scope for foreign borrowing on which the increased expenditures depended. As was pointed out, those expectations proved to be overly optimistic about rising oil prices and stable low real interest rates. No one anticipated that the United States would be able to reduce its inflation and energy import dependence, or that if it did, the results would come not from fiscal stringency but from a radical tightening of monetary policy with rising real interest rates and a domestic recession that would prove to have global consequences.

Dr. Purcell points correctly to growing doubts about the Mexican government's ability to accept economic reality by 1981. It should be emphasized that an important factor was exogenous shocks to oil prices and real interest rates, brought about by policies over which Mexico had no control. Yet it is true that the Mexican government proved stubbornly unwilling to adjust to those shocks in a timely manner. The politics of the presidential system inhibited an effective public critique of its policies, despite severe debates behind closed doors. Unfortunately this situation has changed very little since then, though during the de la Madrid administration, those with a better understanding of market forces had the president's ear in private.

Capital flight from an overvalued peso forced further increases in borrowing, pushing the country well past the limit of prudent indebtedness. Though many of the more thoughtful banks refused additional credit, others continued to solicit participations on Mexico's behalf. But López Portillo's apparent blindness to economic reality was more than a question of macroeconomic illiteracy or a disposition to listen to bad advice. It was also due to his unwillingness to pay a political price for full adjustment that might lose labor support and further tarnish the PRI's populistic credentials in an election year. As a result, the February 1982 devaluation and promises of fiscal stringency were immediately followed by a major government-supported wage hike.

Dr. Purcell treats the transition from López Portillo to de la Madrid too lightly, saying that the latter's "initial approach to the problem did not differ greatly in its goal from that of his two immediate predecessors." In fact, although both Echeverría and López Portillo began their administrations with attempts at greater fiscal and balance-of-payments stability, it was not until de la Madrid's presidency that any major effort at structural reform of the underlying economic system was attempted. While his predecessors brought about radical increases in the role of the state, fiscal deficits, and foreign borrowing, as well as domestic price controls, subsidies, and protection, de la Madrid worked against incredible political obstacles to reduce the public sector role, modify price distortions, and encourage increased international openness and competitiveness of the economy. He accomplished those goals while simultaneously attempting to service a debt incurred by his predecessors, reduce corruption, and increase political openness.

The crisis of 1982 certainly called attention to the need for long-overdue reforms. Yet flaws in the system had been recognized much earlier. The difference is that, before 1982, some of the more extreme advisors called for reforms in the direction of greater state control and central planning, while others urged policies favoring greater attention to market forces, private investment, a reduced role of the state, and fewer distortions in the economy. By 1982, it was evident to most that the state-led model had profound limitations, given the nature of the Mexican system and the realities of the world market. Even today, whatever the economic implications, a sharp move in either direction means a wholesale abridgement of the economic and social entente that served Mexico so well for so long. No one was willing to take that risk until the crisis of 1982 made it apparent that a new approach was essential and that it would have to be implemented as soon as possible, Mexican style.

Even since then, it has been difficult to change the system at its roots.

Although the PRI social pact had led to a gradual encrustation of power and privilege, in many respects it still seems to be working. While state-imposed distortions in the economy have acted increasingly as dead weight on productivity growth, the system remains impressive in terms of its institutional inertia, social self-control, and political allegiance. How else might one explain the willingness of so many millions to accept a drastic decline in real wages, massive exchange rate devaluation, economic stagnation, and triple digit inflation?

Restructuring had not occurred earlier because it meant overhauling a system that "worked" in many dimensions, albeit at a severe cost in terms of economic productivity, political pluralism, regional balance, and distributional justice. It is by no means clear that the debt crisis, which certainly has called attention to the underlying weakness of the economic model, will facilitate the restructuring process. Some reasons are as follows.

The debt itself permitted continued growth of an inefficient industrial structure into the 1980s, providing subsidies, protection, and state infrastructure for activities that could scarcely cover average variable costs after 1982. Today many of the plants erected during the debt-led boom of import substitution operate at a fraction of their capacity, and their managers face a slack domestic market, threats of increased import competition, and uncertainty about external demand. Meanwhile, the program of restructuring demands new investments along lines of unproven dynamic comparative advantage. Such investments require stable medium-term profit expectations without political and economic risk. Those profits will depend on imaginative new domestic and foreign marketing techniques, quality control, and access to capital and intermediate goods, technology, and credit at reasonable long-term rates, at the very time when capital markets are crowded out by the state, interest rates suffer from inflationary expectations, and tax policies are subjected to fiscal uncertainty.

The debt problem affects all of those areas. As a result, although the debt crisis has forced attention to policy reforms in the direction of adjustment and restructuring toward greater openness and economic efficiency, the debt itself stands in the way of investor response to those very policies by increasing economic risk. On the political side, the more democratization that the PRI allows, the greater the short-term political instability and uncertainty surrounding the policy regime, which is bound to affect investor perceptions of political risk. Both issues are implicitly raised in Dr. Purcell's paper but not explicitly addressed. One way out is for the United States to accommodate greater economic restructuring in Mexico, through the provision of stable access for its exports. That strategy will call for political reforms in Mexico which the United States must also accommodate, by a willingness to stand with its neighbor through a process that will at times appear uncomfortably populist, at other times uncomfortably authoritarian, and at all times uncomfortably nationalistic.

We must first appreciate how difficult it is for a country of 80 million people, with a per capita income one-eighth that of the United States, to change a system that has provided a considerable degree of stability and growth for so many decades, now that its economic structure requires a major overhaul and its society calls for more political participation. The current level of debt must be seen as a dark cloud hanging over expectations, even in the most optimistic scenarios. This can be partly offset by an accommodating role of the United States in an expanding economic partnership that allows for a unique and independent Mexican political system. Such accommodation will require a much more positive approach to the debt than is currently the case, in exchange for shared economic growth and social progress in both countries. The trade-off appears to be long-term development dividends against short-term interest payments. Dr. Purcell should be complemented for introducing issues that call for a major assessment of United States' policy towards Mexico.

6

LIMITATIONS OF MEXICAN DEBT-
BASED GROWTH

Robert E. Looney

PHASES OF MEXICAN DEVELOPMENT

Many observers trace the current debt crisis back to the administration of Luís Echeverría, who was in office from 1970 to 1976. Basic dilemmas in his economic policy included the desire to use fiscal policy to reform the social structure without creating an adequate tax base; the desire to raise exports while maintaining a fixed exchange rate in the face of accelerating inflation; the desire to strengthen public sector enterprises while trying to maintain their prices at unrealistically low levels; and striving for greater industrial efficiency under a policy of protectionism.[1] The result was that the public sector deficit expanded to 9.5 percent in 1976, and by 1976 Mexico's public foreign debt was $20 billion. These alternative means of supporting Echeverría's policy of shared development proved unsustainable, however; in 1975 the development strategy collapsed.[2]

José López Portillo, who was in office from 1976 to 1982, began his administration with an IMF stabilization program and a promise of structural change. Once the petroleum revenues began surging, however, attempts at stabilization were abandoned as López Portillo decided to spend his way out of trouble through a massively expensive development program. As the oil revenues increased, foreign borrowing also accelerated, and control over spending became increasingly lax.[3] Instead of cutting back expenditures in the wake of the 1981 decline in oil revenues (which reached only $14.5 billion instead of the $20 billion projected in the budget), the government continued its spending by even heavier foreign borrowing, mainly of a short-term nature. By the end of 1981, the public sector foreign debt jumped to $53 billion, of which $14.5 billion was scheduled for repayment in 1982.[4]

DEALING WITH THE DEBT

During the 1983–85 period, there was significant progress in lowering the relative value of the public debt.[5] The domestic public debt, after having increased 60 percent in real terms during 1982, fell 30 percent between 1983 and 1985, and the public sector deficit decreased from 18 percent of the GDP to 9.9 percent. Also during this period, foreign public debt, in relation to the GDP, fell from 43.9 to 40.6 percent. This reflects a decline in the growth rate of net borrowing, which fell from levels surpassing 7 percent of the GDP in 1981 to 3.1 percent in 1983, 1.5 percent in 1984, and 0.4 percent in 1985.

The country has also made important improvements in public finances, in trimming the size of government and increasing efficiency in public enterprises.[6] The largest part of the reduction in the fiscal deficit came from cuts in government spending on goods and services before interest payments; spending has declined almost 8 percentage points of the GDP since 1981. The system of state subsidies was also completely revised. Between 1982 and 1985, government transfers to public companies in real terms declined by 40 percent. Also, an effort has been made to reduce the gap between the general price levels for consumer goods and the prices of public goods and services, especially in energy. Subsidies on gas, electricity, mass transportation, and basic foods are being phased out.

To stop capital flight, the government has set interest rates well above the inflation rate. The authorities have created incentives for export-oriented companies and companies generating new jobs. They are also divesting many state-run firms.

On another front, the government has enjoyed some success in its debt-capitalization program.[7] Launched in June 1986, this program allows debt to be converted into capital by foreign investors. Conversion is authorized if the applicant can persuade the government that it will create new jobs, increase exports, or introduce advanced technology with its investment. Depending on the nature of the project, the debt is exchanged for pesos at 76 to 100 percent of face value. By late 1986, some $200 million in external debt had been converted under this system.

Debt-for-equity agreements amounted to $850 million in foreign investment in the last nine months of 1986. Primarily because of fears of inflation, the program ceiling for 1987 has been set at $1.5 billion.[8] Optimists contend that this program could liquidate 8 percent of Mexico's external debt and that the country, by offering discounts of 5 to 25 percent to foreign investors wishing to purchase shares in 55 state-run firms that currently face indebtedness and liquidity problems, could get rid of a major source of federal budgetary deficits.[9] It is not at all clear, however, that the program will make more than a token dent in the country's external debt.[10] At most, foreign bankers and Finance Ministry officials estimate the debt swaps will retire about $3 or $4 billion of Mexican debt.

Finally, by joining the GATT, the country hopes to increase trade with the United States, which already accounts for 60 percent of its total trade, and to expand and diversify trade with Europe. Major measures under the GATT agreement include:[11] (1) a protection system that relies primarily on tariffs, in contrast to the previous structure that relied mainly on import licenses; and (2) cutting maximum import tariffs from 100 to 45 percent in 1986 and 30 percent in 1988.

THE 1986 RESCUE PACKAGE

The 1986 crisis initiated widespread debate about the causes, consequences, and costs of the debt. A popular public point of view was that Mexico could not and should not have to face more years of harsh austerity to satisfy the IMF and commercial bankers, but more conservative elements of the Mexican government felt that it was critical that Mexico meet the demands of the IMF and obtain the loans necessary to avoid a default. Others argued that, although the loans were necessary, concessions should be made by the IMF and the international banking community. This faction maintained that Mexico had attempted to restructure its economy and had imposed austerity; the unfortunate collapse of oil prices in 1986, they insisted, should be a responsibility shared by the commercial banks and the international financial institutions.[12]

The rescue package called for the commercial banks to generate approximately $6 billion of new loans. The IMF and World Bank loans were contingent on the commercial bank loans being secured. This package also contained some concessions for Mexico. The World Bank agreed to provide additional credit if real economic growth was less than 3.5 percent in 1987. The IMF loan of $1.6 billion guaranteed additional credit if oil prices fell below $9 billion. In exchange for this jumbo loan package, the IMF required Mexico to continue to sell off and reduce the number of state-owned enterprises, to liberalize trade, to attract more foreign investment, and to reduce its domestic deficit by 3 percent of the GDP.

Critics charge that this package will only address the short-run problem of servicing immediate debt obligations. It will possibly get Mexico through 1987, assuming that the economy generates strong real growth, that oil prices stiffen or even increase, that the global economy continues to grow, and that interest rates do not rise—all questionable assumptions.

Critics assert that adding another $12 billion to Mexico's debt will merely increase the nation's long-term debt service obligations. More importantly, they argue that this loan package will not reverse the transfer of capital from Mexico to the developed nations. Instead it will merely perpetuate this negative flow. The critics also warn that it will simply draw U.S. banks further into the debt quagmire. Moreover, they argue that the Mexican people should not have to suffer through more years of austerity and a further decline in their already low standard of living.

CONCLUSION

It is apparent that when the new president takes office in late 1988, he must tackle the fundamental problem that has confronted the present administration as well as its predecessors: how to regain the high rates of growth that characterized the Mexican economy over the 1955–70 period. Since the early 1970s, successive governments have attempted to solve this dilemma by either exporting oil or increasing the country's external debt. Although there has been some progress in transforming the structure of the Mexican economy, there is little reason to believe that simply decreasing government expenditures will return the country to a self-sustaining high growth plan. As Castañeda notes, whatever policies are chosen, Mexico's next president will need all the foreign reserves and breathing room that can be obtained.

In terms of longer-run policies for dealing with the varied issues surrounding the country's external debt, the options appear to be default, a further variant of the current Baker-type stabilization program agreed to in March 1987, or a combination of these two.[13] The default option can probably be rejected out of hand for political reasons, although it is not apparent that from a purely economic viewpoint there would be any great costs (to Mexico) involved.[14]

Pragmatic Mexicans[15] realized some time ago that political and economic reforms need to be enacted before the country will be able to return to any type of growth path resembling that achieved in the 1955–70 period. Controls on capital flight, privatization of inefficient and corrupt state-controlled industries, a lowering of trade barriers, tax reform, and price controls have been instituted or are being considered.[16] It will be politically impossible to fully implement these reforms without a significant reduction and eventual elimination of the debt burden.

NOTES

1. Travier Márquez, "La Economía Mexicana en 1977 y su Futuro," mimeographed (Madrid: 1977).

2. For a complete account of this period see: Robert E. Looney, *Mexico's Economy: A Policy Analysis with Forecasts to 1990* (Boulder: Westview Press, 1978).

3. Robert E. Looney, "The Mexican Oil Syndrome: Current Vulnerability and Longer Term Viability," *OPEC Review* 4, Winter 1985, pp. 369–88. See also: Robert E. Looney, "Scope for Policy in an Oil Based Economy: Mexican Stabilization Policies in the 1970s," *Socio-economic Planning Sciences* 21:3, 1987, pp. 167–76.

4. An analysis of the events leading up to the 1982 crisis is given in Robert E. Looney, *Economic Policymaking in Mexico: Factors Underlying the 1982 Crisis* (Durham: Duke University Press, 1985).

5. *Wall Street Journal*, August 8, 1987.

6. *Wall Street Journal*, August 8, 1987.

7. In the Mexican case, debt swaps work this way: a foreign company buys Mexican government debt on the secondary international market at the usual discount (in 1987 this was about 55 cents to the dollar) and redeems it within Mexico for pesos. For the highest priority investment projects, defined as the purchase of state-run enterprises, the government will supply pesos at the loan's full face value. In the lowest ranking of the nine investment categories defined under the plan, Mexico will hand over the peso equivalent of 75 percent of the loan's dollar value. Most transactions approved so far have fallen under the third category, which gives a 92 percent rate for projects oriented toward exports or high technology, or projects that will be located in designated industrial development zones. Also included in this category is foreign equity participation in existing Mexican-owned enterprises. The pesos must be used for approved capital investment and not for import financing, foreign debt payment, or as a cheap source of local working capital. The pesos are paid out directly to the foreign investor's local suppliers, creditors, and contractors. Compare with: "How Debt Swaps Work," *Journal of Commerce*, December 16, 1986.

8. "Heels Dragged on Local Debt Swap," *Latin America Weekly Report*, July 16, 1987, p. 4.

9. "Mexico," *Latin America Weekly Review*, October 2, 1986, p. 2.

10. William Orme, "Debt-Equity Swaps as a Passing Mexican Fancy," *Journal of Commerce*, December 16, 1986.

11. *Wall Street Journal*, August 8, 1987.

12. John C. Pool and Steve Stamos, *The ABC's of International Finance* (Lexington: Lexington Books, 1987), p. 113 (hereafter cited as *ABC's*).

13. The more traditional IMF stabilization programs are dealt with in the following: Robert E. Looney and P. C. Frederiksen, "Feasibility of Alternative IMF-Type Stabilization Programs in Mexico, 1983–1987," *Journal of Policy Modeling*, October 1983.

14. See Anatole Kaletsky, *The Costs of Default* (New York: The Twentieth Century Fund, 1985); Arthur MacEwan, "Latin America: Why Not Default?," *Monthly Review*, September 1986, pp. 1–13.

15. See Jorge Castañeda, "Mexico's Coming Challenges," *Foreign Policy*, Fall 1986, pp. 120–160; Carl Migdail, et al., "Mexico is Going to Make It," *Washington Quarterly*, Winter 1986, pp. 171–186.

16. Pool and Stamos, *ABC's*, p. 117.

7

DEBT AND TRADE: A POSSIBLE LINK

Saúl Trejo-Reyes

GENERAL OVERVIEW

Half a decade of "muddling through" on the basis of purely financial
solutions, imaginative as many of them undoubtedly are, has shown
that the debt problem is more intractable than was initially thought.[1]
Even countries that have faithfully swallowed the bitter International
Monetary Fund (IMF) pill do not seem closer to a growth path compatible
with meeting their international obligations and satisfying the needs of
their own populations; the debt of developing countries only continues
to grow.

Public opinion in debtor countries has become unfavorable, especially
in its perception of payment, even under the milder conditions obtained
as a result of major reschedulings, as simply paying more in order to
maintain an international credit rating, which will enable the country to
obtain further credits to be used for debt service. Thus, legitimacy is
impaired, creating a serious long-term problem.

On the other hand, public opinion in some creditor countries still
largely considers debtor governments as sinners who must not only
repent their interventionist spendthrift ways, but also be converted to
free-market economics before they can hope to extricate themselves from
their current predicament. This attitude endures both in government
and financial circles, even though there is no country where this solution
has worked successfully, and despite the fact that Latin American debtors range from Chile and Argentina, which have accumulated the bulk
of their debts uner free-market policies, to Brazil and Mexico, which
have followed more statist policies.

As one writer has said, "America preached budget balancing, even as its own deficit ballooned. We touted the virtues of free trade, while blocking imports of sugar, steel and textiles, the foreign exchange lifelines of much of Latin America. We criticized overvalued exchange rates, while the value of our own currency soared."[2]

As a result of these conflicting viewpoints, the debt problem is increasingly viewed as a zero-sum game, where one side's gains are necessarily the other's losses.

The relationship between trade prospects and debt-service conditions has been repeatedly characterized as crucial by debtor countries. However, it has hardly been recognized by creditors. Neither creditor banks nor their respective governments have been willing to recognize the full implications of their oversight. The problem for the world economy is seen primarily as one of adjusting trade balances and capital flows between the United States and industrial exporters, especially Japan and Western Europe.[3]

For debtors, the need to service their foreign debt implies the generation of trade surpluses of suitable magnitude; this was not achieved by Latin America in 1983 and 1984. In the first year, the combined trade balance for the region was $25.4 billion, and new external payments were $34.9 billion. In 1984 the figures were, respectively, $35 billion and $37.6 billion.[4]

Under current debt-service payment schemes, high rates of inflation in debtor countries are inevitable, since the government's financial requirements imply a permanent pressure on available internal savings and on interest rates. The four-way tug-of-war between government, business, labor, and foreign creditors, for a share in gross domestic product (GDP) is the central element giving rise to high rates of inflation, despite the drastic contraction of public expenditure and economic activity during the last five years. Those high rates of inflation have a direct effect on all internal productive activities and all financial costs, public or private.

Although debt service has a high direct cost in terms of growth, its effect on the level of GDP and on the attractiveness of new investment is much greater. First, the level of aggregate consumption and demand is depressed due to the wage policies required by the adjustment program. Second, the level of interest rates and government's reduced level of expenditures make new investment opportunities for the domestic market much less attractive, as aggregate demand is reduced to a level that makes new investment unnecessary, or at best uncertain. Third, inflationary and exchange-rate prospects, coupled with a shortage of investment opportunities, mean that capital goes mainly into financial speculation or else leaves the country.

THE MEXICAN CASE

The fall of oil prices in early 1986 cost Mexico the equivalent of 40 percent of 1986 merchandise export earnings and made it all but impossible to continue "debt service as usual." Despite a marked increase of nonpetroleum exports, it has not been possible for the country either to resume growth on a permanent basis or to service the foreign debt, except through further increases in the total amount outstanding. Between the end of 1982 and mid–1987, debt rose from $84 billion to close to $100 billion. In 1986, the public sector deficit,[5] amounted to 15.7 percent of GDP, almost double its 1985 level, mostly as a result of the shortfall in petroleum earnings.

A comparison with previous levels of debt-service payments and growth shows that, given the high import elasticity of GDP, debt service directly reduces annual growth by at least 4 percentage points.[6] The effect of debt-service payments has been to transform expectations regarding future economic performance so completely that the average growth rate of GDP fell to zero for the five-year period considered.

The fact that nontraditional exports grew very rapidly raised protectionist pressures on the part of the United States, by far Mexico's largest trading partner. However, even the substantial results achieved meant that, in terms of total merchandise exports, Mexico was still far from its 1981 position in 1986.

MEXICAN DEBT-SERVICE REQUIREMENTS

Mexico cannot resume growth on a sustainable basis without both a reduction in debt-service payments and substantially increased exports. This strategy would allow for the resumption of growth and for increased income for domestic factors of production, which in turn would lead to further growth, without the danger of expansion being brought to a halt through a lack of foreign exchange for imports. In order to achieve such growth, net foreign exchange receipts would have to increase sufficiently to cover both increased import requirements and the replacement of foreign credits by export receipts, so that further increases in debt-service payments would be halted.

The amount of Mexico's foreign debt in mid–1988 will be on the order of $105 billion, which means a net interest burden of approximately $9–10 billion. This is the minimum size of the required current account surplus if one were to set as an objective the prevention of further growth in the total amount of foreign debt. Of course, to the extent that the actual surplus is smaller than $9 billion, the country would need to finance part of the interest burden through additional borrowing; this postponement of the problem will ultimately result in the need for a more drastic adjustment. There is also a growing unwillingness of banks to finance the country except on terms that are politically unacceptable since they require continued austerity and low growth.

One side effect of disruptions of the international economic system in the last few years has been a growing protectionism, which makes it clearly very difficult, if not impossible, for debtors to pay. As the president of Mexico stated recently: "If the world does not allow us to trade, then it cannot demand that we pay [debt service]."[7] Of course, commercial banks are increasingly reluctant, despite scoldings from the Treasury and the IMF, to increase their exposure. It has been pointed out that "even lower [interest] rates and healthy exports will not be enough."[8] Neither will it be possible to find mutually acceptable solutions if an effort is not made to break out of the ever-increasing concern with narrowly defined national interests. Fresh money to meet the interest bill is not the answer.

DIFFERENT TYPES OF PROPOSALS

Proposals for a solution to the debt quandary may be grouped into two broad categories: those that tend to favor debtors and those that favor creditors, although most actors recognize that any solution involves costs for all concerned. The issue here is that the losses are to be shared by both debtors and creditors.

Most solutions offered until now are basically of a financial nature. They have attempted to reduce the burden of debt service during an initial period, after which service payments will rise above their initial trajectory. The hope is, of course, that in the meantime the country's economic prospects, including its foreign-exchange earning potential, will have improved sufficiently to allow the larger payments to be made. The net present value of the future stream of payments after rescheduling may be smaller or larger than that under the initial conditions; that is, either the debtor or the creditors will come out ahead.

The possibility that a purely financial renegotiation will become the first step toward a successful growth recovery strategy depends on export prices and volumes, interest rates, and the growth and development of the debtors' economies. Growth of export income, as well as the lowering of international interest rates, are preconditions for the resumption of growth and thus for reducing the burden of debt service.

For the most part, until the present time adjustment has been effected through an extraordinary reduction in both imports and economic activity, constant currency depreciations, and occasional "maxi devaluations." Between 1981 and 1985, Latin American imports fell from $97.6 to $57.6 billion. This drastic reduction, of course, has affected exports of industrialized countries; in the case of Latin America, U.S. exports have decreased by 40 percent.[9] Thus, if debtors must continue to live under harsh adjustment policies, economic activity in advanced countries will continue to suffer, adding fuel to protectionist trends, and making international growth an increasingly elusive objective. Unless the problem is defined to include trade expansion and industrial restructuring on an international scale, it is not possible for debtors to continue paying debt service indefinitely. They cannot maintain social stability while suffering long-range stagnation and, in many cases, having to face the demands of rapidly growing populations and labor forces.

It is well to point out that it is not only debtors who often seem unwilling to implement the kind of restructuring prescribed by creditors and designed to increase their ability to pay. Creditor countries also seem reluctant to contemplate the policy changes that would foster trade deficits with debtors, which in turn would allow these countries to earn the foreign exchange needed to service their debts. Those trade deficits would have to come from buying the kinds of goods that debtors can export. The immediate problem to be faced here is that the kinds of goods that middle-income debtors are currently able to export are those produced by troubled sectors in the major industrial countries, what the EEC terms "sensitive industries." An additional consideration is that, at present, the United States and Europe are becoming increasingly protectionist as a result of their structural deficits, both with Japan and the Asian NICs, and within Europe, with West Germany.[10]

Helpful as recent debt reschedulings have been in postponing insolvency, they do not address the basic question of how debtors' service capacity will increase as a result of the mandated belt tightening. By addressing only the financial aspects of the problem, they constitute in essence zero-sum solutions. We seem to have reached the limit of the purely financial solutions.

The case of Mexico illustrates the difficulty of achieving a solution under current arrangements, as well as of the impact of the proposed payment alternative. The drop in oil prices early in 1986 means that, under current arrangements, even the best financial renegotiation of the debt is but a postponement of the problem, since public debt-service obligations impose a drastic reduction of profit expectations on any investment made in Mexico. The government must finance service payments from chronically insufficient tax receipts; this means high inflation and continued monetary instability. At the same time, the population, which was 68 million in 1980, is expected to reach at least 100 million by the year 2000, despite a fall in growth rates from 3.4 percent during the past decade to 2 percent in 1986. The labor force, in the meantime, will increase from about 27 million at the present time to 40 to 42 million in 2000.

A PROPOSAL FOR INTEREST PAYMENTS IN DOMESTIC CURRENCY

An alternative form of external debt repayment for debtor countries would consist of paying in local currency a substantial portion of the interest due on the debt owed to commercial banks, for a period of several years. The amount paid in local currency would be used by the creditor banks to set up new firms, either directly or through the sale of their local currency to foreign firms willing to invest in debtor countries. In such a case, banks would immediately recover additional amounts of foreign exchange. The new firms would export a substantial portion of their output to creditor countries, in order to generate the foreign exchange needed both for the payment of dividends and for the eventual resumption of debt-service payments on a conventional basis. Unlike other payment (or nonpayment) schemes, this would be a positive-sum solution.

This proposal addresses two other aspects of the debt problem: the need to increase debtors' payment capacity through exports and the global trade disequilibrium. One result of that disequilibrium is that Europe and the United States have adopted increasingly protectionist policies aimed at Japan and the Asian NICs, but which hamper efforts by debtors to raise their payment capacity. In this case, creditor banks and governments would have to take an active role in protecting the quality of their loan portfolios.

For Mexico, the large decrease in the amount of foreign exchange required for debt-service payments under a scheme linking trade opportunities and payment obligations would mean that the foreign exchange constraint would be relaxed and growth could resume. This strategy would contribute to a return of flight capital, as the economic and political outlook would be drastically improved. Growth, employment creation, and efficient integration to the world economy would follow.

NOTES

1. A recent study sets forth some 20 basic alternatives, from which a number of combinations may be made. The basic proposal developed in this article is briefly mentioned there. See C. F. Bergsten, W. R. Cline, and J. H. Williamson, *Bank Lending to Developing Countries: The Policy Alternatives* (Washington, D.C.: Institute of International Economics, 1985).

2. Jeffrey E. Garten, "Gunboat Diplomacy," *Foreign Affairs* 63, no. 3 (1984), p. 555.

3. See, for instance, a very lucid discussion of the needed adjustments in the American international position, which does not even consider the role of

developing countries' external debt: C. Fred Bergsten, "Economic Imbalances and World Politics," *Foreign Affairs* 65, no. 4 (Spring 1987).

4. CEPAL, *El Problema de la Deuda: Gestación, Desarrollo, Crisis y Perspectivas*, LC/G.1406 (SES.21/10, March 6, 1986), p. 38.

5. This is the economic deficit, measured in current prices. To this figure, one must add government's financial intermediation in order to arrive at its total use of resources.

6. The elasticity of growth of imports with respect to GDP over the period from 1970 to 1986 was approximately 1.9, due to the high levels of imports in the period from 1979 to 1982. If an assumption is made that the amounts paid in debt service during the period from 1982 to 1986 had been used for imports, rather than debt service, then those amonts of imports would have been sufficient to achieve at least a growth rate of GDP equal to the trend value observed during the 1970s, which was about 6.2 percent. In such a case, GDP in 1986 would have been 36 percent higher than its actual level. If fact, imports could have been 60 percent greater than their actual level in that year. Even with an elasticity of imports with respect to GDP of 1.7, which is substantially higher than the level of 1.4 observed empirically, 1986 exports would have been sufficient to sustain that level of GDP.

7. Miguel de la Madrid, *Excelsior* (Mexico City, July 31, 1987), p. 1.

8. William D. Rogers, "The United States and Latin America," *Foreign Affairs* 63, no. 3 (1984), p. 579.

9. U.S., Congress, Joint Economic Committees, "The Impact of the Latin American Debt Crisis on the U.S. Economy," May 10, 1986.

10. If, in fact, Japanese trade surpluses are structural, insofar as they are the result of the very high savings rate observed in Japan, then a global solution will require an even greater degree of adjustment in Japan. The relationship between Japan's savings rate and trade surplus is discussed in: Martin Feldstein, "American Economic Policy and the World Economy," *Foreign Affairs* 63, no. 5 (1985).

8

BRAZIL AND THE DEBT: SOCIAL COSTS

Riordan Roett

The debt is obstructing democratization in Brazil, making the poor poorer and creating pressures that threaten to erupt in social unrest. Unable to earn the foreign exchange needed to service the debt, Brazil has been forced to cut back on needed imports and to drastically cut domestic spending programs, particularly in the social area.

It is in the interests of the United States to help Brazil find a solution to the crisis, not only to regain lost moral authority but also to provide jobs and markets for the U.S. economy. However, rather than seek a comprehensive debt relief program for the third world, leaders of the industrialized countries decided to "muddle through" after 1982. No drastic policy initiatives were needed; Latin American debtor countries would work out their problems with their creditors, principally the private commercial banks, with the participation of the IMF and its traditional formula of domestic adjustment and austerity. Northern pundits and policymakers have argued that this plan was the only way to preserve the integrity of the international financial system. "Radical" solutions, they say, could begin an unraveling process that might prove impossible to stop. The annual industrial summit meetings have consistently ignored the pleas of Latin American leaders for a policy response to the debt crisis.

The choice seems to be between order or ethics. Decision makers from both North and South have chosen to maintain the integrity of the international economic system by sacrificing ethics, thus ignoring (or

The author is indebted to Mr. Richard S. Sacks for research assistance in preparing this chapter.

postponing indefinitely) social justice and equitable distribution. The way in which hemispheric leaders will resolve the "order versus ethics dilemma" will have profound political implications. Preserving order without ethics may prove impossible. The Latin American democracies that have made their debut during the last decade have shown amazing resilience to date, but how long the respresentative regimes will be able to maintain their legitimacy in the face of economic disintegration is uncertain.

THE POLITICAL FRAMEWORK OF THE DEBT

Although democratic regimes prior to the military takeover of 1964 had paid lip service to the needs of the poor, the military government had the resources, for the first time in Brazilian history, to begin to make progress on social issues. But the military ignored social and distribu-tional goals, making huge investments in infrastructure and capital goods industries. They argued that growth must precede development, or that they could not cut the pie before it was baked. Not everyone got a bigger slice of this larger economic pie, and social and economic ine-quities worsened.

The post–1964 authoritarian regimes put almost all political power in the hands of the executive, who was always a general. The Institutional Acts promulgated after 1964 effectively bypassed the 1946 constitution, which was itself replaced in 1967. During the early and mid–1970s, the authoritarian regime ignored even the figment of representative de-mocracy, under little pressure to do otherwise. If eliminating competitive politics was one pillar of the regime's policies, the other was wage repres-sion. The working class was denied its share in Brazil's rapidly expand-ing economy; and as the rich grew richer, the government paid less and less attention to social safety nets.

In 1974, two events occurred that provided the impetus for the *abertura* process. The first was the petroleum price increase that forced the Bra-zilian government to recognize its vulnerability. With growth under pressure, the government decided to keep the economy growing by borrowing money, which was cheap and readily available. Brazil was an excellent credit risk. Its potential was real and, perhaps, finally re-alizable. The second event was the inauguration of General Ernesto Geisel. Perhaps the most competent and creative of the military gov-ernments, Geisel's administration came to office with a game plan for political liberalization.

In January 1978, Geisel designated General João Figueiredo as his successor. Figueiredo implemented a wide-ranging political amnesty that permitted exiled enemies of the regime to return almost immediately to Brazil and participate actively in political life. Committed to political liberalization, Figueiredo had to contend with rapidly changing economic and political circumstances, such as the second petroleum price increase in 1979 and the growing militancy of the political opposition. Figueiredo and his principal advisors confronted a growing cacophony of societal voices as it became clear that the economy was a seriously overheated issue.[1]

By 1979, servicing the foreign debt absorbed about 67 percent of Brazil's export earnings. At first, a belt-tightening program of austerity appeared probable, but it did not have political or societal support. Antonio Delfim Netto, appointed planning minister in August 1979, finally announced austerity and other measures to bring the economy under control. The result in 1981 was a recession that continued into 1985. Foreign borrowing continued apace during this period. Brazil borrowed about $16 billion in new money in 1981 alone.

The crisis erupted in August 1982 with the case of Mexico. The following month, in Toronto, at the annual meeting of the IMF and the World Bank, Brazil received a shock; the country would get none of the $3.6 billion in new loans it had requested without an agreement with the IMF. As the economic situation deteriorated, Brazil had to act decisively to get the financial support it desperately needed. Bypassing Congress, the government decided in July 1983 to restrict salary increases for the next two years to a level 20 percent below the increase of the official cost of living. Other austerity measures were announced. A new letter of intent was negotiated with the IMF as a result of the July measures. The Figueiredo government prepared to enter the last phase of its negotiations with the private commercial banks, but the talks ended inconclusively during the final days of the last military government.

The tortured economic negotiations between Brazil and its creditors in 1982 and 1983 paralleled a series of dramatic political events. The Liberal Alliance, comprised of dissidents from the official party, PDS, joined the longtime opposition party, the PMDB in support of Governor Tancredo Neves for president. Senator José Sarney joined the ticket as the vice-presidential candidate, and in January 1985, the Neves-Sarney team won in the electoral college. The Democratic Alliance (the combined forces of the Liberal Alliance and the PMDB) emerged as a new force in national politics.[2] Yet when the new democratic government entered office, Brazil had no agreement with its creditors.

The political coalition that assumed power in March 1985 was aware that a social agenda is crucial for Brazil's future and of the link between the country's extreme and growing indebtedness and the fragility of its social and political systems. The Year 2000 Plan of Helio Jaguaribe and his colleagues, and the Cruzado Plan of February 1986, sought to tackle social questions as a way to protect and enhance the political *abertura*. However, the 1986 Cruzado Plan is now a defunct letter, and any plans for social change based on it are doomed. President José Sarney is now discovering that restoring the country's economic health while trying to shore up the political system and find social solutions for Brazil's poor is a complex task, if not an impossible one.

THE SOCIAL FRAMEWORK OF THE DEBT

The new government, which would first experience the trauma of Neves' death on April 21, 1985, inherited two problems that the Figueiredo regime had not touched. The first was the debt crisis and its implications for Brazilian development. The second was the dramatic evidence that the state of society had deteriorated as badly as the economy.

One measure of the social crisis in Brazil is income distribution, which in Brazil has always been skewed against the poor. One study indicated that, between 1960 and 1980, the poorest 20 percent of population fell from 3.9 to 2.8 percent of the national income.[3] The economic "miracle" benefited Brazilians in direct relationship to their social class. The higher on the pyramid, the more likely they were to participate in the growth and expansion of the economy. Massive upheavals in the countryside caused urban migration on a scale unprecedented in Brazilian history. The old support systems of family and patron collapsed. While many skilled and semiskilled workers moved into the lower middle class, the unskilled and marginal work force lost what little they had in the countryside.

Failure to include a social component in planning in the 1970s, and a deliberate policy of repressing wages, has created a large and increasingly desperate *lumpenproletariat* in Brazil. Failure to deal with the social agenda during the miracle days pushed social equity issues into the future. The assumption was that income would either trickle down slowly to ameliorate the lot of the poor, or at some unspecified point in the future, the state would have the resources to work on social problems. Neither occurred in the 1970s. By the 1980s, the majority of the population was poorer and more marginal than they had been in the 1970s. Now the desire of the new regime to deal with social issues, in a context of political democracy, is thwarted both by the reality of the foreign debt and the need for continued austerity to finance it. It can either address the social agenda or renege on its international debt obligations. The Sarney administration thought that it would be able to finesse the problem with the 1986 Cruzado Plan, but it failed. The debt is probably the most serious constraint to future growth, and resources are not available to meet the pressing social needs of the majority of the population.

THE SOCIAL AGENDA

Sarney commissioned social scientist Helio Jaguaribe to prepare a national plan, which appeared in 1986 as *Brazil 2000, Para Um Novo Pacto Social.*[4] It starkly addressed the social realities of the miracle years: 53 percent of Brazilians live in poverty; half of the Brazilian population takes home only 13.6 percent of all the salaries earned in Brazil; 10 percent earn 46 percent of total salaries; and the richest 5 percent take home 33 percent, placing Brazil at the head of the World Bank list for the most inequitable wealth distribution. In addition, 27 percent of the population 5 years or older is illiterate; of the population ten years or over, fewer than 18 percent have completed 4 years of primary education and only 5.5 percent have completed the 8-year basic cycle; the national infant mortality rate is 70 per 1,000, twice that in some of the poorest areas.

The social thinking of the Sarney government also found expression in the First National Development Plan of the new Republic for 1986–89 (I PND-NR), which was approved by the Brazilian Congress in December 1985.

This plan stresses the chasm of inequality in Brazilian life:[5] more than 68 million Brazilians live in families with incomes of three minimum wages or less; and of these, some 18 million earn less than the equivalent of one minimum wage (considered to be the level of absolute poverty); during the first half of the 1980s, primary school enrollments increased at rates below population growth, even as the number of students repeating grades increased; in 1984, 11 percent of the urban population obtained hospital treatment and, in rural areas, only 5.8 percent; and approximately 80 percent of all raw sewage receives no treatment whatsoever before being discharged directly into rivers and streams.

Because of poor planning and resources, Brazil today has the highest incidence of polio in all of Latin America. According to estimates, in 1987 only eight of the 23 states of Brazil will have enough vaccine to prevent measles in the childhood population. Large food surpluses are produced for export, to earn foreign exchange required to service the debt, but food production for internal consumption has failed dramatically. While the country is the largest food exporter in the third world, more than 50 percent of Brazilian children suffer from malnutrition. Hugo Assmann, a leading theologian, has written that Brazil is a "country with cattle that never saw people, and people that never saw meat."[6] The Pan American Health Organization (PAHO) has figures that show reported cases of malaria in Brazil increasing from 197,000 in 1981 to 378,000 in 1984.[7] There have been confirmed reports of the reappearance in Brazil of the bubonic plague and of leprosy, and not only in rural areas.

Many Brazilian observers see a clear link between social deterioration and the debt. Debt service has drained resources away from public sector expenditures for social service. The steady drop in health and educational standards has condemned a large part of the population to worsening levels of malnutrition and higher exposure to a wide range of communicable diseases. The absence of investment in education, health, and sanitation, combined with the low purchasing power of the poor, relegates a majority of the population to the margins of Brazilian society. Underfed and underpaid, with inadequate housing and medical attention, millions of Brazilians face a bleak future.

Surveys show that more than one-third of the country's rural population suffers from undernourishment and diseases traceable to neglect, ignorance, or poverty. In the cities, though public health centers have grown, doctors complain that services are severely inadequate.

The government of President Sarney has spoken eloquently of not paying the debt with the hunger of the Brazilian people. Yet the international economic and political realities are such that Brazil now appears willing to work out an arrangement with the IMF that will imply the need for austerity measures, the cutting of federal spending, and the setting of priorities to service both the public and private debt.

Brazil's current recession means a sharply reduced living standard for the majority of its citizens. The hopes of the February 1986 Cruzado Plan failed, and the Bresser Plan of June 1987 was a remedial effort at adjustment, meaning repressed wage levels. It implies the need for dramatic cuts in the social service budget and precedence for trade surpluses over domestic food supply.

THE POLITICS OF THE SOCIAL AGENDA IN BRAZIL

Helio Jaguaribe and his colleagues in preparing the 2000 Project were deeply concerned about the relationship between social poverty and political democracy. If the political system, no matter how perfect in form, cannot respond to the substance of political and social demands, its legitimacy will not last. Arguments about whether a hungry citizen can vote intelligently will soon be replaced with the issue of why such a citizen should bother to vote at all. If voting brings no response to basic human needs, are other avenues open and available for seeking redress?

The current political leaders of Brazil are well aware of the rapid deterioration in the country's social fabric. They are also conscious of the growing possibility of violence and protest against the continuing and deepening poverty. Yet they confront a series of hard choices: whether to address the social agenda of Brazil, which will require scarce resources now dedicated to servicing the foreign debt, or to abandon the foreign debt and run the risk of rupturing Brazil's linkages with the international financial and trade regime.

Even economists have come to understand the difficulty of further cuts in social services. Adjustment in the third world has generally meant austerity, which has been a synonym for a further repression of wages and a precipitate drop in the standard of living of the poorest of society. But the recent Inter-American development Bank study of Brazil's debt argues that:[8]

It would be difficult to defend renewed efforts at austerity . . . income and welfare losses appear to be particularly high, especially when austerity measures are applied in a largely indexed economy . . . thus, the question remains as to how Brazil's long-term need to sustain export growth can be reconciled with the equally pressing need to maintain unemployment at the low levels of 1985–86, while simultaneously taking measures consistent with the objectives of the I PND-NR to improve the distribution of wealth and increase income levels.

A graphic demonstration of the low levels of tolerance for further deterioration in the standard of living, on the part of the poor, took place in Rio de Janeiro in July 1987. An unannounced increase in local bus fares led to a period of burning and rioting unseen since the early 1980s, during the last severe depression.[9] The Rio riots followed soon after an attack on President Jose Sarney and his party during a visit to Rio de Janeiro in which the president's bus was stoned and members of his staff injured. Press reports about the two incidents make the simple point that the new price-and-wage freeze has created a situation in which the social issue has now moved into the streets.

CONCLUSION

The miracle growth years of the 1970s gave Brazil the chance to start solving its social issues, but that opportunity has been lost. In part, domestic political and social demands and pressures were brutally repressed in the name of growth. In a period when the restoration of civilian politics permits a new leadership group to address the issue, the country's resources have already been earmarked to maintain Brazil's creditworthiness. At some point, and in more dramatic ways, the population of Brazil may seek a reassignment of those resources with little concern for Brazil's international commitments or the consequences for the existing political structures of power.

That is the basic argument in favor of a "deal" for Brazil in renegotiating the foreign debt.[10] The country's good faith should not be doubted regarding its commitment to maintaining its creditworthiness. To do so at all costs runs the risk of destroying any possibility of Brazil meeting

its international obligations, while opening the possibility of social upheaval and a rejection of traditional democratic institutions, which would
have profound consequences for Brazil as well as for the hemisphere.

While events in 1987 have confirmed the low level of political competence of the Sarney administration, the fact should not lead to the
conclusion that the Brazilian government's concern for the social agenda
was either exaggerated or misplaced. It is one of the tragedies of post-
military Brazil that the current government has proven so inept in coming to grips with realities. The writing of the constitution during 1987
and the continuing incoherence in the political party system have coincided with President Sarney's vacillations in establishing a creditable
national government. The political drift in Brasilia will only postpone
the government's ability to deal with the pressing development needs
of the population. Yet those needs will not disappear. They continue to
identify a coherent economic strategy.

The tortured negotiations between Brazil and its creditors may obscure
Brazil's social imperative, but they cannot negate it. Either this government, or its successor, will retake the initiative in linking Brazil's continued growth to a response to legitimate social needs. That response
will inalterably be part of the search for political legitimacy in Brazil. A
successful strategy by Brazil in dealing with its social problems at home
will best serve United States' interest in the region. A developed and
growing Brazil is the best hope for a mature and responsible Brazil
regionally and globally. The stakes are high. The continuing unwillingness of the industrialized countries to provide debt relief to countries
such as Brazil is shortsighted and may prove to be a costly mistake in
the future.

NOTES

1. For a review of the economic development of Brazil in the 1970s, see:
Regis Bonelli and Pedro S. Malan, "Industrialization, Economic Growth, and
Balance of Payments: Brazil, 1970–1984," in *State and Society in Brazil: Continuity
and Change*, eds., John Wirth et al. (Boulder and London: Westview Press, 1987).

2. For a discussion of the issues involved in the transition, see: Ben Ross
Schneider, "Framing the State: Economic Policy and Political Representation in
Post-Authoritarian Brazil," in *State and Society in Brazil: Continuity and Change*,
eds., Wirth et al. (Boulder and London: Westview Press, 1987); Silvio R. Duncan
Baretta and John Markoff, "Brazil and Abertura: A Transition from What to
What?" in *Authoritarians and Democrats: Regime Transition in Latin America*, eds.,
James M. Malloy and Mitchell A. Seligson (Pittsburgh: University of Pittsburgh
Press, 1987).

3. See Guy Pfeffermann, "The Social Cost of Recession in Brazil," mimeographed (Washington, D.C.: The World Bank, n.d.).

4. Helio Jaguaribe et al., *Brazil 2000: Para Um Novo Pacto Social* (Rio de Janeiro: Editora Paz e Terra, 1986).

5. James Dinsmoor, "Brazil: National Responses to the Debt Crisis" (Report to the Inter-American Development Bank, Economic and Social Development Department, Country Studies Division, May 15, 1987).

6. From Hugo Assmann, "Democracy and the Debt Crisis," *This World*, no. 14, (Spring/Summer 1986), pp. 83–88.

7. Pan American Health Organization (PAHO), *Health Conditions in the Americas, 1981–1984* (Washington, D.C.: PAHO, 1986), vol. 2.

8. James Dinsmoor, "Brazil: National Responses to the Debt Crisis" (Report to the Inter-American Development Bank, Economic and Social Development Department, Country Studies Division, May 15, 1987).

9. *VEJA, No. 983*, July 8, 1987 captures both the drama and the political significance of the events in Rio de Janeiro in its cover headline, "Fury in the Streets: in the Riots in Rio, the Violent Face of the Crisis."

10. For this argument, see the testimony by Albert Fishlow and Riordan Roett, "Hearings on the Brazilian Debt Crisis," United States House of Representatives, Subcommittee on Banking, Finance, and Urban Affairs, April 23, 1987.

9

THE ARGENTINE DEBT CRISIS AND THE CONSOLIDATION OF DEMOCRACY

Carlos H. Waisman

This work discusses the domestic aspects of Argentine responses to the debt crisis since the reestablishment of liberal democracy at the end of 1983. It begins by considering three ideal typical responses: confrontation with the creditors, accommodation via a stabilization plan, and a radical restructuring of the economy. Afterward, it examines Argentine policies and the prospects for the future in the light of these patterns.

RESPONSES TO THE DEBT CRISIS AND LATIN AMERICAN DEVELOPMENT

The study of these responses is a matter of more than practical or conjunctural interest, for Latin American societies are at a crossroads: their basic social groups and their governments face a situation that forces them to consider a variety of possible policy responses, which will shape the economic and social structure of their countries for decades to come.

The degree to which the response to the crisis involves an element of choice varies according to the balance of power and interests in each society and the degree of autonomy of each state. Yet this is one of the rare instances in the development process in which external factors force decisions about the position of a society in the international economy. Thus, what politicians and the media have labeled as the debt crisis is properly a crisis not only in the conventional sense, that is, a situation of high uncertainty, but also in the more precise sense of being a turning point, a situation in which a decisive change is about to take place.

Parallels drawn between the current global situation and the crisis of

the 1930s are inexact, for the economic and political effects of the debt
question are so far limited to Latin America and some other developing
areas, but it is not an overstatment to argue that this is the first such
turning point in the developmental trajectory of Latin American countries since the Depression and World War II.

At that time, as a reaction to the constraints and opportunities derived
from the international crisis, Latin American societies were transformed
by complex processes that shaped their evolution up to the present. The
Cardenas administration and the development of the PRI in Mexico, the
Vargas regime in Brazil, the Peronist government in Argentina, and the
Popular Front in Chile were just the political manifestations of these
processes. The case of Argentina is remarkable. It responded to the crisis
and the war, like other Latin American countries, by turning its economy
inward, namely, by import-substituting industrialization; unlike most
other Latin American countries, it also reacted by turning its state downward, that is, by establishing a corporatist state. These two shifts represented a radical departure from the model of economic and political
evolution that the country had followed between the midnineteenth
century and the Depression: a relatively open economy, which included
a significant development of manufacturing, and an expanding liberal
democracy. The combined effects in the postwar period are well known:
a sharply fluctuating or stagnated economy and an unstable and authoritarian polity. The consequence of the Depression and the war was,
therefore, a reversal of development.[1]

A crisis of this type thus may lead to either progressive or regressive
economic and political responses, if development and democracy are
considered "progressive." A detailed discussion of these responses is
beyond the scope of this work, but it will be useful to consider the three,
ideal, typical economic responses mentioned earlier (confrontation, stabilization, and restructuring) and one likely political consequence of any
of these three responses, namely, centralization of power.

From a strictly financial point of view, what is critical in the debt
question is not the amount of the debt itself, but the debtors' willingness
and ability to pay it back. This suggests three patterns of economic
responses by the debtor countries. The first, confrontation, entails a
refusal to make payments on the debt in a manner consistent with the
creditors' (governments', agencies', and banks') estimate of the country's
ability to pay. The short-term consequence of a policy of this type is the
maintenance under domestic control of resources that would otherwise
be transferred to the creditors (at the likely cost, however, of massive
capital flight). However, the long-term effect is the disruption of the
country's ties with international trade and finance, and in an extreme
type of confrontation, the suspension of ties with the international cap-

italist economy. There are no cases in the current crisis of a country resorting to the most radical instance of this response, debt repudiation. Policies such as those of Peru, which limits payments to a low percentage of its export income, or to a lesser extent Brazil, which has unilaterally suspended payment on interest, would be mild versions of this pattern.

Cooperation with the creditors through the application of an IMF-style stabilization plan is the typical adaptive response. Since the goal of such a policy is to correct disequilibria in the balance of payments, it entails neither a withdrawal from the world economy, as in the first pattern, nor a change in the country's position in it, as in the third pattern. This policy is the manifestation of a country's willingness to pay according to its ability, and it is usually the counterpart of concessions from the creditors. Thus, its implementation leads to a strengthening of the bonds between debtor and creditors. The responses to the crisis by Mexico, Argentina (since mid–1985), and other Latin American countries exemplify this road.

Restructuring the economy, finally, would be a step forward; its objective is neither withdrawal nor reestablishment of the status quo ante, but a more functional (and thus stronger) level of integration into the international economy. In the context of the most Latin American countries, restructuring would involve a transition from the semiautarkic model of industrialization exemplified by import substitution to an export-led type of industrial growth.

Only through the growth and diversification of its exports can a country service its debt and increase its autonomy in the international system at the same time.[2] Policies of export diversification have been attempted with varying degrees of success in several Latin American countries since the 1970s,[3] but there is no instance so far of a country in the region using these policies as an effective response to the debt crisis.

These economic roads have political causes and consequences. Clearly, the selection among the three patterns is a function of the relative power of different groups and of the power of the state vis-à-vis the society (for example, the first response presupposes a highly autonomous state, and the other two a considerably less autonomous one), as well as of external opportunities and constraints. Regarding domestic political consequences, an important one has been mentioned: the implementation of severe versions of any of these economic policies would be conducive to a medium to high level of centralization of power. The reason is that such implementation would negatively affect the central interest of major social groups, and the ensuing polarization could lead to military rule. Thus, the debt crisis renders problematical the future of the fragile new democracies of South America. Even mild versions of confrontation would lead to the impoverishment of all classes in the society, and the proposition that stabilization policies lead to, or have an elective affinity with, authoritarian rule is widely accepted among students of Latin American politics.[4]

Countries such as Argentina, which have highly mobilized and organized interest groups and a praetorian tradition, are particularly vulnerable to the destabilizing consequences of polarization. In fact, not even actual polarization, but the perception by economic elites or the armed forces that their central interests were in imminent danger has in the past triggered preemptive coups d'etat. Economic crises, which by definition involve high levels of uncertainty, are likely to produce both situations of actual polarization and cases of inaccurate evaluation by elites of the degree of threat to their interests. As I have pointed out elsewhere, in crisis situations, two mechanisms that lead to distorted political knowledge among elites are likely to operate, contributing to a preemptive closure of the political system. The mechanisms are the exaggeration of the revolutionary potential of the lower classes and a flawed understanding of positive and negative international demonstration effects.[5]

There is no reason to assume that history predicts the future, for Latin American societies today have different social structures and institutions than they did half a century ago. However, it is interesting to recall that a wave of such coups swept the continent at the time of the Depression; according to Claudio Véliz, 17 governments were overthrown in the region between 1929 and 1932.[6]

THE ARGENTINE RESPONSE AND ITS POLITICAL CONSEQUENCES

The Argentine debt (about $54 billion, as of this writing) is the third largest in Latin Ameica, and it is one of the highest in relation to exports (see Table 9.1). The payment of interest alone amounts to over 40 percent of export income.

The significance of these ratios should be assessed in the light of the composition of Argentine exports. Unlike Brazil, which successfully diversified its foreign trade in the 1960s and 1970s, Argentina is still dependent on the export of the commodities through which it became integrated into the world economy in the late nineteenth century. While Brazil competes successfully in markets as diverse as those for shoes, arms, and passenger planes, Argentina can sell only grains and beef on the open markets. In 1983, manufactured goods accounted for only 16 percent of Argentine exports, a figure that includes, I assume, processed foodstuffs. The same year, 56 percent of Brazilian exports by value consisted of nonagricultural products, while manufactured goods accounted for 40 percent of the total. Countries such as Mexico and Uruguay were

Table 9.1
Gross Debt and Interest on Debt in Relation to Exports, 1986–87

	Debt-to-Export Ratio		Interest-to-Export Ratio	
	1986	1987	1986	1987
Argentina	536	554	47	43
Brazil	425	471	40	39
Chile	402	370	36	28
Mexico	413	366	35	31
Peru	497	551	31	35

Source: Morgan Guaranty Trust Company, *World Financial Markets* (June–July 1987), pp. 4–5.

also more successful than Argentina in this regard; their manufacturing exports were 27 and 29 percent of the total, respectively.[7] The problem for Agentina is not just the vulnerability inherent in trade specialization, but the fact that the commodities in which the country has specialized have weak markets, with downward real prices and unfavorable prospects, a topic to which I will return.

Since the reestablishment of liberal democracy at the end of 1983, there have been two phases in the Argentine response to the debt crisis. In the first, which lasted up to the middle of 1985, the government proclaimed its intention to honor the country's financial obligations, but it also stated that it would not do so at the cost of a recession. Economic policy aimed at expanding employment and economic activity and maintaining real wages, and debt negotiations contained a significant element of confrontation. For most of this first phase, the Alfonsín administration refused to carry out an adjustment program as demanded by the IMF, and it approached negotiations with the creditors with considerable brinkmanship (tough bargaining, impasses leading to last-minute "rescues," etc.). The government also endeavored, without much success, to form a coalition among debtor countries.

Expansionary economic policies were a total failure.[8] Real gross domestic product (GDP) grew by 2.4 percent in 1984, but it shrank by 3 percent in the first semester of 1985. Inflation, which was 400 percent at the beginning of the new administration, jumped to an annualized rate of 1,500 percent in the middle of 1985. At that time, the accumulated balance of unpaid trade credits and overdue interest on the debt amounted to 40 percent of the export income for that year. Real wages increased in 1984 by 28 percent with respect to 1983, but they fluctuated sharply in the first half of 1985 (even dropping, in the beginning of the year, to 13 percent below the wage level of 1983).

In June of 1985 there was a sudden turn. The previous economic team, made up of economists from the Radical party, was replaced by a group of technocrats and academics. The new economic program, the Austral

Plan, consisted of five basic elements: (1) higher taxes, higher prices for firms in the public sector, and a reduction in public spending, in order to cut the deficit by four-fifths in the remainder of the year (from 12.5 to 2.5 percent of the GDP); (2) the promise to finance the deficit exclusively with external credit; (3) a temporary wage and price freeze; (4) a sharp drop in interest rates; and (5) the introduction of a new currency, the austral.[9] This policy went beyond the creditor's expectations; it was characterized as a shock stabilization plan,[10] which was "harsh even by IMF standards."[11]

As far as the debt is concerned, the accumulation of reserves allowed the government to normalize interest payments. A cooperative relationship with the creditors was established, and agreements providing for rescheduling, new lending, and debt-equity swap schemes were successfully negotiated. In government discourse, hints about the possibility of a moratorium abated, while appeals to creditor banks and governments for concessions in the restructuring of the debt and calls for a "Marshall Plan for Latin America" became paramount. Argentina ceased being the maverick debtor, and for the past two years, it was hailed by bankers and American officials alike as a model of domestic reform and responsible debt management.[12]

The immediate effects of the program were a drastic fall in the inflation rate (from 30 percent in June 1985 to 6 percent in July and 3 percent in August), and a drop in the GDP, which declined by 6 percent in the second semester. In two months, from May to July 1985, real wages were reduced by 15 percent to the level of 1983, when Alfonsín came to power. The only unqualified success was the reduction in the deficit. Inflation began mounting again a year after the new program was implemented (it passed 5 percent in July 1986). In order to check inflation and improve the balance of payments, new measures were announced in February and July 1987, the most important of which were a devaluation, further increases in prices for the public sector and in taxes, a new wage and price freeze, and a reduction in export taxes. The government also formulated plans for the privatization of some firms in the public sector and for a partial liberalization of trade.

As of this writing, Argentina is again under three-digit inflation. Monthly rates in the third quarter of 1987 were in the 10–15 percent range, with prices and wages, it should be remembered, still theoretically under control. The GDP grew by almost 6 percent in 1986, thus more than compensating for the drop in the previous year, but in the first half of 1987, according to current estimates, the rate of growth was close to 2 percent. Most likely, the upturn that followed the Austral Plan will prove to be another instance of the sharp fluctuations that characterize the Argentine economy. The average growth of the GDP in the first three years of the Alfonsín administration was 1.2 percent, roughly the same as the rate of population growth.

Real wages under the Austral Plan fell by 11 percent in 1986 and by 10 percent in the first eight months of 1987.[13] In order to interpret these data, it is important to keep in mind that the standard of living of the working class had deteriorated substantially under the military regime. Adolfo Canitrot and Jorge Schvarzer have estimated that between 1975, the year prior to the military coup, and 1980, real wages fell by a third, and the share of wages in the GDP declined from almost one-half to about a third.[14] There was a further drop in the early 1980s, but wages in 1983 were at the 1980 level.

Against this background, labor response appears to be unusually mild, by Argentine and Latin American standards. The common sense expectation that unions would take advantage of the reestablishment of democracy and the subsequent reduction in the costs of political mobilization to regain some of the terrain lost has not materialized. Likewise, the reaction to the drop in wages that followed the application of the Austral Plan was moderate. To be sure, there have been six or seven general strikes since the beginning of the Alfonsín administration, and there were also several periods in which labor unrest reached considerable magnitude, leading to mass demonstrations, strikes in public services, and even the seizure of a major Ford plant. However, the intensity of labor mobilization was low in comparison with the three previous democratic experiences, in the 1960s and 1970s. In all these situations, high levels of social polarization set the stage for the military coups that overthrew elected governments—a relationship that was not always accidental, for in some cases, a segment of the union leadership formed part of the coup coalition.

The reaction was also moderate at the specifically political level. The first congressional elections in the Alfonsín administration took place a few months after the beginning of the Austral Plan, and the Radicals won a plurality. Moreover, the Peronists lost in these elections a substantial proportion of the votes they had obtained in 1983. Most importantly, labor mobilized resolutely on the side of the constitutional authorities during the military mutiny of Easter 1987. There was considerable friction between the government and the unions in 1986, but for several months in 1987, a union leader of orthodox Peronist background was appointed as labor minister, an action that was widely interpreted as the manifestation of an accord between the government and a segment of the union movement. This accord, under the circumstances, reflected the acquiescence on the side of these unions to the constraints imposed by the stabilization policy. Later, labor went along with the decision by the government to open a round of collective bargaining negotiations, from which the discussion of wages would be excluded.

These are pragmatic actions on the part of labor, and they do not imply a subordination of the unions to the government. Throughout the period, labor leaders fought hard to prevent a slide of real wages, and the government endeavored to maintain the pre-Alfonsín and post-Austral Plan wage level. Moreover, the political outlook may be changing. In the second congressional elections, which were held in September 1987, the Peronists won a plurality, and the Radicals lost about a third of the votes they had received in 1983. But the fact remains that, after four years of the Alfonsín administration, the praetorian struggle for redistribution that characterized previous situations of hyperinflation and stabilization under democratic rule has not taken place.

ACCOUNTING FOR THE LOW LEVEL OF POLARIZATION

Since this behavior contradicts the substantial body of literature cited earlier, a discussion of its possible causes may be of interest. The two most obvious hypotheses for the explanation of labor moderation are political: first, this moderation would be a consequence of the characteristics of the main political actors in this conflict, the government, and labor; and second, it would be an effect of political learning. In addition to these political factors, there are social ones: there have been, in the past 20 years, substantial changes in the Argentine social structure, and these changes have had an adverse impact on the power of the labor movement.

The first of the factors mentioned is plain; the Alfonsín administration is a more effective player of the political game than any the three previous elected governments Argentina has had in the past three decades. There are three reasons for this. First, this government is more legitimate, in the eyes of labor and the population in general, than two of these previous administrations (those of 1958–62 and 1963–66; the third civilian government was the Peronist one of 1973–76). These two governments came to power as a result of elections from which Peronists were excluded, and thus they were regarded by the labor movement as illegitimate. Alfonsín, on the other hand, won by an absolute majority in open elections. Moreover, the fact that the Alfonsín administration is committed to the preservation of liberal democracy in its two dimensions, participation and contestation (a statement that cannot be made in relation to any elected government since the Depression) is a significant determinant of its legitimacy, regardless of the extent to which democracy in itself is a value for the labor leadership. In the second place, the Alfonsín administration is more cohesive than at least two of these previous regimes (those of 1958–62 and 1973–76). Third, this government has displayed a great deal more tactical sophistication than its elected predecessors (with the possible exception of Peron's brief administration of 1973–74) in bargaining with labor and the political opposition.

The second reason of a political nature is that the Peronist movement of the 1980s is a much less effective political contender than the Peronism of the 1960s and 1970s. The crisis of Peronism, which is manifested by its current organizational fragmentation and ideological turmoil, is the consequence of two factors: the painful (and delayed) assimilation of the tragic events of the 1970s and the unresolved succession crisis.

Internal organizational and ideological divisions within Peronism are the inevitable legacy of the emergence of a radical Left in the 1960s and 1970s, the violent conflicts between this Left and the Right, the demoralization produced by the anarchic experience of the Isabel Perón administration of 1974–76, and the passive acceptance of the military regime by the Right at the time when the Left was destroyed and a large segment of Peronism and labor were subject to considerable repression. In the late 1980s, the Left is no longer a significant factor, the right is much less powerful than in the past, and a large liberal democratic segment (the Renovating wing) has developed within the party; but old antagonisms linger, and new ones appear as a consequence of diverging interpretations of this complex experience.

The most important cause of the current weakness of Peronism is the fact that the movement is still in a process of transition, both organizationally and ideologically. The death of Juan Perón produced not only a succession crisis, but also a need to redefine the nature of the movement. There was no alternative leadership in place, and it could not be otherwise; charisma is seldom inherited, and its routinization takes time. Moreover, routinization implies a bureaucratic succession, and this entails the conversion of a diffuse "movement" into a modern party, which can only be a party of labor and the poor, in alliance with a segment of the middle class and the intelligentsia, that is, a typical labor or social democratic party. Large segments of the labor and political wings of the movement are evolving toward a model of that type, but it is still uncertain whether this transition will encompass the whole of Peronism.

This organizational transformation, in turn, presupposes an ideological redefinition: once the founder of its doctrine, its interpreter and arbiter, is dead, the inconsistent Peronist ideological amalgam ceases to be viable. A modern party does not require a coherent doctrine, but a traditional Peronism, which admitted both a neofascist interpretation (in its origins) and a Marxist one (more recently), and also various intermediate possibilities, would be an inadequate programmatic base for a social democratic party in a liberal democratic regime. Corporatist and moral economy arguments are still strong in Peronist discourse, but conventional liberal and social democratic themes have become more frequent than in the past. In any case, Peronism is in flux and this impairs its effectiveness.

The last political factor I mentioned is political learning. Not only the contenders have changed, but also the rules that constrain their interaction. The current shift toward moderation and compromise is the consequence of two aspects of the collective experience of the Argentines in the recent past: the delegitimation of the military as a political actor and the delegitimation of nondemocratic political formulas.

For most Argentines, the military regime of 1976–83 was a traumatic experience, both because of its economic policies, which affected adversely the interests of labor and the weaker segment of the capitalist class, and of its reckless disposition to use force on a large scale, both domestically and internationally. The government, labor, and all the other social groups recognize now that the military can no longer be defined as the benign arbitrators of political conflict, as outsiders who reestablish "order" whenever the level of polarization is too intense; or as the rescuers to which a group could resort whenever its basic interests were threatened in the conflicts over the distribution of income. This realization is a powerful inducement for restraint and compromise. In fact, the military regime's only positive by-product is this reactive secularization of Argentine politics.

The other important aspect of political learning is the delegitimation of nondemocratic political formulas.[15] The legitimacy of any political regime is always a function of the legitimacy of its alternatives. The range of these alternatives varies, according to the direct experience that different groups have had with specific regimes and to the vicarious experiences they may have acquired through international demonstration effects to which different societies, and groups within each society, may have had access. In Argentina, all of the alternatives to liberal democracy considered desirable or acceptable by the major social forces have been tried in the last decades and have failed: restrictive democracy, corporatist popular regimes, and both "soft" and "hard" military rule. Even the socialist option, espoused by a segment of the intelligentsia in the 1960s and 1970s, lost whatever glamor it had, both as a result of direct experience (the catastrophic consequences of the "armed struggle" of the 1970s) and of vicarious ones (the failure of Allende's "peaceful road" in Chile and the disenchantment of the European intelligentsia with "really existing" socialist regimes). None of the other nondemocratic models in the world today is considered worth following by significant groups. As a consequence, liberal democracy enjoys substantial legitimacy, largely by default; its legitimacy is based, to a large extent, on the fact that all the other plausible roads were followed with negative results.

As I stated earlier, there is also a social cause of labor moderation: the working class was weakened by changes that took place in the social structure in the past two decades. As the political system is in transition, so is the social structure. While the political system is in a process of (still uncertain) institutionalization of democracy, the social structure is becoming more underdeveloped. Thus, the political transition renders Argentina more similar to the advanced capitalist democracies, while the social transition moves the country closer to the traditional Latin American pattern. Since this latter process weakens labor and the inefficient capitalists, it contributes to moderate the struggle for the distribution of income and thus facilitates the institutionalization of democracy. Nevertheless, it will be a democracy in which the interests of labor and the other components of traditional populist coalitions weigh less than in the previous constitutional experiences since World War II. Perhaps it is because most Argentines are becoming poorer that they can also become freer (and thus "formally" freer). A dialectician would call this the paradox of underdeveloped democracy.

From the late nineteenth century to the midtwentieth century, the social structure of Argentina resembled more those of the so-called lands of recent settlement (the British dominions) than that of typical Latin American countries such as Brazil or Mexico. Argentina had a small rural population devoted to labor-extensive agriculture, a large secondary sector, no significant labor reserve (in fact, a labor shortage), a large educational system, and the high rates of upward mobility that a dynamic economy made possible. In all these respects, the profile of Argentine society was closer to that of advanced capitalist countries than to the one that prevailed in Latin America (in fact, until the 1960s, Argentina looked more "developed" than most of Mediterranean Europe).[16]

When stagnation set in, as a consequence of the autarkic industrial policies that followed in the postwar period, the Argentine social structure took on the traits of underdevelopment. Looking at the society from the bottom, as the issue under consideration requires, the underlying process is one of the marginalization: its two aspects are the growth of the informal sector and the reduction in the size of the working class. Both imply a considerable rate of downward mobility.

The expansion of the informal sector is indicated by the growth of the "independents," other than family labor, in the labor force. Most of these are self-employed individuals holding low-productivity jobs in manufacturing and commerce. Their share of the active population has increased from 16 percent in 1960 to almost 25 percent in 1980.[17] On the other hand, the industrial working class has shrunk, as a consequence of the liberalization of trade in the late 1970s; employment in manufacturing went down by 26 percent from 1976 to 1980.[18] Today, the largest Argentine unions are no longer of blue-collar but of white-collar workers, a large proportion of whom are government employees.

These two processes interact: not only is the working class smaller, but also the unions are weaker because the existence of a significant labor reserve reduces their ability to control the labor supply. At the individual level, workers are deterred from engaging in risky forms of collective action by the presence of a growing stratum of urban poor, and by the knowledge of the existence of widespread downward mobility.

THE UNCERTAIN FUTURE OF STABILIZATION POLICIES
AND THE SPECTER OF CONFRONTATION

The paradox of underdeveloped democracy may be true, but the consolidation of democracy still requires positive reinforcement, that is, the new regime must at some point show its efficacy,[19] meaning the ability to improve, or at least bring back to "historic" levels, the standard of living of key groups in the society, labor in particular. Otherwise, intense mass mobilization and the ensuing polarization may recur; in that case the future of stabilization policies and eventually of democratic rule will be problematic. Prospects for polarization exist for two reasons: first, as time goes by, some of the factors accounting for the current low level of social conflict could lose their effectiveness; and second, should that happen, some other aspects of Argentine society conducive to polarization will become salient.

First of all, it should be clear that a new regime may legitimate itself by showing its efficacy in noneconomic areas, or by dealing with economic issues that do not involve growth or distribution. The Alfonsín administration took significant steps in that direction: the rule of law was reestablished, basic political rights are respected, the leaders of the military regime and a small number of the officers accused of massive violations of human rights were brought to court (the others being granted amnesty only in the face of a military upheaval), a food distribution program for poor families was started, university enrollment has expanded, a divorce law was enacted, etc. At this point, there is little room left for the kind of noneconomic efficacy that would enhance support for the government, especially among the lower classes.

With the passage of time, some of the causes of moderation and compromise are likely to weaken. In the first place, the legitimacy and effectiveness of the government may decline. Its legitimacy has suffered as a consequence of the economic situation and the results of the last congressional elections, in which the Radicals got little more than a third of the total vote. Moreover, its freedom of maneuver is likely to diminish because of two factors. The first is the growing autonomy of the armed forces, which after having blocked the prosecution of officers accused of human rights violations, are beginning to reactivate as a political actor.

For example, top officers openly ask for a vindication of the performance of the military in the "dirty war," and they hint that their next demand will be a total amnesty. It is clear that the government has failed to place the military under control, and there is no reason to expect that their political mobilization will be limited to professional demands. The second factor that will restrict the effectiveness of the government is the fact that, after the recent elections, the Radicals do not have a majority in any of the two houses of Congress. Thus, they will need to make coalitions either with the Peronists (thus weakening or abandoning the stabilization policy), or with the small parties on their right (thus intensifying the conflict with labor).

The second factor conducive to polarization is that the cohesion and thus the effectiveness of Peronism are likely to increase. Its recent electoral victory and the fact that presidential elections will be held in 1989 are powerful incentives in this direction. Should the Peronists come to power, it would be very hard for them to apply a stabilization policy. This would never be accepted by their labor base, which remains quite independent from the Peronists' political leadership; labor may have weakened in Argentine society as a whole, but it is still the backbone of Peronism. As for the debt policy in general, the Peronist public position is one of confrontation with the creditors. A recent meeting of the Renovation wing, the liberal democratic segment of the party, called for a moratorium and for solidarity among the debtors, and opposed debt-equity swaps.[20] I am sure that the leaders of this faction understand very well the costs of internal populist policies and of confrontation with the creditors, but pressures from below will push them toward these policies, should they win the next election.

Thirdly, the effects of political learning may also fade as time goes by. It is not difficult to imagine a scenario in which the memories of fear and repression under the military abate among groups other than the intelligentsia, and in which inefficacious democracy joins the long-lost political formulas having a low level of legitimacy in Argentine political culture.

Thus, the prospect is that unless the new democratic regime shows a modicum of economic efficacy, the government will lose legitimacy and effectiveness, Peronism will increase its power, and the restraining effects of political learning will weaken. Should that happen, the stage is set for a resumption of praetorianism and instability. The underlying structural causes have not been modified by the transition to liberal democracy. These causes are basically two characteristics of Argentine society: first, it combines a stagnated economy with a society made up of highly mobilized and organized social forces; second, its polity includes strong interest groups that are imperfectly controlled by political parties, and a partially autonomous state apparatus (the military).

The first of these characteristics produces praetorianism, in Huntington's sense. In addition to the two conflict groups, workers and capitalists, that struggle for the distribution of income in the context of a stagnated society, it is important to add a third key group, the intelligentsia. Its radicalized segment formed the Peronist Left and the guerrilla organizations in the 1960s and 1970s. The social matrix that produced this intelligentsia is still there: a mass system of higher education. According to the *World Handbook of Political and Social Indicators*, Argentina had in the 1960s a higher rate of enrollment in higher education than any West European country except the Netherlands.[21] In 1983, when Alfonsín came to power, the rate was one-fourth of the population aged 20 to 24, which was still at West European levels.[22] Since then, enrollment has increased substantially.[23]

In order to assess the political significance of this mass university system, it should be remembered that Argentine higher education is not divided into undergraduate and graduate levels; all graduates receive professional degrees and thus have the corresponding professional aspirations and the potential for frustration in a stagnated economy with a very large professional stratum. It is true that the dropout rate is very high, but the majority of students who attend for many years without ever graduating (many because they must work full time) are likely to feel dissatisfied as well, and to blame society for their inability to complete their studies.

Most of the frustrated intelligentsia will eventually adapt to the situation, in most cases by lowering goals to realistic levels, and a small proportion will emigrate; nevertheless the potential for radicalization of this group is substantial. Since other sources of frustration operate among workers and the urban poor (for example, the recent drop in wages, job insecurity, and descent into the informal sector), the structural conduciveness for the formation of radical mass movements remains high.

The second characteristic of Argentine society noted earlier, the fact that it contains strong interest groups that are inadequately controlled by political parties and a partially autonomous military apparatus, is what produces the authoritarian responses to polarization. I have already pointed out that Peronist unions are quite autonomous with respect to the political leadership of the party. This autonomy is greater in the case of business, for Argentina lacked, for the past half-century, a conservative party representing business interests and capable of developing a mass following. In the past few years, a center-right party, the Union of the Democratic Center, has been growing (it got 6 percent of the vote in the last congressional elections), but it is still unclear whether it will survive its founder and evolve into a mass organization. Lacking strong political brokers with an ability to mediate and refine social conflict, the different groups have contended nakedly for the surplus, thus converting Argentina into an extreme example of the praetorian situation.

The other side of the equation is, of course, the fact that the military, from the 1940s to the present, have been relatively autonomous from the government. They have acted as the "regulators" of the praetorian game by seizing power whenever the level of legitimacy of an elected administration was low. The Alfonsín government missed the opportunity to subordinate the armed forces. At the beginning of the Alfonsín administration, when the military was in disarray as a consequence of the failure of its previous regime and of its defeat in the Malvinas/Falklands war, the administration failed to move to transform the military into a professional organization under civilian control. It would be impossible to do so now, when the government is weaker and the armed forces are already politicized.

The fact that the mechanisms that in the past produced authoritarian outcomes are still in place does not mean, of course, that they will necessarily be reactivated. The key issue is, again, whether elected governments can show sufficient efficacy. This would facilitate the absorption of much of the frustration generated by stagnation among workers, the urban poor, and the intelligentsia, and also the formation of a strong party system in which all the major social groups are represented. This is unlikely in a situation in which interest payments on the debt amount to more than 40 percent of the country's export income. If this pressure does not change, the most likely scenario is the intensification of social conflict. This could lead to the abandonment of the stabilization policy, perhaps as a result of a Peronist victory in the next presidential election and a high level of polarization. Protracted and very intense polarization could again, as it did in the past, produce government paralysis or the perception of a threat of mass radicalization; these states would be conducive to another round of military intervention, even though the threshold of resistance for this possibility would be quite high.

Regardless of whether this happens, the armed forces are likely to have some influence in politics, especially under a Peronist administration. Their orientation toward the debt question will depend on how their current internal crisis is resolved. The military, like many other organizations in Argentine society, are in a state of flux. The chain of command has weakened to an unprecedented degree: in the mutiny of April 1987, army units refused to follow orders of their commanders and repress the rebels; in one unit, reportedly, officers voted whether they would obey their superiors. As in the 1960s, statements and analyses attributed to different groups of officers are circulated among politicians and journalists. At all levels of their hierarchy, the military are trying to assimilate the two defeats they suffered: one internal (the revulsion caused by the large-scale violation of human rights in the last military regime), and the other external (in the war with England). The latter, in particular, is leading many of them to rethink the naive and Manichaean view of the world that prevailed in the Argentine armed forces.[24] Assumptions about the position of Argentina in the Western alliance and about the nature of U.S.-Argentine relations are openly questioned.

The fact that this ideological reevaluation takes place at the same time that the country is choked by the debt could be conducive to the revival of the military "nationalism" that emerged as a consequence of the Depression. In that period, the economic crisis and the realization that Argentina was an informal member of the British Empire led a faction of officers, one of whom was Juan Perón, to seek in fascism an ideological framework for the understanding of the nature of the country and of its position in the international system. This was the key group in the pro-Axis regime of 1943–46, which engaged in a sharp confrontation with the United States, to the extent that Argentina was treated almost as an enemy nation during much of the war and in the early postwar period. This was the regime from which Peronism sprang. Ever since that time, there have been "nationalists" in the armed forces, and the reemergence of an organized faction with a coherent antiliberal ideology (which would be more akin to contemporary third world nationalism than to old-fashioned fascism) is a real possibility. Such a faction would find ready allies within Peronism for a confrontational policy in relationship to the debt.

INDUSTRIAL RECONVERSION AND THE FAILURE OF POLITICAL LEADERSHIP

The urgency of the debt question should not obscure the fact that it is not the source of the Argentine economic crisis. The country's economy has stagnated since the 1970s: from 1973 to 1984, the average annual growth rate of the GDP was 0.4 percent, the poorest performance in South America and a retrogression in per capita terms, since the annual population growth was 1.6 percent in that period.[25]

This is the culmination of the slippage that began in the postwar years. At the outbreak of World War II, the Argentine per capita GDP was comparable to that of France; in the 1960s it was still higher than that of Japan; and today is in the same range as those of Brazil, Chile, and Mexico.[26] The cause lies, as pointed out earlier, in the autarkic industrialization policies followed during the postwar period. These policies led to the formation of a dual economy, in which the foreign exchange produced by an internationally efficient agrarian sector is absorbed by a noncompetitive manufacturing sector tied to a relatively small internal market. Once the captive market was saturated, growth could only be based on the expansion of agrarian exports.

Argentina failed to develop internationally competitive manufactures, in the manner of Brazil; but it also failed to specialize in an export commodity with oligopsonistic potential, as was the case with Mexico. Long-term prospects in the international markets for corn, wheat, and beef are not encouraging. Real prices for these commodities are in a downward trend, due to a major expansion of production capacity in the past decade, both in advanced countries and the Third World. To paraphrase Barbara Insel, the world is "awash in grain,"[27] and the outlook is for a grain surplus for the foreseeable future. This is not only due to subsidization in many countries but also to technology. In the past few years, yields have improved substantially, and new varieties can be grown in environments that were previously considered marginal. These developments will be intensified by the coming biotechnological revolution. As for beef, the demand for this quite wasteful source of proteins will be restrained not only by changing tastes and the concern for health in advanced countries, but also by the expansion of a very efficient substitute, the poultry industry, in rich and poor countries alike.

Thus, for Argentina to grow again, it must replace the old policy of import substitution with a new one of export promotion and the development of competitive manufacturing. Should this be done, the negative effects of the debt problem will only be conjectural, and the structural limits to the consolidation of democracy will disappear.

A serious program of export diversification would entail the need to import substantial amounts of machinery and technology. However, the country's ability to import is squeezed by three factors: the stagnation of exports; the import needs of the existing noncompetitive industries, which require foreign intermediate inputs and machinery; and the service of the debt. The other potential source of funds, foreign capital, is unlikely to be available in large amounts in the current economic situation. The only possibility left is reconversion: some of the existing industries would have to be phased out, and competitive manufacturers would expand or start anew.

The impediments for such a course are enormous. They are political, rather than economic or technical. In an ideal world devoid of political constraints, it would not be difficult to design a set of policies aimed at changing the position of the country in the world economy. Neither of the two "pure" mechanisms for industrial reconversion, industrial policy and trade liberalization, seems to be, by itself, appropriate for the Argentine context, whatever their abstract merits. Industrial policy ("picking the winners") would be very risky, for the selection of criteria are even less obvious in a society like Argentina than in an advanced capitalist economy. Most of the country's industries are noncompetitive, and many of its manufacturers (for example, of footwear or textiles) would face protectionist pressures in rich countries. Market mechanisms such as trade liberalization may be more effective in the abstract. However, in the Argentine economy, in which most imports would have better quality or lower prices than their domestic counterparts and in which most firms are small and technologically backward, extensive trade liberalization would lead, as happened in the late 1970s, to large-scale deindustrialization. (The negative results of trade liberalization at that time, however, were compounded by overvaluation of the currency.) An intermediate road would be most effective; it would combine the phasing out of the most inefficient industries, financial support and labor-retraining programs for industries with some export potential, and a gradual and segmented liberalization of trade.

The political obstacles for a program of this type are obvious: in Argentina, the efficient and the popular are negatively correlated. Few democratic governments could muster enough power to carry out a policy that affects the central interests of most capitalists and workers, and this prospect appears even less likely in a recently established but already beleaguered democracy. Hothouse capitalism generates a typical collective action problem. The existing situation is highly unsatisfactory for all the actors: capitalists, workers, and the state. However, reconversion would imply for all of them, in the short run, costs that are certain and definite. In the long run, there would be large gains for the state and for many, but not all, members of the capitalist and working classes (there would be losers in any case, namely the most inefficient capitalists and a segment of labor), but these gains are uncertain and diffuse. The status quo wins.

Yet this is one of those situations in which forward-looking political leadership could make a difference. The debt crisis could be used as a catalyst, as a constraint that could help change the way in which key groups in the society define their interests. In short, it could be a blessing in disguise.

Three aspects of the debt crisis are conducive to such a redefinition of group interests. First, the imperative nature of the debt crisis is evident: it requires action. Secondly, the debt crisis is widely perceived as a turning point. It could be presented as one of those major ailments that can only be effectively cured with major surgery, that is, the restructuring of the Argentine economy. Stopgap measures will not do. In the third place, the fact that there is a correlation between a solution to the debt crisis and positive developments in the two major issues facing Argentine society, namely economic growth and the consolidation of democracy, could be understood by all the major social groups. Major sectors of both the capitalist and the working classes could be led by political leadership to the conclusion that the barriers to growth and the difficulties in the institutionalization of democracy are the consequences of the fact that the current pattern of integration of Argentina into the world economy is inviable, and that overcoming them require the re-establishment of a "virtuous" relationship between the country and the world economy.

However, opportunities do not translate automatically into policies. It is unlikely that Raul Alfonsín (or any successor, for that matter) would embark on a project of this type on a large scale. The reason is not a lack of intellectual understanding of the problem: probably Alfonsín himself, and certainly Juan V. Sorrouille, the economy minister, and the members of the policymaking team, would agree with the previous discussion. Sorrouille coauthored a book on the Argentine economy that contains an interpretation along these lines.[28] Recently, he argued that "in a previous moment of its history the Argentine economy could grow under the rules of the game of a semi-autarkic model . . . [but] nowadays the country will not attain efficiency in production and in the allocation of resources unless it accepts the challenge of international competition."[29] These principles are having an impact on policy. Some significant steps are being taken to liberalize trade (against, as could be expected, the intense opposition of industrialists). In the past months, import licenses were lifted for some textile, petrochemical, and other products, in some cases as an anti-inflationary measure. A loan from the World Bank will enable the government to finance some imports, and the recent standby agreement with the IMF calls for the progressive elimination of import licenses.[30] Nevertheless, the government insists on the limited scope of these measures. It is obviously aware of the political limits to the liberalization of trade, and it will endeavor to prevent the mobilization of business and labor around this issue.

What would be needed in this instance is a large-scale reconversion plan to enable the country to use a large share of its export income for the development of export industries. In the democratic regime, this is possible only with the support of most capitalists and workers. This presupposes a strong dose of political engineering. Paradoxically, Argentina requires, in order to unmake the wrong choices made by the Peronists in the 1940s, a coalition similar to the one that reshaped the country at that time. This also includes a strong political leadership, which does not necessarily mean an individual leader, and much less so a personalistic leader with a nondemocratic ideology, as was then the case. In the 1940s and in the context of another crisis of the international system, a very sophisticated political entrepreneur named Juan Perón formed a coalition between workers and capitalists, and convinced these two groups that their interests would be best served by isolating the country's industry from the world economy. The result was stagnation and illegitimacy. The coalition I have in mind for the current crisis would have a similar social composition, but its objective would be the opposite; the outcome would be, hopefully, different as well.

Yet the Alfonsín administration has a more modest horizon. Its central concern is the institutionalization of democracy, and Alfonsín has many times defined his criterion of success as the ability to transfer office to an elected successor. This moderation, is not, unfortunately, an expression of realism, for the future of democracy is intertwined with the solution of the economic crisis. My impression is that the debt crisis will be a missed opportunity for Argentina.

NOTES

1. I discuss this process in another work: Carlos H. Waisman, *Reversal of Development in Argentina: Postwar Counterrevolutionary Policies and their Structural Consequences* (Princeton: Princeton University Press, 1987) (hereafter cited as *Reversal of Development*).

2. A change of this type is inconsistent with the first type of response, confrontation, whose outcome is marginalization from the world economy, but under certain circumstances it may be a by-product of a stabilization plan. However, a restructuring of exports is neither a necessary policy component nor a necessary consequence of a policy aimed at overcoming balance-of-payments disequilibria.

3. For a critical discussion of the experience of Chile and other countries in the Southern Cone, see: Alejandro Foxley, *Latin American Experiments in Neoconservative Economics* (Berkeley: University of California Press, 1983).

4. See Carlos Díaz Alejandro, "Southern Cone Stabilization Plans," in *Economic Stabilization in Developing Countries*, eds. William Cline and Sydney Weintraub (Washington, D.C.: Brookings, 1981); Robert Frenkel and Guillermo O'Donnell, "The 'Stabilization Programs' of the IMF and their Internal Impacts," in *Capitalism and the State in U.S.-Latin American Relations*, ed. Richard Fagan (Stanford: Stanford University Press, 1979); Stephan Haggard, "The Politics of Adjustment: Lessons from the IMF's Extended Fund Facility," in *The Politics of International Debt*, ed. Miles Kahler (Ithaca: Cornell University Press, 1986); Robert R. Kauffman, "Democratic and Authoritarian Responses to the Debt Issue: Argentina, Brazil, Mexico," in *The Politics of International Debt*, ed. Miles Kahler (Ithaca: Cornell University Press, 1986); Thomas Skidmore, "The Politics of Stabilization in Postwar Latin America," in *Authoritarianism and Corporatism in Latin America*, ed. James Malloy (Pittsburgh: University of Pittsburgh Press, 1977).

5. I have dealt with these mechanisms in Waisman, *Reversal of Development*, ch. 7.

6. Claudio Veliz, *The Centralist Tradition in Latin America* (Princeton: Princeton University Press, 1980), p. 279.

7. Data are from the World Bank, *World Development Report 1986* (New York: Oxford University Press, 1986), p. 199.

8. See Morgan Guaranty Trust Co., *World Financial Markets*, February and September/October, 1985; Naciones Unidas, Comisión Económica para America

Latina y el Caribe, *Nota sobre la Evolución de la Economía Argentina en 1985*, (Buenos Aires: Naciones Unidas, 1986) (hereafter cited as *Nota sobre la Evolución*); Naciones Unidas, Comisión Económica para America Latina y el Caribe, *Tres Ensayos sobre Inflación y Políticas de Establizacion* (Buenos Aires: Naciones Unidad, 1986), especially see pp. 144–147 (hereafter cited as *Tres Ensayos*); United Nations, Economic Commission for Latin America and the Caribbean, *Economic Panorama of Latin America 1986* (Santiago, Chile: United Nations, 1986) pp. 15–22.

9. See Daniel Heymann, "Inflación y Políticas de Establización," *Revista de la Cepal* 28 (1986), pp. 67–98 (hereafter cited as "Inflación"); Morgan Guaranty Trust Co., *World Financial Markets*, September/October 1985; Naciones Unidas, *Nota sobre la Evolución*.

10. Heymann, "Inflación," p. 88; also in Naciones Unidas, *Tres Ensayos*, p. 135.

11. Morgan Guaranty Trust Co., *World Financial Markets*, September/October 1985, p. 7. For a similar statement, see also Miles Kahler, "Conclusion: Politics and Proposals for Reform," in *The Politics of International Debt*, ed. Miles Kahler (Ithaca: Cornell University Press, 1986), p. 267.

12. See, for instance, the enthusiastic endorsements from Barber C. Conable, the president of the World Bank; Ronald Reagan; and William R. Rhodes, the chair of the committee of creditor banks dealing with the Argentine debt, in *Clarín Económico*, edición internacional, May 11–17, 1987.

13. *Clarín Económico*, January 4, 1987; October 11, 1987.

14. Adolfo Canitrot, "Teoría y Práctica del Liberalismo. Política Antiinflacionaria y Apertura Económica en la Argentina, 1976–1981," *Desarrollo Económico* (Buenos Aires) 21, no. 82 (1981), pp. 131–190 (hereafter cited as "Teoría y Práctica"); Jorge Schvarzer, *Martínez de Hoz: la Lógica Política de la Política Económica* (Buenos Aires: CISEA, 1983), p. 130.

15. Carlos H. Waisman, "The Legitimation of Democracy Under Adverse Conditions: The Case of Argentina," in *From Military Rule to Liberal Democracy in Argentina*, eds. Monica Peralta-Ramos and Carlos H. Waisman (Boulder: Westview Press, 1986).

16. I discuss these matters in *Reversal of Development in Argentina*, ch. 3.

17. See Juan M. Villarreal, *El Capitalismo Dependiente: Estudio sobre la Estructura de Classes en la Argentina* (Mexico: Siglo XXI, 1978); *Clarín Económico*, July 8, 1984.

18. Canitrot, "Teoría y Práctica," pp. 185–186.

19. A classical point is made by Juan Linz, *The Breakdown of Democratic Regimes: Crisis, Breakdown, and Reequilibration* (Baltimore: Johns Hopkins University Press, 1988), ch. 2.

20. *Clarín Económico*, edición internacional, May 4–10, 1987, p. 3.

21. Charles L. Taylor and Michael C. Hudson, *World Handbook of Political and Social Indicators*, 2d ed. (New Haven: Yale University Press, 1972) pp. 229–231.

22. World Bank, *World Development Report 1986*, p. 237.

23. According to a source, enrollment has doubled since 1983. See *Clarín Económico*, edición internacional, July 6–12, 1987. I think this is an exaggeration.

24. See the statements and material from interviews in Carlos J. Moneta, "Fuerzas Armadas y Gobierno Constitucional Después de las Malvinas: Hacia una Nueva Relación Civil-Militar," *Foro Internacional* 36, no. 2 (1985), pp. 190–213.

25. World Bank, *World Development Report 1986*, p. 183.

26. See Waisman, *Reversal of Development*, p. 6.

27. Barbara Insel, "A World Awash in Grain," *Foreign Affairs* 63, no. 4 (1985), pp. 892–911.

28. Richard D. Mallon and Juan V. Sorrouille, *Economic Policymaking in a Conflict Society: the Argentine Case* (Cambridge: Harvard University Press, 1975).

29. *Clarín Económico*, edición internacional, May 4–10, 1987, p. 6.

30. See *Clarín Económico*, edición internacional, May 18–24, 1987; June 22–28, 1987; July 13–19, 1987.

10

NOTES ON THE ARGENTINE DEBT CRISIS

Carlos Alberto Carballo

Argentina has been strongly affected by the debt crisis. Since 1980, per capita gross national product (GNP) has dropped more than 50 percent, gross domestic investment to half the previous historical average, and the country struggles with hyperinflation. Debt service has grown from 48 percent of exports in 1981 to 72 percent in 1987. Only a fraction of debt services has been paid out of the trade surplus, despite a severe shrinkage of imports, permanent recession, and lack of investment. As a consequence, the foreign debt has risen from \$36 billion in 1981 to \$54 billion in 1987.

An outstanding feature of the Argentine debt is that it was not caused by a foreign trade deficit. Arms acquisitions were important, but flight of capital accounts for more than 50 percent of the total debt. It is sometimes said that capital flight has been halted, but the black-market price of dollars tells a different story.

Why is the flight of capital so strong and persistent? Political and economic instability, lack of propitious business opportunities, side effects of the informal economy, and the possibility of windfall profits by speculation on financial markets were important factors.

The Austral stabilization plan, launched in June 1985, promised an end to inflation, which is now back to well into the triple-digit figures. The elections held on September 6, 1987, had bad results for the Alfonsín administration. Debt was an issue in the campaign, with the Peronist party proposing a tougher stand, whether or not this issue was an important factor in voting decisions. We know that dissatisfaction with economic policy was strong; recent Gallup polls inform us that 80 percent of the population feels that economic policy was bad or very bad.

Very important transformations are needed in the economy to reestablish growth. They go very deep into the economic and social structure and, of course, a great deal further than a mere opening of the economy. An opening of the economy without a reorganization of the state, sensible exchange rates, and an accommodation of the whole internal economy to market incentives could be very dangerous.

There is no substitute for sensible administration of public enterprises and the state bureaucracy. For instance, tax evasion substantially orients economic activities. At present, capital-intensive companies are paying the bulk of sale, income, capital, and social welfare levies. It is not strange that investment goes to areas such as trade and services that are able to avoid that tax burden. The needed reorganization will meet with terrible obstacles. Many years of going the wrong way have created a network of interests, social groups, and cultural values that are not easy to remove.

On the other hand, public opinion is every day more aware of the futility of going on with a state of affairs that does not offer a better future. That desire for change gives the possibility for a real transformation of the Argentine economic and social systems. As I see it, the road is going to be long and full of detours. Some of them can include unrealistic approaches to the debt situation. Notwithstanding, I feel that it is "high noon" for changes in Argentina.

The most appropriate commentary, however, would be a little story. A man was being examined as candidate for a position as guard at a railroad crossing. He was asked what he would do if he saw two trains headed for a collision and had no way of signaling them to stop. He answered that he would call his wife and say, "Come here, we're going to see a wonderful train collision."

11

VENEZUELA, CENTRAL AMERICA, AND THE CARIBBEAN

Gary W. Wynia

While most of the chapters in this volume focus on the region's largest economies, they are not the only ones that suffer from debt burdens. Smaller countries also merit brief comments.

Venezuelans have tried hard to resist subjugation to a bargaining process in which they increasingly find themselves at a disadvantage as their debt rises. Unlike most of their neighbors, they have averted mediation by the IMF. In 1986 their foreign debt reached $30.8 billion, the fourth largest in Latin America. In February of that year they signed an agreement with creditors to refinance $21.2 billion of debt maturing between 1982 and 1986. It became operational in October 1986 but still had to be renegotiated in 1987 because the fall in oil prices did not allow the country to comply with the original terms.

In 1986 Venezuela had about $15 billion in foreign exchange reserves and a large coffer for a country of its size, something that made it easier to survive without severe belt-tightening measures until oil prices fell in midyear. It was a real shock, for after receiving $14.8 billion from oil revenues (90 percent of the nation's export earnings) in 1985, Venezuelans anticipated $12.6 billion in 1986 but received only $7.5 billion.[1]

In midyear, President Lusinchi announced a 21-point austerity program, devaluing the bolivar and restricting imports. Most controversial was his attempt to convert $7 billion of private sector debt into government bonds that would pay 5 percent over 15 years, far less than was owed to foreign creditors. Led by Chase Manhattan, three major banks retaliated by halting lines of trade credit in an attempt to block what they considered a very costly precedent in debt conversion. In the end they succeeded, for in December 1986, Lusinchi abandoned the bonds scheme in favor of a complicated plan that did less damage to creditors than to Venezuelan business. This was an excellent example of the leverage still wielded by major creditors.[2]

Throughout 1986, Venezuelans refused to have dealings with the IMF, yet followed some of its recommendations, such as devaluing the bolivar by 48.8 percent in December. For a time Venezuela crawled along, its authorities working hard within OPEC to raise international oil prices, and succeeding somewhat in 1987. Success finally came in the wake of the Brazilian halt of payments in February 1987, when Venezuela and its creditors reached new terms on most of the debt.

Central American countries are, for the most part, the "basket cases" of debt management in the hemisphere. This is hardly surprising given their relatively low capacity to generate wealth and their heavy dependence on few exports. Several patterns are obvious today.

First, their interest payments, though not taking as much from export income as they do in Mexico, Brazil, and Argentina, are still relatively high on a per capita basis in what remain poor economies. Second, interest on debt is increasingly no longer being paid in full. Third, creditors have, for the present time, tolerated noncompliance, no doubt convinced that the Central American countries will not set precedents for the larger nations and therefore do not create cause for exceptional concern, unlike similar behavior from, say, Venezuela or Mexico. Fourth, the region's economies have been helped by better coffee prices and the lowering of oil prices in 1986, but this improvement is still too little to generate enough growth to allow full payment of debts.

Costa Rica has the highest per capita debt of the region at $1,630 per person. About 25 percent of its export income goes to pay interest on its foreign debt, making frequent renegotiation of terms essential. Since mid–1986, Costa Rica has paid only about $3 to $5 million a month in interest, well short of the $12 million due. It has talked sporadically to individual banks, but is in no hurry to sit down and negotiate. In the meantime, thanks to the high price of coffee, the fall in oil prices, and U.S. aid, the economy grew about 2 percent in 1986, continuing a trend that began in 1983 after two years of negative growth.[3]

Nicaragua's chances of servicing its $4 billion debt look remote. It has suffered a sharp drop in farm production for export and a large increase in its trade deficit. Though high coffee prices and low oil prices have helped somewhat, its economy did not grow in 1986 for the third straight year, and its prospects for the future do not look much better as long as its civil war continues to interrupt rural production. It is estimated that real money wages fell by 45 percent in 1986.[4]

Honduras has also fallen behind in interest payments by about $15 million on its $2.4 billion debt. Yet more than its southern neighbors, it is trying to reschedule its debt. Meanwhile, El Salvador is able to make payments on its $2.1 billion debt with substantial aid from the United

States. Even if there should be an increase in earnings from coffee, it will continue to need such aid. Austerity measures have generated substantial protest.

Prospects for recovery in the Caribbean are not much better than those in Central America, though the means being employed domestically to cope with debt problems are a bit more diverse. In the Dominican Republic, the debt of $3.6 billion was rescheduled in 1985, but because the country must spend nearly 40 percent of export income on debt payments, its economic growth will be seriously constrained for some time to come. Starting in 1985 the country experienced its first economic decline in almost two decades. Since it relies on sugar for about 40 percent of its export earnings, it has been hurt by low sugar prices during the past few years. The tightening of U.S. sugar quotas has not helped either. Nevertheless, prospects are improving somewhat. At least new president Joaquín Balaguer, elected in May 1986, managed to launch an IMF-style austerity program, achieving most of its initial objectives by the year's end. The economy grew by 2 percent in 1986, but real wages fell by 9 percent; unemployment stayed around 30 percent, and riots were not unknown.

Jamaica's debt of $2.1 billion will consume about 25 percent of export earnings over the next couple of years. The fall in oil import prices in 1986 has partly compensated for the fall in bauxite income, and inflation fell because strict monetary policies were followed. Jamaica is also one of the few countries drawing some benefit from the U.S. Caribbean Basin Initiative, which has allowed it to expand its agricultural and manufacturing exports to the United States. Still, economic growth was less than 1 percent in 1986. Protests were common and more are feared.[5]

Cuba is a case apart. It owes $3.7 billion to Western creditors and $18 billion to the Soviet Union and East European countries. It stopped paying interest on its hard currency debt in the summer of 1986, and its chances of servicing it any time soon look remote. The fall in oil prices has hurt its ability to reexport Soviet oil, a major source of income in the face of falling sugar prices. Moreover, its production of only 6.5 million tons of sugar in 1986 (after 8 million in 1985) has forced it to buy sugar in order to comply with deals made with Soviet bloc countries. A halt in fresh money from Western creditors is forcing a slowdown in imports from Western economies.

NOTES

1. *Miami Herald*, April 21, 1986.
2. *New York Times*, July 21, 1986; *Wall Street Journal*, February 23, 1987.
3. *The Economist*, March 14, 1987, p. 76.
4. *The Economist*, March 14, 1987, p. 76.
5. *Miami Herald*, April 21, 1986.

12

CAN THE MICE ROAR? SMALL COUNTRIES AND THE DEBT CRISIS

Howard J. Wiarda

In 1982 the Latin American debt "situation" exploded into the Latin American debt "crisis." The twin oil shocks of 1973 and 1979, declining demand for many Latin American products, rising interest rates, lenders who had too many petrodollars to lend but who failed to discriminate among borrowers, Latin American borrowers whose projects were extravagant and sometimes dubious, and a U.S. government eager to allow private loans to serve as a substitute for declining public assistance were just some of the many factors that contributed to today's international debt crisis.[1]

While the focus of international attention has been for obvious reasons on the large debtors (Argentina, Brazil, Mexico, and Venezuela), there has been little serious examination of the smaller debtors. On a per capita basis, their debts are quite as onerous as those of the larger countries, and often more so. Yet because their debts loom smaller in the global scheme of things and do not have the possibilities of undermining the banks or the international financial system as the large debtors do, only limited attention has been devoted to them.[2] The question we ask here is whether the smaller debtors have been able to maneuver in the current debt crisis with as much adroitness as the larger ones, and hence whether they also have the same possibility of lifting this burden as the larger countries.

THE DEBT CRISIS AND ITS MANAGEMENT

The Latin American foreign debt has the potential to be disastrous for: the banks that hold the debt; the Latin American governments (mostly new democracies) that must repay it; the international financial system that is threatened with collapse if the debt is not paid; and the U.S. government (and ultimately the U.S. taxpayer), which may have to face the dismal and politically unpalatable prospect of bailing out all of the previous three.[3]

The size of the debt is staggering: about $400 billion, with $40 billion more per year (approximately) being added in new interest. Brazil owes around $120 billion, Mexico $100 billion, Argentina $60 billion, and Venezuela $40 billion. Those are the large debtors. Yet on a per capita basis, Costa Rica's debt burden is the continent's heaviest.

Before proceeding further, it is necessary to tackle some myths about the debt. First is that the debt will ever be paid back in full with anything resembling real money (as distinct from that which is "cranked off" the local treasury printing presses). The debt is so large that it is inconceivable that much more than a trickle of interest (and virtually no principal at all) will be repaid. All the parties, of course, know that the debt cannot and will not be paid back, though no one can admit it publicly, or the whole house of cards that supports the present strategy of managing the debt crisis will be blown away.

Second, even though everyone knows that the debt cannot be paid back, Latin America cannot be permitted actually to default. That would stigmatize the area as "uncivilized," a label that it has been trying to live down for hundreds of years; it would make the region ineligible for new loans; no new capital would come in, thus curtailing development; it might result in the seizure of Latin American assets; and it would subject the area to a broad range of financial and political penalties. The cost of outright default to Latin America would be severe.

Third, even though the banks also know that these loans are uncollectible, they cannot entirely write them off as such. If they did, the banks would no longer receive even the interest on the Latin American loans anymore, which is what the banks at this stage are chiefly interested in; the term used for paying interest is "servicing" the debt. Additionally, the bank's stock would plummet, and management would come under severe criticism from shareholders. Some of the banks themselves with an especially high Latin American debt exposure relative to their assets (these are the large, so-called money-market banks, including the Bank of America, Chase, Citibank, and Manufacturer's Hanover) might even have to fold. This last threat was greater two years ago than it is now, when the banks are making comparatively large profits and are thus better able to write off some of their uncollectible Latin American loans.[4]

Fourth, the U.S. government must help maintain the myth that the debts are payable and therefore only a financial matter between debtors and creditors. The alternative is for the United States to say that the debt is a political matter (it is, of course), in which case the U.S. government would have to be drawn into this act far more deeply than it wants to be. For once the United States admits that the debt is unpayable and is therefore a political matter, it is the U.S. government that would also have to step in to keep Latin America solvent, to keep the banks from going under, and to prop up the international financial system. We may be assured that "bailing out" what will surely be presented as corrupt Latin American regimes and rich U.S. banks is not a platform that politicians in either the Congress or the White House will want to run on in the next election. The implication is that it is the "poor, long-suffering" U.S. taxpayers who will be left "holding the bag" for all these other "deadbeats."

Yet if the debt cannot be paid while at the same time default has to be avoided, how then is this debt situation to be dealt with? The answer is that the debt can be "managed." Then we need to carry the analysis a step further by asking what managing the debt means to the various actors involved.

To the banks, managing the debt means keeping the Latin American loans on the books as at least potentially collectible even though only a trickle of interest may be coming in and no principal at all. It means continuously rolling over the debt, foregoing some fees, lowering interest rates where possible, and making new loans available. It means ignoring due dates, glossing over nonpayment, and acting as though several of the countries of the area (particularly the smaller of the less important ones) were not already in de facto default. The banks seem to be willing to do virtually anything about the debt within reason, except admit that their loans to various Latin American countries are no good.

To the Latin American governments, managing the debt means some limited belt tightening, some efforts (albeit not always very strenuous) to impose austerity, efforts to increase and diversify exports, constant renegotiations with the banks regarding what is called "repayment," and continuous promises that the debt will in fact be repaid. In this way, Latin America seeks to remain "creditworthy" but without ever paying back any principal and, in some cases, very little in the way of interest either.

For the U.S. government, managing the debt means constantly talking optimistically as if it believed these debts would be paid, putting pressure on the banks to keep making new loans available so as to enable the Latin American governments to at least make interest payments, and arm-twisting agencies such as the World Bank and the Inter-American Development Bank to make more loans to Latin America available. It means prodding the Latin American governments to make structural reforms in return for these new loans, constantly searching for a "new handle" to make the debt issue go away or at least attenuate its impact, and goading the other parties to the dispute to keep up all the fictions previously noted. Meanwhile, the United States has redirected its foreign assistance activities away from major development projects and toward the servicing of debt.[5]

Hence, all the parties to the debt crisis have a strong interest in maintaining the idea that it is manageable. To do otherwise would be to admit that the debt is unpayable, the loans cannot be collected, the Latin American governments and some of the major U.S. banks are unsound and unstable, the international financial system is insecure, and that the American taxpayer will ultimately have to shoulder the burden. The plan, in short, is to play for more time, keep postponing the day of reckoning, and hope that the slender threads by which the entire strategy hangs do not snap and that meanwhile world economic recovery will enable Latin America to grow out of the crisis.

Yet the situation is not static. While the process and "system" of managing the debt described here have been in effect since 1982, each of the parties has made significant strides toward getting out from under this burden. The banks have been converting their Latin American debt holdings into paper and selling it off, trading debt for equity in the countries affected, lobbying for legal and tax changes that will enable them less painfully to absorb their losses, raising domestic interest rates as a way partially to make up for lost revenues from Latin America, and meanwhile rolling up enormous profits in the last two years so as to be able better to absorb the losses from their Latin American loans while at the same time looking for other ways to pass their losses onto the U.S. government and onto the taxpayers. Many bankers (though not usually the big money-market ones) say that if they have five good years (they have already had three), they will be largely out from under the Latin American loan burden; others say that if they can only collect interest for a couple more years (again, having had several good years of collecting interest at or near 20 percent), they will come out of this crisis not altogether badly. Hence their concern is that the debts continue to be serviced and not that the loans have to be paid back.[6]

The Latin American governments have also learned a variety of lessons. For one thing, they have learned that the International Monetary Fund is not nearly so draconian now as compared with its earlier reputation, and that the requirements that the IMF imposes in return for pronouncing a country creditworthy can be gotten around. Second, large debtors like Brazil have learned that the sheer size of their debt, and its destructive capacity if unpaid, give them considerable power and room to maneuver in international negotiations. Third, the Latin American governments have learned that the United States has a powerful political and strategic stake in their survival and will not let them collapse politically nor economically; that position gives them considerable leverage.

Fourth, they have learned that the austerity and structural reforms demanded by the United States and the IMF can be turned on for a time and then relaxed or avoided altogether. At the same time, the Latin American countries have diversified their exports, cut waste, and streamlined and made more efficient their public bureaucracies.

The United States also has a tough balancing act to perform; it wants to help solve the crisis but also wants as much as possible to stay out of direct involvement. Hence, the United States has maintained a generally hands-off attitude publicly, while stepping in massively but on an ad hoc basis in genuine crises (for example, the Mexican bailout of 1982). At the same time, through the Baker Plan and its several subsequent corollaries, the United States has nudged all the parties toward some more general and comprehensive solutions. The United States has put massive pressure on the reluctant private banks to keep the loan funds flowing, has similarly put pressure on the Latin American governments to keep interest payments coming in, and in the meantime is both working toward some changes in its tax laws to help ameliorate the crisis and prepare the groundwork for eventually having the U.S. taxpayers absorb these losses, either through new taxes, inflation, or a special agency that will take over some of the debt.[7]

It is clear from the foregoing discussion that there are various levels (some public, some private) at which the Latin America debt is being met and that there is considerably greater movement on the part of all the parties to the crisis than usually meets the eye. The presumption is not that as a result of these activities the debt crisis will entirely be resolved, but that its dimensions will be lessened over time and that it will become less severe and go into what economist Albert Hirschman, in another context, called a "quasi-vanishing act."[8] The fact of the matter is that the debt crisis has already begun to loom less large, and all the present players in the game have learned to play it quite well.

Most of what I have said so far applies to the large debtors, Argentina, Brazil, Mexico, and Venezuela, whose debts are so large that they have received the main attention from the banks and the United States. Do these general comments concerning the management of the debt apply in the same way to the smaller debtors? In addition, what leverage (if any) do they have in this game, to what extent are they ignored in the preoccupation with the big debtors, and what will be the outcome of the crisis on these smaller countries?

SMALL DEBTORS

The position of the small debtors is inherently different from that of the large ones. Not only is the size of the large nations' debt far greater in absolute terms but also their behavior, the context in which they operate, and the ways in which they are treated by others are different.

We begin by reviewing the actual debt situations of the smaller Latin American countries, then move to a discussion of how the small debtors are treated by the banks and the international financial community, and finally explore the capacity and limits of political bargaining of these smaller countries.

Bolivia has a total external debt (1985 figures) of $3.97 billion and a gross national product (GNP) of 2.6 billion.[9] The country has exports of goods and services of $737.5 million, imports of $1.11 billion, and international reserves of $492 million. Bolivia's ratio of total external debt to exports is 538.5 percent, its ratio of debt to GNP is 152 percent, its ratio of reserves to debt is 12.4 percent, and its ratio of reserves to imports (in months) is 5.4. Generally if a country's debt is more than twice its exports, there is cause for alarm;[10] in Bolivia's case the debt is more than five times its officially registered exports (the drug trade makes these figures not entirely accurate). Bolivia has not been servicing its debt since 1985 and is widely viewed as being in de facto default; however, in recent months, there have been signs of improvement in the Bolivian economy and new loans have accordingly also become available.[11]

Costa Rica has a total external debt of $4.19 billion and a GNP of $3.32 billion, exports of $2.27 billion, imports of $1.64 billion, and reserves of $525 million. Its ratio of debt to exports is 330 percent, its ratio of debt to GNP is 120 percent, its ratio of reserves to debt is 12.5 percent, and its ratio of reserves to imports is 3.8 months. Costa Rica is clearly in better shape than Bolivia but is also in deep trouble.

The Dominican Republic has a total external debt of $3.3 billion and a GNP of $4.3 billion. Its exports in 1984 were $1.38 billion, its imports were $1.8 billion, and its reserves in 1985 were $346 million. Its ratio of debt to exports was 222 percent in 1984, the ratio of its debt to GNP was 76.6 percent, the ratio of its reserves to debt was 10.5 percent, and the ratio (1984 figure) of its reserves to imports was 1.7 months. The Dominican Republic's debt service ratio worsened beginning in 1982, but a stabilization program carried out by President Salvador Jorge Blanco beginning in 1985 helped to improve the situation. Currently, there is a great deal of uncertainty concerning the future direction of the national accounts.[12]

Ecuador has a total external debt of $9.2 billion and a GNP of $11.7 billion. The total value of its exports is $3.3 billion, of its imports $3.4 billion, and of its reserves $854 million. Ecuador has a debt-to-export ratio of 283 percent, a debt-to-GNP ratio of 79 percent, a reserves-to-debt ratio of 9.2 percent, and a reserves-to-imports ratio of three months. Once again, as with the other countries, Ecuador's ratio of debts to exports is uncomfortably high, and since 1984, it has not been paying the interest on its loans. Like Bolivia, Ecuador is widely considered to be in de facto default.

Strife-torn El Salvador has a comparatively small foreign debt of $1.7 billion, mostly owed to the U.S. government, and a GNP of $3.7 billion. Its exports in 1984 were $954 million, while its imports were $1.3 billion and its reserves $333 million. In 1984 El Salvador's ratio of debt to exports was 179 percent, its ratio of debt to GNP was 43 percent, its ratio of reserves to debt was 18 percent, and its ratio of reserves to imports was 2.8 months. El Salvador has both the lowest debt of any of the countries encountered so far, and is the only one whose ratio of debt to export is less than 2 to 1. This position is due in part to the immense U.S. assistance to the country in the last decade; it is not a sign of a healthy and robust economy.

Guatemala has a total external debt to $2.6 billion and a GNP of $10.8 billion. Its exports total $1.2 billion, its imports $1.5 billion, and its reserves $471 million. Guatemala's ratio of debt to exports is 217 percent, its ratio of debt to GNP is 24 percent, its ratio of reserves to debt is 18 percent, and its ratio of reserves to imports is 3.9 months. Guatemala therefore occupies something of a middle position in our listing, with a quite robust economy and a worrisome, but not entirely fatal, debt-to-exports ratio.

Honduras has a total external debt of $2.7 billion and a GNP of $3.2 billion. Its exports amount to $966 million, its imports are $1.3 billion, and its reserves are $111 million. Some critical ratios in the Honduran case are: debt-to-exports, 281 percent; debt-to-GNP, 85 percent; reserves-to-debt, 4.1 percent; and reserves-to-imports, 1 month. Honduras in this area, as in many others, ranks close to the middle among the smaller Latin American countries; it is not in the best position but not the worst either.

Jamaica has a total external debt of $3.75 billion and a total GNP of $1.7 billion. Its exports are just over $1 billion yearly, while its imports are $1.2 billion and its reserves total $161 million. The principal ratios in Jamaica's case are: debt-to-exports, 346 percent; debt-to-GNP, 218 percent; reserves-to-debt, 4.3 percent; and reserves-to-imports, 1.5 months. Unlike many of the countries considered here, Jamaica's debt-service ratio went up in 1985.

Nicaragua's debt of $5.6 billion is the largest of the Central American countries. Its GNP was $2.8 billion prior to the recent depression. The figures on Nicaragua's imports, exports, and reserves, as well as its principal ratios that are based on these figures, are hard to come by, outdated, and sometimes grounded in different criteria than those of the capitalist countries of the region. For what they are worth, the figures show exports of $846 million in 1983, imports of $993 million, and reserves of $220.5 million. Nicaragua's ratio of debt to exports for 1983 was 845 percent—the highest in the hemisphere. Its ratio of debt to GNP for 1985 was 197.6 percent. The ratio of reserves to debt in 1983 was 5.6 percent, and the ratio of debt to imports for that same year was 2.7. Nicaragua is in trouble, not only because of the size of the debt and debt-service ratio, but also because its principal benefactor, the Soviet Union, seems increasingly reluctant to provide new economic assistance.

Panama has a debt of $4.5 billion and a GNP of $4.3 billion. Its exports are $6.38 billion, imports $6.44 billion, and reserves $98 million. By comparison with the other Central American countries, Panama's debt ratios are quite good: the ratio of debt to exports is 73.8 percent, and the ratio of debt to GNP is 107.7 percent. Its ratio of reserves to debt, however, is a low 2.1 percent and its ratio of reserves to imports is 0.2 months.

Paraguay, which has practiced a more conservative and traditional economic policy, has a total foreign debt of $1.78 billion. Its GNP is $2.7 billion. Its exports amount to $1.2 billion, its imports are $1.4 billion, and its reserves $559 million. Paraguay has a comparatively low ratio of debt to exports of 151 percent and a very low ratio of debt to GNP of 65 percent—the lowest in the hemisphere. Paraguay's ratio of reserves to debt is 31 percent—and its ratio of reserves to imports is 4.7 months. One could almost conclude from these figures that Paraguay has no serious debt problems.

Uruguay has a debt of $3.9 billion and a GNP of $4.7 billion. Its exports total $1.3 billion, its imports $1.45 billion, and its reserves just over $1 billion. Uruguay's ratio of debt to exports is a troublesome 295 percent, but its ratio of debt to GNP is 83 percent. Its ratio of reserves to debt is 26.4 percent, and its ratio of reserves to imports is 8.6 months. Uruguay has a debt problem, but it is not so serious as those of some other countries.

What is immediately striking about these figures is the variation in the debt situation that exists between these 12 cases. We commonly gloss over these differences in treating the area as a whole. The "good performers" in the area are stigmatized along with the "poor performers," and the result is a lack of confidence, or of new investment, in the area as a whole. The situations of all the small Latin American countries are summarized in Table 12.1.

The major commercial banks have already largely written off the debts of a number of the smaller countries. They consider Bolivia, Ecuador, the Caribbean countries, and *all* of Central America to be in de facto default and no longer worth worrying about. The dollar amounts are so small compared with those of the larger countries that the banks have made a decision to concentrate on the latter. Yet that decision, quite rational from the banks' point of view, has the result also of practically guaranteeing that there will be virtually no new loan money for these

Table 12.1
Summary of Small Country Debt Situations

Country	ExDebts (total)	GNP	ExG&S	ImG&S	Res	Debt/Ex (%)	Debt/GNP (%)	Res/Debt (%)	Res/Imp (mos)
BOLIVIA	3.97b	2.6b	737.5m	1.1b	492m	538.5	152.0	12.4	5.4
C. RICA	4.9b	3.32b	2.27b	1.64b	525m	330.0	126.0	12.5	3.8
DOM REP	3.3b	4.3b	1.38b	1.8b	346m	222.0	76.6	10.5	1.7
ECUADOR	9.2b	11.7b	3.3b	3.4b	854m	283.0	79.0	9.2	3.0
EL SALV	1.7b	3.7b	954m	1.3b	333m	179.0	43.0	18.0	2.8
GUAT	2.6b	10.8b	1.2b	1.5b	471m	217.0	24.0	18.0	3.9
HONDURAS	2.7b	3.2b	966m	1.3b	111m	281.0	85.0	4.1	1.5
JAMAICA	3.75b	1.7b	1b	1.2b	161m	346.0	218.0	4.?	1.5
NICAR	5.6b	2.8b	846m	993m	220.5m	845.0	197.6	5.6	2.7
PANAMA	4.5b	4.3b	6.38b	6.44b	98m	73.8	107.7	2.1	0.2
PARAGUAY	1.78b	2.7b	1.4b	1.4b	559m	151.0	65.0	31.0	4.7
URUGUAY	3.9b	4.7b	1.3b	1.45b	1b	295.0	83.0	26.4	8.6

Source: World Bank, *World Debt Tables: External Debts of Developing Countries* (Washington, D.C.: 1986–87 edition).

smaller countries from the private banks. Why should they pour money into countries on which they have already given up? Furthermore, in the urge to concentrate on the large debtors, there is little discrimination between the smaller countries. All are condemned (or better, ignored); good performers such as Paraguay or Panama, medium performers such as Costa Rica or the Dominican Republic, and poor performers such as Bolivia or Ecuador are all treated alike. As a result, all suffer as a function not of merit but largely and simply of smallness.

DEALING WITH THE SMALL COUNTRIES

In part at least, the problems of small debtors receive less attention because the banks and the U.S. government are almost constantly involved in working out rescheduling packages and new loan monies for the larger countries.[13] Argentina, Brazil, Mexico, and Venezuela have received the bulk of the attention, leaving little time left for the smaller countries.

At the end of 1984, the "big four" debtors (Argentina, Brazil, Mexico, and Venezuela) owed U.S. banks about $70 billion. All of the other countries owed a total of $19 billion to the U.S. banks, of which more than 60 percent was owed by medium-sized debtors: Chile, $7 billion; Colombia, $3 billion; and Peru, $2 billion. The smaller debtors owed only about $7 billion in total to U.S. banks. In short, even when the debt of all the smaller countries is combined, it still comes to only a small fraction of what the larger debtors owe.

Because of the small size of their debts and hence the lack of any threat on their part to the banks, the small countries have received far less generous treatment from the banks. The large countries' grace and repayment periods have usually been considerably more generous than those for the smaller countries, fees and spreads are typically lower for the big debtors, and the banks have been far more willing to grant multiyear reschedulings to the large debtors than to the small.

To cite only a few examples, during the early rounds of rescheduling in 1982–83, the small countries typically received grace periods ranging from one to three years while Mexico got four. Repayments were expected usually from the small countries in five or six years whereas Mexico got eight years, even though the per capita debt burden was higher in the small countries than in Mexico, and even though Mexico had a far greater capacity to repay, with a GNP per capita approximately twice that of the smaller countries of the area.

The same or greater differences existed with regard to fees and spreads. Mexico's fee (the up-front amount charged by banks for rescheduling commercial bank debt) was one percent, while those of the smaller countries were all at least 25 percent higher. Similarly, spreads were smaller for the larger countries (less than 2 percent) than for the smaller ones (consistently more than 2 percent). As the debt crisis worsened in later years and the pressure mounted, the banks dropped many of these fees for small as well as big countries; yet the spread still remained larger for the smaller countries than the big ones, and the repayment periods for the large debtors also remained longer.

In addition, private commercial banks have been far less willing to offer new loans to the smaller countries than to the larger ones. The logic is that new loans will enable the larger debtors to continue paying their interest charges and thus maintain the fiction of creditworthiness. That is, after all, what the banks are mainly interested in: collecting the interest, thus servicing the debt, and enabling the banks to continue these loans on the books as "performing." However, sometimes it took enormous pressure on the part of the U.S. government to get the banks to join in these new loan packages for the larger countries, leaving no enthusiasm whatsoever on the part of the banks for additional "bailouts" of the small countries. Some debtors such as Honduras were given no new bank loans for a time; with the others, the banks have been very stingy and have only stayed in the game in limited ways, in these cases because they have been cajoled and badgered by the U.S. government into doing so.

To put it bluntly, the private banks have in effect given up on collecting interest or principal from Bolivia, Ecuador, or the countries of Central

America. These countries are in de facto default, that is, they have not paid any or only a minimum of interest for a given period, and the banks regard their loans as uncollectible. The banks do not say that publicly, since they do not want to start a chain of defaults that would jeopardize their chances of collecting from the large debtors. However, if it were not for the heavy arm-twisting by the Federal Reserve Board and Department of the Treasury, which occasionally pries some additional loan funds out of the banks, the banks would have entirely written off these small and "hopeless" debtors long ago.

Not only have the banks given the small countries less favorable rescheduling packages or been unwilling to advance any new loans, but the small debtors are confronted with a variety of other problems that make their possibilities for recovery considerably less than for the larger countries. In the first place, the economic decline of most of the smaller debtors actually predates the onset of the debt crisis. It seems reasonable to suggest, therefore, that even were the debt burden on these countries to be lifted, they would very likely still be in a position of very limited growth, no growth, or negative growth and thus would continue with severe economic problems.

Second, these countries have very small domestic markets that are insufficient to stimulate much new production. They remain heavily dependent on a few export commodities (sugar, coffee, bananas, and tin) whose prices globally are likely to remain very low, and hence they all have severe balance-of-payment problems that would remain even if there were no debt problem.

Third, because the standard of living is generally lower in the smaller countries than the larger ones, and because the smaller countries (except Costa Rica) lack even the limited institutional infrastructure that the big ones have (such as social security, unemployment insurance, and various social "safety net" programs), the effects of the debt in the small countries have been more severe. Standards of living have declined more dramatically in the small countries than in the large ones; health and education services have declined disproportionately; under- and unemployment are worse; and malnutrition, disease, and sheer misery are considerably worse.

These special circumstances make it more difficult for the small countries simply to grow out of their debt situations, which is, in fact, the only long-term solution, in the same way as the bigger countries. Underdeveloped, with small markets, not in a very strong nor effective position internationally, and underinstitutionalized domestically in both an economic and political sense, they are simply not equipped in the same way as the large countries to take advantage of the worldwide economic recovery that began in the mid–1980s.

BARGAINING CAPACITY OF THE SMALL COUNTRIES

Despite the disadvantages they suffer from the result of their small size, their underdeveloped character, and the small size of their debts, the small countries are not without bargaining capacity in international political and economic arenas. Some, in fact, have proven adept at enhancing their positions regardless of their small size and relative unimportance globally. Here I shall point out some of the means by which small debtors have employed leverage to their own advantage.

First, the small countries have employed what may be termed the "free-rider" or "piggyback" effect.[14] The small countries have often been successful in arguing that they should receive the same, or nearly the same, treatment as the large countries in terms of interest rates on loans, fees, spreads, time of repayment, etc. Differences remain between small and big debtors, but the small countries may actually benefit—even though they had nothing to do with it—from an advantageous agreement worked out with an Argentina, Brazil, or a Mexico. Seen in this light, being small an actually be an advantage; in fact, smallness can cut either way depending on the circumstances.

Second, the small countries have learned that the banks will not mobilize against small debtors in the same way they will against the big ones. Countries such as Bolivia, Ecuador, and several of those in the Caribbean and Central America are in de facto default, and yet nothing very bad happens to them. They do not suffer penalties, their assets are not seized, they are not stigmatized as "uncivilized" in the family of nations. The banks choose to ignore these de facto defaults in the small countries because they do not want to jeopardize their chances of collecting when it really counts, from the large debtors. Actually there is a penalty that these small de facto defaulters pay in that de facto default cuts their chances for new lending from the banks and closes off concessional loans. Yet what might be called the "gunboat consequences" of default (for example, seizure of airplanes of the national airlines when they land at Miami and other penalties) are also quite improbable; the only issue in stopping payments indefinitely is that of real resources flow. As Bolivia, Ecuador, and Central America illustrate, even that problem can be overcome with time if other compelling arguments (discussed later) come into play.[15]

Third, there is a "small country effect" by which the small debtors may actually come out ahead. For example, on a per capita basis, the small countries get more aid from the U.S. Agency for International Development than do the large ones. It does not cost very much to be relatively generous with the smaller ones.[16]

Fourth, some of the small debtors have played cleverly on their "nice little country" image. This is especially true if they are islands of democracy in a sea of turmoil, that is, the circum-Caribbean countries. The best players of this game have been Costa Rica and Jamaica, countries whose leaders are always on the phone to President Reagan, Vice President Bush, or the high U.S. officials pleading their respective cases. The Dominican Republic has also played this game quite well, though not so cleverly as the other two.

A fifth factor I shall call the "situational effect." A good part of the banks' response to the debt crisis in these small countries is determined by when, how, and under what circumstances trouble first occurred. Costa Rica got into debt trouble early in 1981–82, and the banks made things difficult for that country. Then the Mexican crisis broke, and the banks became worried about the demonstration effect of Mexico's inability to pay and the need for a massive bailout of the other countries. The banks were no longer so concerned with the actual debt situation of small countries such as Costa Rica but only with the demonstration effect. After that, they simply paid Costa Rica less attention. In the meantime, of course, Costa Rica took on special importance in the Central American context.[17]

The sixth factor may be especially hard for Americans to understand. That is, that some small debtors may intentionally botch their standby arrangements with the International Monetary Fund for the purpose of subsequently prying still greater concessions out of the U.S. government. This is especially likely to be the case if they think that Washington worries and cares about the stability of their political system. For example, in the Dominican Republic there is considerable evidence that former President Salvador Jorge Blanco purposely provoked the strike and food riots of 1985 in which scores of people were killed. He did this both out of vanity (to prove to the U.S. Embassy and the IMF that his analysis of the implications of raising food prices was the correct one) and as a conscious way of playing on the Americans' fear of provoking "revolution" in another country close to Cuba. The results were just those that Jorge had predicted: the damage from the riots was not too severe and the United States was scared into giving more aid under better terms. This technique may well backfire of course, especially in the hands of a weak president; in Jorge's case, it helped his party to lose the next presidential election in 1986.

The democracy theme, the seventh factor, has been an important one on which the small countries have cleverly played, especially since they know that the United States has put so many of its foreign policy marbles into that basket. Costa Rica, the Dominican Republic, Bolivia, Panama, Ecuador, El Salvador, Guatemala, and Honduras have all been able to extract mileage out of their democratic credentials, out of their arguments that they are bastions of democracy in a continent verging on chaos. If the United States does not support them with loan funds and a guarantee in one form or another of their loans with the private banks, they argue that they will "go down the tubes" (interestingly, in many small country capitals this is the very English-language expression that local politicians use). Of course, it is the U.S. government's obligation, for sound strategic reasons, to see that such a collapse does not happen.

The anticommunist issue, the eighth factor, is an old and rather tired one by now, but it is still used effectively by many countries. The revolutions in Grenada and Nicaragua, the rising Soviet presence in Latin America, and the guerrilla insurgence in El Salvador, Guatemala, Colombia, and Peru all gave fuel to those Latin American politicians who are good at playing the anticommunist game and who know that the issue, after being largely dormant since Che Guevara's death in Bolivia, can evoke a panic response in the U.S. government. None of this is to say that there is no real or serious communist threat anywhere in Latin America.[18] But it is also to say that many Latin American politicians are quite good at exaggerating and manipulating the threat for their own advantage.

Ninth, there is the Central American violence, which has refocused U.S. attention on Latin America. This is not to pass judgment on the validity of the so-called "domino theory," but it is to say that there are sufficient worries in the U.S. government about the dominoes falling to give the dominoes themselves considerable leverage. All the countries of Central America, to say nothing of Mexico, have used the domino theory as a way of getting greater assistance and concessions from the U.S. government, including getting the United States to put pressure on the private bank holders of their debts.

In fact, if one runs down a list of all the small country debtors discussed here, one finds that each one of them has some special feature that it has used to achieve special favors, better terms, or more loan money from the U.S. government, if not out of the private banks. Bolivia is a struggling democracy, has a strong left-wing threat, is the focus of the U.S. government's antidrug campaign, and occupies a strategic location in the heartland of the continent. Costa Rica is a bastion of stability in turbulent Central America, is close to the Panama Canal, lies on the border with Nicaragua, and has been steadily "milking" the fact that it is the most democratic country in the region.

The Dominican Republic has cleverly played upon its new openings to Cuba to get further concessions from the United States; it also is a struggling democracy that the United States would not want to see go under. In addition, the Dominicans are still skillfully making the Americans pay for the revolution and U.S. intervention of 1965.[19]

Ecuador is another struggling democracy whose overthrow would embarrass the United States; Ecuador's president has played on his free enterprise views to endear himself to the Reagan administration. In El

Salvador, the United States has invested so much time, commitment, and money in the last few years to thwart the guerrilla challenge that El Salvador will not be permitted to go under no matter what happens.

Guatemala is a critical country, a struggling democracy, has the largest economy in Central America, a serious guerrilla challenge, and is the last domino before Mexico. Honduras is the launching pad for U.S. activities directed against Nicaragua and is critical for the success of the entire U.S. Central American policy. Jamaica is the focus of the Caribbean Basin Initiative, faces a serious left-wing challenge, and its prime minister is always on the phone to Chase Manhattan or Washington. Nicaragua is outside of the U.S. orbit, which is one of the key reasons why it is in so much trouble politically and economically.

Panama occupies a strategic location because of the Canal, is a critical commercial as well as drug center, and has extracted favors from the United States for maintaining some semblances of democracy. Paraguay has followed a conservative fiscal policy and is not strongly threatened by its foreign debt situation. Yet in the past, Paraguay's authoritarian regime has stressed its stability, anticommunist outlook, and strategic location to qualify for U.S. aid. Uruguay is similarly not in a fatal debt stranglehold, but its struggling democratic government has also been able to squeeze some assistance out of the foreign aid budget and has been able to get better terms from the banks.

Seen in these lights, the small debtors may not be in such a disadvantageous position as some of the literature suggests. There are general properties common to all the small countries, or to several of them as members of a group (for example, the countries of Central America), by which they have qualified for greater aid from the United States or a better deal from the banks. There are also special circumstances unique to each of them individually by which the small countries have taken advantage of their location, strategic importance, international position, or particular domestic circumstances to garner some greater aid or favors from either the U.S. government or the banks, both public and private.

CONCLUSIONS AND IMPLICATIONS

Size can cut both ways. In the present international debt crisis, there are obvious disadvantages to being small. The major disadvantage of small size is that the debts are sufficiently insignificant in comparison with those of large nations so that no one—and certainly not the big money-market banks whose fate may hang on what happens to the large debtors but not the small ones—pays much attention. Small size may be an advantage at times, as well as a disadvantage, depending on many things, including the particular circumstances of each individual country and what I earlier called its situational variables.

One is reminded of the metaphor used by ex-Guatemala president Juan José Arévalo in the title of his book, *The Shark and the Sardines*.[20] Sharks do not always eat sardines, and clever sardines may manipulate the shark. One should not underestimate the political capacities of the "sardines" of Latin America. In any event, all the parties to this crisis must absorb some losses while simultaneously gradually pulling themselves out from under the crisis. In this way, the debt crisis will probably not be resolved but will atrophy and become less severe over time.

NOTES

1. For more complete discussion of the causes and consequences of the debt crisis, see Howard Wiarda, *Latin America at the Crossroads: Debt, Development, and the Future* (Boulder: Westview Press and American Enterprise Institute, 1987) (hereafter cited as *Latin America at Crossroads*).

2. The best analysis is by Christine A. Bogdanowicz-Bindert, "Small Debtors, Big Problems: The Quiet Crisis," *Policy Focus*, no. 2 (Washington, D.C.: Overseas Development Council, 1985) (hereafter cited as "Small Debtors").

3. The analysis here follows that of Wiarda, *Latin America at Crossroads*.

4. Based on interviews with bankers responsible for managing their international debt portfolios.

5. Based on interviews with Latin American government and U.S. embassy officials during five extended research trips to Latin America in 1985 and 1987.

6. Based on interviews with U.S. bank officials. It should be noted that, in 1987, when Citibank and other major banks set aside funds to help cover their Latin American debt losses, they emerged in a stronger, not weaker, bargaining position.

7. Japan has put forward plans to create a special agency that would consolidate all Japanese public and private bank loans to Latin America; some U.S. officials have suggested a similar plan, for example Henry Kissinger, *O Estado de São Paulo*, June 25, 1987.

8. Albert Hirschman, *A Basis for Hope: Essays on Economic Development in Latin America* (New Haven: Yale University Press, 1971), ch. 14.

9. All the figures in this section are based on World Bank, *World Debt Tables: External Debt of Developing Countries* (Washington, D.C., 1986–87 edition). All figures are for 1985 (the most recent available) unless otherwise indicated.

10. This is a rule of thumb suggested by American Enterprise Institute economist John Makin.

11. See the work of Jeffery Sachs, "Managing the LDC Debt Crisis," in *Brookings Papers on Economic Activity*, eds. William C. Brainard and George L. Perry, (Washington, D.C.: Brookings Institution, 1986), pp. 397–440.

12. Based on field research in the Dominican Republic in March–April 1987.

13. The analysis here and in the following paragraphs reflects closely that of Bogdanowicz-Bindert, "Small Debtors."

14. Mancur Olson, *The Logic of Collective Action: Public Goods and the Theory of Groups* (Cambridge, Mass.: Harvard University Press, 1965).

15. Joan Nelson of the Overseas Development Council has provided useful

information on these themes in various private discussions; see also her superb paper on "The Political Economy of Stabilization: Commitment, Capacity, and Public Response," *World Development* 12, no. 10 (1984), pp. 983–1006 (hereafter cited as "Political Economy").

16. Based on field work and interviews with U.S. embassy officials in Costa Rica and the Dominican Republic in 1985 and 1987.

17. Nelson, "Political Economy."

18. A recent assessment is Howard J. Wiarda and Mark Falcoff, *The Communist Challenge in Central America and the Caribbean* (Washington, D.C.: American Enterprise Institute and the University Press of America, 1987).

19. Based on field work and interviews in the Dominican Republic during March–April 1987.

20. Juan José Arévalo, *The Shark and the Sardines* (New York: Stuart, 1986).

13

A SMALL COUNTRY'S DEBT: THE CASE OF COSTA RICA

Felix Delgado Quesada

Noneconomic considerations frequently prevail in the negotiations and decisions regarding the foreign debt. On the one hand, there is a very widespread belief among the debtor countries that the international financial organs are not really independent from the private commercial banks, and neither of these from governmental authorities. Furthermore, commercial banks commonly concentrate on short-term financial implications, to the neglect of the broader interests of not only the debtor countries but also the banks themselves. At the same time, the interdependence of the different parties has increased to the extent that it interferes with the needed flexibility. There is a lack of perception necessary to attack the situation in a global context.

Thus far, the problem has been treated on a case-by-case basis. This is unrealistic. The number of countries with debt problems has continued to grow during this decade, which means that they encounter more generalized difficulties than is usually admitted. More importantly, the debt problem of some countries could occur and persist only because other countries have a global balance-of-payments surplus and are building up reserves. The case-by-case approach is also defective in that it fails to consider the general framework in which international economic relations are maintained. There are external problems that especially affect small countries, such as Costa Rica, which are very open to the outside world and are seriously burdened by debt. The "oil shock" and

Mr. Delgado was compelled to cancel personal participation in the conference because of strenuous negotiations with the Costa Rican bank committee, but he sent this chapter, which is translated by the editor.

recurrent international financial instability are examples of those external difficulties. For this reason one should consider the need for a new world economic order.

It is surprising, however, how fully the unqualified case-by-case approach is supported by leading world economic powers and multilateral organizations whose basic responsibility is for the good functioning of international economic and financial relations. There are, of course, many important differences between the various groups of debtor countries. Productive capacity, degree of diversification of exports, ability to generate revenues in foreign currency, degree of integration in financial and commercial markets of the world, and flexibility of the political system are examples. Thus, the indebted African countries are different from the small Latin American debtors, and these in turn from Brazil and Mexico,.

A surprising aspect is the asymmetry with which the banks apply the case-by-case approach. It is not considered permissible to treat differently very different countries. In this way the "precedent problem" has become the magic word for the commercial banks when an unorthodox proposal for handling the debt is suggested. This has been prominent in the recent experience of Costa Rica.

One can reasonably deduce that the fundamental reason that the banks insist on the case-by-case approach is to prevent a union of debtor countries, which might give them more negotiating strength and harden their positions regarding service of the debt.

There is also a contradiction in the way that the rules of the market are conceived. In discussing the interest rate to be applied to a restructuring of a country's debt, the banks strongly insist that the market rate should be applied. However, they do not accept the judgment of the market in fixing the amount owed. The market value of the notes of many countries is below half of the nominal value of the obligations. In those cases, the effective interest is not that of the market but more than double. This reality should be taken into account while avoiding deliberate action of the debtor to depress the price of its paper more than is called for in view of its medium- and long-term economic prospects.

The foreign debt problem has made necessary complicated negotiating processes. On the one hand, the banks normally demand a financial stabilization program supported by the IMF. Since internal problems are more than short range, it is necessary to go on to structural reforms, which have become a prime concern of the World Bank. Agreements with bilateral creditors, in or out of the Paris Club, are also required as part of the IMF program. In all of these, there is no single defined objective, but the various actors pursue their own objectives, which are often different. The banks try to extract as much as possible in the short term. The fund is interested in avoiding restrictions on payments and normalizing financial flows from the debtor countries. The World Bank wants to promote a market economy. This conflicts frequently with the debtor country's objective of combining fulfillment of foreign obligations with sustained growth, not only in the short term but also in the long term.

This complex scheme of interrelations, known as "cross conditionality," is unfavorable for the debtor country. In the specific case of Costa Rica, it has meant many long series of negotiations, repeated short-term adjustments that cause what has been called "adjustment fatigue," and a radical change in the functions of ministers of finance and presidents of the central bank (who have to neglect internal affairs to give more and more time to complex foreign problems). The worst of the problem is that it fosters a climate of uncertainty that frightens investment away and thus reduces possibilities of medium- and long-term growth, as well as of meeting foreign obligations.

In conclusion, while the debtor countries must assume their share of responsibility for the creation of the debt, the creditors must do the same. An orderly market mechanism for the repurchase of the debt in some manner might be a reasonable solution. Furthermore, the prolonged and exhausting negotiation processes (commonly annual or semi-annual) should be replaced by calculations of medium- and long-term ability to pay, with a formula to permit the debtor country to pay out a suitable proportion of whatever economic improvement they can achieve thanks to the sacrifices that the creditors are prepared to accept.

The failure of the strategy followed through this decade and up to the present, which is shown by the growing gravity of the debt problem, makes clear the need for a long-term focus instead of the short-term approach of the IMF and its essentially short-term adjustment programs.

14

CHILE AND DEBT-EQUITY CONVERSION

James M. Livingstone

In response to the sharp increase in reserve provisions by the large U.S. money center banks, much has been written recently about the potential contribution of debt-to-equity conversions in solving the developing countries' debt problem. It is clear, however, that while debt-to-equity conversions can now play a larger role in the alleviation of the debt problem, they are not a solution. To the extent that they stabilize the debt or reduce the rate of increase, then the process buys time for the troubled debtor countries to make the necessary structural adjustments. Debt-to-equity conversions can also contribute to the adjustment process through the promotion of investments that might not otherwise have taken place, as well as through the transfer of technology and the reallocation of resources to the private sector.

This chapter analyzes the potential contribution of debt-to-equity conversions to the alleviation of the developing nations' debt problem, using the program in Chile as a model. The program in Chile is by far the most successful to date in terms of the absolute amount converted as well as the share of the external debt that has been converted. As of August 1987, over 10 percent of the country's total external debt had been converted to various forms of investment. These conversions have helped to stabilize Chile's debt over the past two years. As a result, since the implementation of the program in May 1985, Chile has saved about $200 million in interest payments, and the debt burden as a share of gross domestic product (GDP) has dropped sharply.

ORIGIN OF CHILE'S DEBT PROBLEM

Chile's economic crisis of the early 1980s was caused by a combination of macroeconomic mismanagement, internal financial disarray, and the world economic recession. The major policy mistakes were the fixing of the exchange rate and, at the same time, the opening of the capital account of the balance of payments. The fixed exchange rate during 1980 and 1981 resulted in a sharp appreciation of the peso that encouraged imports and discouraged domestic production and savings. The consequence was a balance-of-payments gap that reached 10 percent of GDP in 1981. High domestic interest rates encouraged overseas borrowing but did not raise domestic savings substantially. Between 1977 and 1981, the external debt of the private sector increased by over $9 billion. At the end of 1981, the private sector debt without any official guarantee accounted for over 65 percent of the total external debt, with 85 percent owed to foreign commercial banks at floating rates.[1] With no general controls, the authorities had very little idea of the explosion of private external obligations. The massive increase in external debt to a level equal to $1,460 per capita resulted in debt-service payments absorbing almost 60 percent of export earnings in 1981.

At the same time, in 1981 and 1982 Chile was hit by the world recession, suffering a terms-of-trade loss over $0.5 and $1.3 billion in each year, respectively.[2] Faced with an increasing resource gap and a sharp loss of international reserves, the authorities finally devalued the exchange rate by 15 percent and adopted a crawling peg system in June 1982. However, the devaluation was insufficient and speculation continued. The authorities allowed the peso to float in August, and after it depreciated another 30 percent, they reestablished the crawling peg system in September 1982. The authorities also imposed restrictions on foreign exchange transactions.

The devaluation increased the large external debt of the private sector by almost 70 percent in peso terms. With dollar liabilities and a peso income stream, much of the private sector as well as the financial system was bankrupt. In December 1982, the authorities attempted to implement a short-term stabilization program with the help of the International Monetary Fund (IMF). However, the stabilization program was cut short by the growing insolvency of the financial system, which resulted in the massive withdrawal of short-term external credit lines. This situation forced the authorities to intervene among the debtors and the largest private commercial banks and to seek a restructuring of the debt maturity profile with external bank creditors as well as a new-term money facility. The external financial package, completed in July 1983, also called for the restoration of the short-term commercial bank credits to their pre-January levels. This agreement with the banks, as well as additional resources from the IMF, allowed Chile to stabilize the economy and to begin the long road toward economic recovery in late 1983.

CHILE'S DEBT-TO-EQUITY CONVERSION PROGRAM

Saddled with an external debt equal to more than 130 percent of its GDP, Chile faced a long-term structural adjustment process to improve debt-service capacity. However, cash flow analysis revealed that additional reliance on external finance had to be limited to avoid falling into a deeper debt trap. Recognizing that the country simply had too much debt, the authorities decided to utilize the secondary market that had developed for trading developing nations' debt paper to encourage the conversion of the debt into equity and to promote the return of financial assets held abroad. The discount offered on the debt paper in the secondary market basically allows the investment to take place at a preferential exchange rate.

Chile's debt-to-equity program was initiated in May 1985 in response to market demands from domestic entrepreneurs and foreign investors. In recognition of the potential adverse impact of monetary emissions and the spread between the official and parallel exchange rates, the monetary authorities designed a program within a legal framework that helps protect the domestic economy against potential monetary and exchange-rate difficulties.

The rules for the debt-conversion process were divided into two main chapters (18 and 19) of the Central Bank of Chile's foreign regulations to capture the two distinct types of allowable transactions. The two types of transactions are as follows.

Chapter 18 allows the conversion of debt for any purpose. This chapter is primarily used by residents, but also nonresidents, for the prepayment of debt at a discount, as a cheap method to finance working capital, or to reinvest on favorable terms assets held abroad. Transactions under this chapter do not require Central Bank approval; however, there is also no right of access to foreign exchange for the later remittance of earnings or capital. As residents can acquire foreign exchange through the parallel exchange market to purchase debt instruments on the secondary markets in London and New York for conversion under this chapter, the Central Bank manages the volume of transactions through an auction system to limit the impact on monetary emissions as well as on the spread between the official and parallel exchange rates. The system has worked well. Chile has one of the lowest inflation rates among all developing countries, and the spread between the official and parallel exchange rates has rarely exceeded 10 percent.

The advantage to resident investors of funding investments for working or fixed capital under chapter 18 is based on the discount factor in the secondary markets less the cost of the auction bid ("cupo"), the spread between the official and parallel exchange rates, and the discount for long-term instruments in the domestic market. Based on recent values for these factors, the effective ultimate benefit ranges from 5 to 9 percent.

Chapter 19 permits the conversion of debt into approved investments, with subsequent access to foreign exchange for the remittance of earnings and capital subject to specified time constraints. This chapter is used primarily by foreign investors wishing to convert debt instruments they hold directly into equity investments or to purchase instruments on the secondary markets for conversion into equity. The investment may be in any firm, not just that of the original debtor. Under chapter 19, each transaction must be approved by the Central Bank. In assessing each transaction on a case-by-case basis, a major consideration of the Central Bank is whether the investment would take place without the benefits of the preferential exchange rate under the conversion program. The Central Bank also tries to encourage that some part of the investment be made on a cash basis. The Central Bank has rejected debt-to-equity swap transactions for some major projects on the basis that Chile has a comparative advantage in the production of the particular item. Thus, the projects are expected to be undertaken anyway on purely economic terms.

THE SUCCESS OF CHILE'S CONVERSION PROGRAM

As of the end of August 1987, over $2.1 billion has been converted under the various chapters within the program. This amount equals 10 percent of Chile's total external debt of $21 billion. Chile's program is the most successful to date in terms of the absolute amount converted and especially in terms of the share of debt converted.

Most of the early transactions in 1985 and 1986 were primarily for the prepayment of debt, the change from foreign to local currency of debt by residents through the return of assets held abroad, and for conversions under chapter 18. However, a couple of recent large foreign investments in the forestry sector have sharply raised the amount of conversions under chapter 19 as well. Over the next several years, conversions under chapter 19 are likely to far surpass the other categories in view of the recent action taken by Chile's major creditor banks with regard to general loan-loss provisions, and particularly in view of the Federal Reserve's changes in regulations governing U.S. banks' ability to convert debt paper directly into productive assets. The medium-term exposure of U.S. banks after adjustment for guarantees totals over $3.5 billion.[3] Thus, there is still a large potential for conversions.

The benefits to Chile of the debt-conversion program have already been significant. It is playing a major role in Chile's structural reform in three ways: by stabilizing the level of external debt, by promoting the return of capital flight, and by encouraging investment that otherwise might not have occurred. As a result of the conversions, Chile's external debt has stabilized at the year-end 1985 level of about $21 billion, despite current account deficits in each of the last three years in excess of $1 billion financed primarily with further external borrowings. The debt burden as a share of GDP has already declined from over 130 percent to less than 120 percent.

Since the beginning of the program in mid–1985, Chile has also saved about $200 million in interest payments.[4] This cash-flow effect has a compound benefit because the additional interest payments would have added to the external debt through the external financing of higher current account deficits in 1985 and 1986. Furthermore, in 1987 interest payments on this additional debt would make again the current account deficit larger than would otherwise be the case. This benefit is especially important for a country like Chile with an excessive amount of external debt. An improvement in creditworthiness over the medium term is dependent on the delicate balance between structural adjustment and the need for further external funding. The stabilization of the debt is, in effect, "buying time" for Chile to restructure the economy.

The debt-conversion program has also encouraged the return of capital. An estimated $400 to $500 million has been repatriated to Chile to take advantage of the debt prepayment and investment opportunities offered by the program.[5] This amount equals almost 15 percent of the total $2 to $3 billion in capital flight from Chile in the early 1980s.[6] Perhaps the most important aspect of the conversion program is that it is promoting investment in Chile that might not otherwise have occurred. Over the past three years, Chile has received new foreign direct investment on a cash basis of only $177 million, compared with over $2 billion through debt conversions.[7] Furthermore, much of this investment is going into the capitalization of export promotion/import substitution industries that are helping Chile's structural adjustment process toward improved debt-service capacity. This investment is also bringing greatly needed new technology to Chile's industrial base. An excellent example is the recent investment from debt conversions in Chile's forestry sector by two major New Zealand firms.

The ultimate amount of Chile's debt converted will be determined by the foreign investment climate in Chile, the continuation of prudent macroeconomic policies, and particularly the availability of viable projects. However, in view of the potential investment opportunities, the maximum limit for debt-to-equity conversions in Chile is expected to be near $3.5 to 4 billion. This amount represents almost 17 percent of Chile's total outstanding external debt. Based on recent trends this amount could be reached in late 1988 or early 1989. As a result, the absolute amount of Chile's debt at the end of 1988 will be less than or very close to the year-end 1985 level, and the debt-to-GDP burden will have dropped to about 100 percent from a peak of over 130 percent at the start of the program in mid–1985. Thus, the conversion program will have made a significant contribution to the improvement in Chile's creditworthiness and long-term economic viability. Furthermore, Chile will enter the 1990s with a new dynamic export-oriented private sector that will be the driving force behind a higher potential growth path.

There are a number of reasons for the particular success of Chile's debt-to-equity conversion program. First, the government has established a clear legal framework for the conversion process, taking into account different types of transactions by residents and nonresidents. Second, Chile has one of the most liberal foreign investment policies among the developing countries, and only the petroleum and uranium industries are off-limits. Third, Chile has followed a stable set of prudent macroeconomic policies for a number of years. Fourth, the central bank has put in place an effective auction system to limit the impact on the spread between the official and free-market exchange rates for transactions involving residents. The fifth factor is that the local currency receipts from the conversion transactions are issued by the central bank in the form of long-term local financial instruments, which are discounted in the domestic market for actual local currency. This method limits the impact on monetary emissions and inflationary pressures. Chile's inflation rate for the past two years has been below 20 percent. Finally, the sixth factor is that the central bank redeems debt for conversion at face or close to face value of the debt instrument.

In summary, Chile has implemented a system to maximize the amount of conversions, while minimizing the potential adverse impact on the domestic economy.

OTHER DEBT-TO-EQUITY CONVERSION PROGRAMS

Following the success of Chile's conversion program, a number of other countries have established their own programs and still more countries are looking into the possibility. The other countries with programs in place include Mexico, the Philippines, Ecuador, Costa Rica, Jamaica, and recently Argentina and Venezuela. Among the countries with programs under review are Guatemala, Brazil, Nigeria, Uruguay, Colombia, and the Dominican Republic. The other programs, however, are not likely to be as successful as Chile's in terms of the share of debt converted. In response to economic and political pressures, most of the other countries' programs contain a number of restrictions and are not as well designed as Chile's to maximize the amount of debt converted. They are more focused on strict debt-to-equity swaps, rather than debt conversion for a multitude of purposes, including debt prepayment, working capital financing, and varied investments. Thus, use of the

Chilean example as a broad scale for the potential size of conversions in other countries is likely to be optimistic. Among the major restrictions in some of the other programs are:

1. Limits on the total amount of conversions per month or per year. The Mexican program limits monthly conversions to $100 million, and the Argentine program restricts the amount of conversions to $300–400 million per year. In contrast, Chile's program only limits monthly conversions under chapter 18, primarily involving residents, to control the spread between the official and parallel exchange rates. There are no limits on chapter 19 transactions, which involve mainly investments by nonresidents.

2. Declarations of several sectors of the economy as off-limits for debt-to-equity conversions by nonresidents. The Philippine, Mexican, and Argentine programs all have restrictions regarding investment in a number of sectors of the economy. In Chile, only the petroleum and uranium industries are off-limits.

3. Limitations of conversions to investments only in "productive" assets. This excludes the use of debt conversions as a cheap method to finance working capital or to prepay debt.

4. Limitations as to the type of "eligible" external debt accepted for conversion. The Mexican program, for example, is restricted to external public debt.

5. Requirement that each amount of debt converted be matched by a specified share in cash. The Argentine program requires that each dollar of debt converted be matched by a dollar investment in cash.

Most of the other countries' programs do not have separate types of transactions for residents and nonresidents. Moreover, Chile has not been as concerned with the potential consequences regarding foreign domination of the economy or the subsidy element involved for foreigners or nationals that stashed capital abroad. Thus, the real limitation to the contribution of debt conversions to the mitigation of the developing nations' debt problem will come more from imposed restrictions on the supply of available opportunities for political reasons than the supply of debt instruments available for conversion.

POTENTIAL GLOBAL CONTRIBUTION OF DEBT CONVERSIONS TO THE DEVELOPING NATIONS' DEBT PROBLEM

The ultimate size and contribution of debt conversions to the developing nations' debt problem will be determined by several major factors: (1) the ability and willingness of banks to sell or convert debt instruments from their own portfolio, absorbing the loss with loan-loss provisions or primary capital; (2) changes in regulations allowing banks, particularly

U.S. banks, to invest a larger amount of equity in nonfinancial activities and to hold equity positions for a longer period of time; and (3) the investment climate fostered by developing countries, including the scope of debt-conversion programs implemented.

The first two factors are in the process of adjustment by the banks themselves and regulatory bodies in a number of countries. Thus, the main factor that will determine the contribution of debt conversions within the devoloping nations' debt problem is the policies of debtor countries themselves.

The recent large increase in loan-loss provisions by the major U.S. banks to a level equal to 25 to 40 percent of their developing country portfolio places the banks in a much better position to sell, swap, or convert their debt and to absorb the losses associated with the discount. This action will greatly increase both the eventual supply of and demand for debt instruments for the sake of conversion. Assuming that U.S. banks were willing to sell or convert 15 percent of their $90 billion troubled developing nation portfolio and banks from other countries 25 percent then the potential supply of debt instruments for conversion purposes could reach almost $65 to $70 billion. This amount equals about 20 percent of the total $300 billion in bank debt of the troubled debtor nations.

Meanwhile, the Federal Reserve has liberalized its Regulation K to allow U.S. banks to acquire up to 100 percent ownership in a foreign nonfinancial firm provided that: (1) the firm is in the process of being transferred from the public to the private sector; (2) the firm is in a heavily indebted, less developed country; (3) the shares are acquired through a debt-for-equity conversion process; (4) the shares are held by the bank holding company or a subsidiary; and (5) the equity position is divested within five years.[8]

A major part of the problem facing the heavily indebted developing countries is the sharp slowdown in investment inflows. The net resource flow from direct investment, as well as from other private credit sources, has been negative in every year since 1982.[9] The large negative private outflows have far exceeded the positive net official inflows, requiring the gap to be financed by the drawdown of official reserves and significant adjustments in the balance on goods and services. In the case of just direct investment, the accumulated net outflow between 1982 and 1986 totaled over $9 billion. A reversal of this trend is an important part of the overall solution to the developing countries' problem.

However, foreign investors clearly perceive the risks to investment in developing countries to be greater now than before the onslaught of the debt crisis. Thus, a return of large foreign direct investment inflows is not to be expected unless the higher perceived risks are offset by higher potential returns or are somehow mitigated. The formation of the Multilateral Investment Guarantee Agency (MIGA) under the auspices of the World Bank is an attempt to encourage the flow of direct investment to developing countries by mitigating some of the risks.[10] This agency would insure direct investments made in developing countries against noncommercial risks, including breaches of contract, blockages to remittances, expropriation, and losses resulting from civil unrest or war.

Debt-conversion programs can also play a major role by providing a higher potential return. They allow investment to take place at a preferential exchange rate that translates into a higher potential return. A number of arguments have been made that countries through debt-conversion programs are merely subsidizing investment that would have taken place anyway. Perhaps this situation may be true in some cases. However, something needs to be done to increase direct investment flows. The current rates of return are not sufficient to raise inflows back to the 1982 peak in view of the perceived risks.

Furthermore, central banks have the ability to manage the problem through the debt-conversion approval process. In the case of Chile, the central bank does not approve debt conversions for any project thought likely to take place anyway based on Chile's comparative economic advantages. For example, debt conversions have not been approved for any copper projects, as Chile is the world's lowest cost producer and most projects have a relatively high profit margin.

The ultimate size and contribution of debt conversions to the debt problem will be determined more from the "opportunites" side. It will depend on the countries' ability to accept market realities in formulating programs that maximize conversion opportunities within tolerable political parameters. Annual debt conversions equal to about 1.5 to 2.0 percent of a countries' stock of debt are considered manageable, providing the country implements an appropriate monetary policy.[11] This implies that annual debt conversions for all the troubled countries could be about $4.5 to $6.0 billion.

In 1988, the deeply indebted countries are projected to register a combined current account deficit of over $18 billion.[12] Assuming this deficit is financed totally from additional external borrowings, the total external debt (bank and nonbank) of these countries can be expected to increase over 3 percent to almost $577 billion in 1988. However, if these countries were to implement effective debt-conversion programs, the increase in external debt could be reduced to a rate of only 2 percent. This rate is below the expected growth of these countries' real GDP. Thus the ratio of debt to GDP would improve slightly. Over a number of years, debt conversions assisted by structural adjustment measures could make a significant contribution to the reduction of the debt burden and the return of access to international financial markets.

NOTES

1. World Bank, "Chile, an Economic Memorandum," mimeograph, Washington, D.C., September 24, 1984.

2. World Bank, "Chile, an Economic Memorandum."

3. Federal Financial Institutions Examination Council, *County Exposure Lending Survey*, Washington, D.C., April 24, 1987.

4. Roberto Toso, "Debt Conversion Schemes: The Chilean Experience" (Paper by the New York Financial Representation Office of Chile, Central Bank of Chile, January 19, 1987), unpublished.

5. Estimate of Central Bank of Chile.

6. *The Economist*, March 7, 1987, pp. 87–90.

7. Republic of Chile, "Economic Memorandum," February 25, 1987.

8. The Federal Reserve Board, "Press Release," August 12, 1987.

9. United Nations, *World Economic Survey 1987*. New York, 1987.

10. IBRD, Convention establishing the Multilateral Investment Guarantee Agency, International Bank for Reconstruction and Development, October 11, 1985, p. 2.

11. Wolfgang Spieles, "Debt-Equity Swaps and the Heavily Indebted Countries," *Inter-economics*, May/June 1987, p. 123.

12. International Monetary Fund, *World Economic Outlook*, April 1987, p. 162.

15

PERUVIAN STATEMENT

Carlos E. Melgar

Though the developing countries may presently owe money to the more developed countries, they also are historic creditors of the industrialized nations. We should not forget that poverty and backwardness in our countries are, to a great extent, the result of the exploitation and spoliation to which they have been subjected by developed countries, and which today finds in the foreign debt its most sophisticated and inhuman expression.

The government of Peru does not have the intention to adopt a position of revolt, default, or isolation in relation to the international financial community regarding the problem of its debt, but on the contrary, acknowledges its obligations and reaffirms its intent to honor them.

Peruvian officials maintain that the problem of indebtedness is an issue derived from the unfair and asymmetric international relations existing between North and South America, and that it must be solved by the parties involved: creditors, debtors, multilateral financial organizations, and creditors from the international banks.

The government of Peru honors the coordinating consultations undertaken by the countries forming the Cartagena consensus, which is oriented toward the creation of a political dialogue with creditors about the problems of indebtedness and the establishment of basic criteria for a solution. However, Peruvian officials recognize that negotiations related to the debt of each country must be conducted according to its own specific situation and do not pretend, consequently, that the solutions applicable to Peru form a model for confronting the debts of other developing nations.

By the same token, Peru recognizes that it is the responsibility of the government of each country to decide and implement, in exercise of its sovereignty, the economic policy most fitting to its own realities, needs, and possibilities.

Consequently, the government of Peru cannot accept that this economic policy be dictated by other states or by financial organizations such as the International Monetary Fund.

At the same time, the experience acquired in the last few years has taught that many of the measures proposed by the IMF bring recession, devaluation, and inflation to countries such as Peru and entail serious economic, political, and social consequences that only exacerbate their already precarious situations.

For those reasons, the Peruvian government has proposed that debtor countries deal directly with the governments of creditor nations, the international financial organizations, and the private banks concerning the debt involved in each case.

This position raises questions, both ideological and pragmatic, since the criteria generally recommended by the IMF do not take into account the political and social reality of each country; their implementation not only becomes impractical and inadequate, but also creates problems even greater than those they were intended to solve.

THE CASE OF PERU

Even though the amount of the foreign debt of Peru, $15 billion, is much smaller than that of other developing countries such as Brazil, Mexico, or Argentina, its impact on the national economy is much greater for several reasons: it is equivalent to 80 percent of Peru's gross national product (GNP); it is equal to almost six times the amount of Peruvian exports for last year; in the last few years, Peru experienced a decrease of the GNP and of the per capita income of the population; the capacity of Peru to repay is almost nonexistent; and the social situation of Peru does not leave any margin for further economic adjustments.

It should also be emphasized that Peru is presently and literally at war in two fronts—war that is being fought at a high cost and virtually without any help from anywhere.

Peru is violently at war with the traffic in narcotics, with almost no resources to match those of the well-funded, well-armed international criminals. It should be noted that in 1985 the Agency for International Development recommended, in a 360-page report, an initial investment of $660 million for agricultural development of the Huallaga Valley to substitute coca for viable crops. In order to fight this drug war, whose ultimate casualties are youngsters in the United States, Peru has received under $7 million in American aid last year.

Peru is also under vicious attack by the Shining Path guerillas, a Maoist organization so barbaric and cruel that it could make the Khmer Rouge of Kampuchea look reasonable, and it seems to be linked to narcotics traffic as well.

When the indebtedness crisis in developing countries began in 1982, it initially received a treatment that was strictly financial. This financial treatment took place through the policies of adjustment implemented at the IMF's request. Far from having a favorable impact, the policies imposed were the cause of recession and the destruction of the productive structure of developing countries, and tremendously worsened their situation.

In this context, the rise of interest rates above their historic levels brought an increase in the cost of servicing the debt, which, together with the loss of income for developing countries as a result of impairment of the terms of exchange, the plummeting of raw materials' prices, and the protectionist policies of the industrialized countries, created a situation of grave crisis expressed in the growing incapacity of the debtor countries to repay. In the face of this dilemma, which originated a process of net transfer of resources from the developing countries (among them Peru) to the developed ones, the government of Alán García adopted, since July 28, 1985, the position of using only 10 percent of the revenue coming from exports to service and pay Peru's foreign debt.

This sovereign and nationalistic position assumed by Peru regarding the problem of the debt has been picked up by various political and diplomatic authorities who have recognized the eminently political nature of the problem and the necessity to implement, between debtors and creditors, a political dialogue ruled by the principle of mutual responsibility, which can make it possible to reach a permanent global solution to the problem.

Finally, in face of the worsening problem of the debt, the developing countries are becoming aware of the necessity of joining efforts with the creditors, at times under the auspices of international organizations, in ongoing renegotiating processes. Only in a world in which development and justice can become a reality, will peace and well-being for all mankind be achieved. To give a structural solution to the problem of the foreign debt essentially entails the creation of a new international economic order based on justice and the right to development of all nations without distinction.

16

CASTRO'S DEBT CRUSADE

William Ratliff

Almost every time Fidel Castro orated in 1985, it was to call upon Latin Americans to band together and repudiate their foreign debts. His campaign eased off in 1986, chiefly because he got very little support from the hemisphere's other political leaders. Commentators pointed out the Cuban leader's own apparent hypocrisy, for while he was loudly calling on other Latin American governments to renounce their debts, he was assiduously renegotiating his own with the Paris Club. Still, his campaign continued, though more subtle than before, as the crisis deepened.

Fidel Castro claims that he has been warning about the consequences of the debt longer than any other world leader, and this may well be true. In a talk before officials of the Economic Commission on Latin America, held on November 29, 1971, for example, he asked how in the future governments were going to pay their mounting debts and still develop their countries, indeed, to maintain even a minimum level of subsistence.[1] When addressing the United Nations General Assembly in September 1979, as president of the Nonaligned Nations, he said the debts of the "relatively least developed countries . . . are impossible to bear and have no solution. They should be cancelled."[2] Castro also told a Brazilian journalist in 1985 that he had been "concentrating on the debt crisis since 1982," the year Mexico sought debt relief and raised the specter of default if major concessions were not forthcoming.[3]

The crusade began in December 1984, when Castro stated that the Latin American countries generally could not repay their debts and set in motion a campaign that nearly consumed Cuban officials and the Cuban media during the following year. The centerpiece was to have been a Continental Congress on the Foreign Debt in Havana in mid–

1985. This was originally conceived as a summit of Latin American presidents, but no president attended. Castro then went to the masses and called for the creation of broad fronts against the debt. This theme was followed through in meetings during the summer of 1985, including the Fifth Latin American and Caribbean Journalist Seminar, the Latin American Press Forum, and the Congress of the Federation of Latin American Journalists.[4] The chief newspaper, *Granma*, published dozens of pages on the debt, in addition to a series of feature articles.

The essence of Castro's position is that the foreign debt of the third world countries in unpayable, immoral, even illegal. He calls it a cancer "that multiplies, that kills off the organism" and "must be destroyed totally through surgery. . . . Anything that deviates from that idea is simply deviating from reality. Given that reality, all technical formulas, all palliatives won't improve the situation. They will only serve to make it worse." Castro goes on to state that the challenge is to unify those who are oppressed to inform themselves and the industrialized world that the debt problem is a political one with millions of lives in the balance. The resources to solve it, and to create a New Economic Order that will be more equitable and help overcome the poverty of the Third World, can easily be taken from military spending of the Western powers without costing the average person anything. If ordinary people in the developed world knew they had nothing to lose by this change, Castro argued, they would support it immediately.[5]

In fact, Castro is slightly more evenhanded in his proposal regarding the debt than his critics sometimes acknowledge. At one point, he suggested that the socialist world should set an example: "The more developed countries within the socialist world should contribute and should struggle for the development of poorer countries. . . . I believe the principle of pardoning the debt should come from here, to erase the debt. We have not reached that stage yet, but the stage will come where the debts should be erased."[6] Castro set an example in January 1985 when he "forgave" $70 million that Nicaragua owed Cuba for the construction of a sugar mill.

The campaign was more subdued in 1986 and 1987, though the subject was often discussed.[7] When Brazil announced its decision to suspend most interest payments on its commercial debts in February 1987, Castro wrote to Brazilian president José Sarney of Cuba's absolute solidarity with the decision, adding that "governments cannot passively accept strangulation of their economies." In a press interview, he added, "This is the moment to turn the history of Third World peoples around" and concluded that "whether there are negotiations or not it will be the debtors who will have the last word from now on."[8]

Castro became less strident for several reasons. Some Latin American leaders with good nationalist credentials challenged and condemned his position. For example, in 1985 Argentine foreign minister Dante Caputo said Castro's stand was "against the principles upon which our international economic, financial, and commercial relations are based," to which, as indicated earlier, Castro would be the first to agree. Two years later, Caputo added that to proclaim "I won't pay" is "a childish prescription, the romantic expression of ideologies. . . . "[9] Some other Latin American leaders have said much the same.

The most dramatic confrontation was the exchange in mid–1985 between the Cuban leader and the recently inaugurated Peruvian president Alán García, a revolutionary socialist who has tried to remain more truly nonaligned than Castro. García is the first populist of continental appeal to appear on the Latin American Left in many years, an attractive democratic leader whose youthful vitality stands in contrast to the aging dictator in Havana. García proposed to put no more than 10 percent of export earnings into debt payment, the most radical commitment by a chief of state in the hemisphere short of Castro's calls for complete renunciation of payments. But Castro's congratulatory message to the Peruvian president was petulant, lecturing him that "should you really decide to struggle in a serious, firm, and consistent manner against (Peru's) Dantesque tableau of social calamities and liberate your fatherland, as you have promised in public, from domination by and dependence on imperialism, the sole cause of this tragedy, you can count on Cuba's support." García replied, alluding to Cuba's economic dependence on the Soviet Union, that "we have no special privileges from any power, because we do not struggle against one dependency with the weapons of another hegemony." In response, Cuban UN representative Isidoro Malmierca lamented that "a Latin American voice would repeat the same vile slander, the rotten arguments coined in Washington."[10]

The second problem was what was commonly perceived as Castro's hypocrisy regarding debt renunciation. Colombia's chief of the National Planning Department alluded to this when he said, "The attitude of the Cuban government is indeed strange. It talks about the problems of other countries with such assurance, but it does not have the modesty of talking about its own experiences, using the argument that its debt is not bound by the usual commitments and obligations as an excuse."[11] It is well known that about a quarter of Cuba's GNP comes from the Soviet bloc, that Cuba received about $4 billion in Soviet military aid and $20 billion in economic aid between 1980 and 1986—more economic aid than the Soviet Union gave to all other countries in the world combined—and that the present Cuban debt to the Soviet Union is about $10 billion.[12]

In addition to his debt to the Soviet bloc, Castro owes an estimated $3.5 billion to nonsocialist banks, loans that he has tried hard to keep in order. In July 1986, as the Cuban financial sitution deteriorated, Cuba reluctantly suspended payments on its debts while continuing to negotiate feverishly with the Paris Club, seeking better terms on its previously rescheduled debt and some hundreds of millions of new dollars. After Cuba suspended payments, insurance companies of Japan, Canada, and other countries ended their coverage for Cuban shipments. The new Soviet leader, Mikhail Gorbachev, refused to come up with more money even though Cuban foreign currency receipts were cut drastically by the falling price of the Soviet oil that Cuba was reselling on the open market. At the end of 1986, Castro announced that convertible currency from trade would fall from $1.2 billion to $600 million in 1987, and severe austerity measures were imposed. Meanwhile, Cuba kept trying to negotiate new debt terms with its creditors.[13]

Castro claims there is no hypocrisy involved. Cuba has a debt to the socialist countries, he admits, though he says it is nobody's business how large it is. He says Cuba pays no interest on that debt, though his critics argue that he repays the Soviet bloc for its aid in other ways, most importantly through his foreign policy. As for the debt to nonsocialist countries, Vice President Rafael Rodríguez gave the Cuban position as follows: (1) Cuba has made some mistakes in the implementation of development plans, but the plans were not mistakes, and none of the money misspent went into the pockets of military leaders or cheats, as in other Latin American countries; (2) banks did not loan to Cuba "solely for business purposes," as they did to other countries, but made a moral commitment when they bucked U.S. economic and political pressures; and (3) most of the debt was not contracted with the United States or Western European capitalists, but with countries that cannot be described as fully developed or where capitalism has reached its final phase; for example, more than half is owed to Spanish, Argentine, and Mexican government banks.[14]

CONCLUSIONS

Castro has been excluded from active leadership on the formal governmental level in resolving the Latin American debt crisis. For example, in March 1987, the Peruvian prime minister proposed that the Organization of American States (OAS) was the "ideal forum" for discussion of problems of economic growth, the debt, and democracy; since Cuba does not belong to the OAS, it is effectively excluded from such deliberations.[15]

Castro is undoubtedly correct when he says the Latin American countries will never be able to pay back their debts, indeed, that many cannot continue servicing what they now owe. Some solution must be found.

Other countries, without a patron who will bail them out, have tried to find a way out of the crisis without the drastic step of simply renouncing their debts, often displaying considerable political skill in doing so. Castro has recognized the disease, but it remains to be seen whether all the medicines being considered by others will fail, as he claims.

Castro is also correct in arguing that, for the Latin American countries, the debt problem is at root political, not economic. He is right that throughout Latin America the decisions that led to borrowing in the first place, the uses made of the money when it arrived (aside from what was simply siphoned off to foreign bank accounts), and thus the policies that led to the crisis, flowed from political decisions regarding the need for national development and the best ways to achieve it. However, the political aspect Castro neglects is that ideologically motivated decisions are frequently wasteful and contribute little or nothing to real growth.

Noneconomic political convictions have led to a variety of counterproductive economic policies in many Latin American countries, among them the idea that foreign equity investment, often seen as imperialistic, must be restricted beyond limits acceptable to foreign investors. Because of the barriers to investment, the only remaining source of needed developmental funding is foreign aid or loans. Aid to Latin America has seldom been very substantial, and a realistic appraisal of attitudes in the developed world suggests that it probably won't be in the foreseeable future. Loans have been gigantic but little of the money has been used productively.

One of the developmentally hopeful changes in recent years is that Marxist-Leninist governments led by the People's Republic of China, are increasingly looking to decentralization and individual initiative to restore sagging economies. Fidel Castro has stubbornly turned in the opposite direction, toward tighter centralization and antimarket measures. Elsewhere in Latin America there has been some movement toward opening and privatization of the economy, as in Chile, Brazil, and Mexico.

Yet restructuring and changing perspectives could take decades, if they come at all. Even well-advised governments may be pressured by politically motivated critics to remain dependent on or revert to statist policies that will cause further decades of frustration.

So far Castro's crusade against foreign debt has not drawn public support from Latin America's political leaders. But it has made inroads with some politically directed religious figures, labor leaders, teachers at all levels, and assorted other influential intellectuals.[16] In addition, he has brought the default option to the attention of a broader public who may in time—whether in democracies or dictatorships—bring pressure of one sort or another on government leaders to turn toward default.

Thus, if borrowers and creditors do not find some way to resolve the debt crisis to almost everybody's relative satisfaction, Castro may yet turn out to have been something of a prophet.

NOTES

1. See "Palabras del Primer Ministro de Cuba, Commandante Fidel Castro Ruz, en la CEPAL," in *Fidel en Chile* (Santiago: Editorial Quimantu, 1972), p. 238.

2. Quoted from Fidel Castro, "Meeting on the Latin American and Caribbean Foreign Debt," *Tricontinental*, no. 103, 1985, p. 6.

3. See *Folha de São Paulo*, cited in Radio Marti, Office of Research, *Cuba: Quarterly Situation Report*, April–June 1985, chapter 6, p. 1 (hereafter cited as *Quarterly Report*).

4. See Radio Marti, *Quarterly Report* 2, July–September 1985, pp. 8–9.

5. See Fidel Castro, "Meeting on the Latin American and Caribbean Foreign Debt," *Tricontinental*, no. 103, 1985.

6. Fidel Castro's comments to a Venezuelan journalist on September 17, 1985, at the Latin American Press Forum on the Financial Crisis, cited in Radio Marti, *Quarterly Report*, July–September 1985, chapter 2, p. 4. Also see remarks to the press on September 22, 1987 in Foreign Broadcast Information Service (FBIS), Latin America, September 28, 1987.

7. See, for example, address to Sixth Ministerial Meeting of the Group of 77 in Havana, *Granma Weekly Review*, April 26, 1987.

8. See *Granma Weekly Edition*, March 8, 1987; *EFE*, February 24, 1987, cited in FBIS, Latin America, February 24, 1987.

9. See *DNY*, August 2, 1985, cited in Radio Marti, *Quarterly Report* 2, July–September 1985, chapter 2, p. 8; *Gente*, April 2, 1987, cited in FBIS, Latin America, April 10, 1987.

10. See Radio Marti, *Quarterly Report* 2, July–September 1985, pp. 9–10. Relations subsequently improved. In June 1987, the Cuban paper *Granma* carried an exclusive interview with the Peruvian leader, who made some points that agreed with Castro; *Granma Weekly Review*, June 21, 1987.

11. See *El Siglo*, August 31, 1985, in Radio Marti, *Quarterly Report* 2, July–September 1985, p. 8.

12. Juan del Aguila, "Cuba," in *Latin America and Caribbean Contemporary Record, 1984–85*, ed. Jack Hopkins (New York: Holmes & Meier, 1986), p. 678.

13. See *New York Times*, July 11, 1986; Radio Marti, *Quarterly Report* 3, July–September 1986, pp. 13–16. For a detailed list of several dozen austerity measures, see *Granma*, December 27, 1987.

14. Interview carried on Havana Tele-Rebelde Network, March 24, 1987, described in FBIS, Latin America, March 25, 1987.

15. See *EFE*, March 2, 1987, cited in FBIS, Latin America, March 3, 1987.

16. For example, the declaration of the Latin American and Caribbean Workers' Conference held in Campinas, Brazil, in May 1987 exactly follows Castro's line. See *EFE*, May 20, 1987, in FBIS, Latin America, May 22; *La Hora*, May 22, 1987, in FBIS, Latin America, June 4, 1987.

17

TO LEND OR NOT TO LEND

Alfred J. Watkins

Since the beginning of the debt crisis in August 1982, debtor nations have transferred more financial resources to their creditors in the form of interest and principal payments than they have received in the form of new loans. Virtually everyone agrees that these financial transfers should not be allowed to persist, at least not at the rate of the past few years. Otherwise, politicians in debtor nations may soon be forced to choose between their nation's economic growth and making another round of interest payments.

It is no exaggeration to say that the glue holding the debt-containment strategy together has been the promise that those transfers would be reduced, thereby permitting debtor nations to grow while also paying interest. That promise has been used to justify whatever creditor nation policies happen to be in vogue at any particular moment, whether they be the austerity policies of the pre-Baker Plan days, the growth-with-structural-adjustment policies of the Baker Plan, or the "menu of options" approach now coming into vogue. The argument invariably was that if debtor nations persevered for just a little while longer, making another round of interest payments and accepting another round of net outflows, their creditworthiness would be restored and the financial markets would be willing to lend them more money.

For debtors, the prospect of regaining voluntary access to the international capital markets had been the proverbial pot of gold at the end of the rainbow. Because they believed that the new money spigot would once again be opened, politicians in debtor nations have, by and large, placed great value on maintaining good relations with the international financial community, servicing their debts and swallowing the bitter medicine prescribed in the name of restoring creditworthiness.

In creditor countries too, the claim that debtor nations would forfeit their access to the international capital markets has been one of the most powerful political arguments against the various debt relief plans before Congress.[1] According to the critics of these congressional proposals, commercial banks will refuse to resume lending to debtor nations if Congress forces the banks to write off a portion of their sovereign loans or reduce interest rates to below market levels. If debtor nations cannot tap the existing international pool of external savings, where will they get the capital to reactivate their economies, increase their purchases of U.S. products, and restore their living standards?

Thus, for both debtors and creditors, the issue of renewed commercial bank lending is crucial. Debtors expect that new loans will be their reward for good behavior. And creditors know that the prospect of new loans is the primary reason that debtors have been well behaved. Even Peruvian president Alán García, perhaps the most rebellious of the debtor nations' leaders, has made an effort to service the debts of creditors willing to continue extending additional loans. Clearly, most creditors have a vested interest in maintaining at least the illusion that new loans might be made available.

Yet will new loans be forthcoming in the amount that will be needed to head off radical unilateral actions by the debtors? If commercial banks won't provide the necessary funding, who will? And what will happen if a political stalemate in creditor countries prevents the public sector from filling any financing gap left by the private financial markets?

Nevertheless, this chapter assesses the prospects of renewed commercial bank lending to debtor nations. The analysis will proceed in three stages.

The first part will start with a brief summary of what commercial bankers have been saying about the prospect of renewed commercial bank lending to debtor nations. On the assumption that actions speak louder than words, it will conclude with an analysis of what they have been doing.

The second section will examine the secondary market for commercial bank loans. The purpose of the analysis is to determine how the secondary markets might react to a new round of sovereign loans, either by the commercial banks or official creditors. Will new loans enhance the value of old loans, or will they merely push the mountain of debt forward, making an ultimate resolution of the crisis even more remote?

The third section will examine the factors that induced commercial banks to get into sovereign lending in the first place, and whether those inducements still exist despite the dramatic financial market changes since the beginning of this decade. Finally, the conclusion will assess how these developments will probably affect the outcome of the debt crisis.

PROSPECTS OF RENEWED COMMERCIAL BANK LENDING

Judging from their public statements, commercial banks have not evinced any great eagerness to get back into the developing nation syndicated loan business or to provide the bulk of the balance-of-payments support that debtor nations will need for the remainder of this decade and the next. More importantly, since the onset of the debt crisis, private capital market financing of developing nations' current account deficits has virtually dried up, especially for those countries with the largest external debts. Thus, despite all the press attention lavished on commercial bank innovations such as debt-equity swaps and multiyear reschedulings, the fact remains that only a steady infusion of public capital has kept the debtors at least minimally afloat.

Commercial banks appear to be of two minds concerning the question of new loans to sovereign borrowers. On the one hand, even as they were increasing their loan-loss reserves earlier this year, all banks pledged allegiance to the Baker Plan, reiterating their willingness to provide additional financial support to those debtor nations implementing appropriate adjustment policies.

On the other hand, those same commercial bank executives have been declaring in no uncertain terms that they do not intend to continue financing the current account deficits of debtor nations. See, for example, Morgan Guaranty's latest issue of *World Financial Markets*,[2] in what is perhaps one of the best leading indicators of commercial bank sentiment, the Institute for International Economics (IIE) calculated that the most indebted developing nations will need approximately $20 billion per year of new external financing if they are to restore growth and not fall behind on their debt-service obligations.[3] Whereas the Baker Plan relies on commercial banks to provide most of these funds, the IIE study suggests that this task should now be assumed by such public sector financing institutions as the World Bank, the regional development banks, and the various creditor nation export financing agencies.

The Institute for International Finance (IIF), a research consortium established in 1984 by the leading commercial banks, has also questioned the wisdom of having the banking system provide balance-of-payments financing for indebted developing countries. As a recent IIF report notes:

As private sector intermediaries with primary responsibilities to depositors and shareholders, banks never envisaged playing the leading role in providing permanent balance of payments finance. Yet, by 1986 this had become their "assigned" role. . . . In light of experience since 1982, commercial banks cannot continue to accept this responsibility, because it is incompatible with their fiduciary obligations. . . . Commercial banks cannot play the role of "lender of last resort," filling a residual financing gap.[4]

Commercial banks' complaints about their role as "lender of last resort" ring somewhat hollow in view of the fact that they have not been a significant source of developing nations' financing since 1982. Expressions of fealty to the Baker Plan have not been matched by new loan commitments.

During the "salad days" of syndicated lending in the late 1970s and early 1980s, most of the external capital flowing to the developing countries came from the commercial banking system. Between 1978 and 1981, for example, the 15 heavily indebted countries included in the Baker Plan borrowed approximately $180 billion. Approximately 90 percent, or $161 billion, of the total was supplied by private creditors, primarily commercial banks. The remaining supplies of external funds were obtained from official creditors such as the World Bank and from reserve-related liabilities such as loans from central banks.

Commercial banks not only provided most of the new funds, but also, in each of those years, their loans exceeded the countries' trade deficits, interest payments, and current account deficits. Consequently, debtor nations had a net inflow of funds.

However, the difference between the debtors' receipts of new commercial bank loans and the value of their total interest payments went from a surplus of $20.3 billion in 1981 to a deficit of $14.8 billion in 1982. The resulting gap between commercial bank disbursements and the developing countries' interest payments was filled, in part, by a $10 billion improvement in the countries' merchandise trade balance and, in even larger part by a $13 billion increase in reserve-related liabilities, that is, drawings from the IMF, bridge loans from central banks, etc. Whereas borrowing from these sources had averaged only 10 percent of commercial bank borrowings in the years before the debt crisis, by 1982 reserve-related borrowings amounted to just under 50 percent of commercial bank disbursements.

The precipitous decline in commercial bank lending to the Baker 15 countries and the resulting need to fill the financial vacuum with public capital did not stop with the mid–1982 onset of the debt crisis. In 1983, as private sector lending declined by $33 billion from its 1983 level, the gap between the private sector's lean disbursements and the debtor nations' interest payments widened to $44 billion. A $26 billion infusion of capital from public lending sources helped fill part of that gap, as did a $25 billion improvement in the 15 countries' combined trade balance.

As recently as April, 1987, the IMF was not forecasting any large-scale revival of commercial bank lending for either 1987 or 1988. In 1987, the IMF expects that private sector loans to the Baker 15 countries will amount to only $8.9 billion, most of which represents disbursements on Mexico's $6 billion and Argentina's $2 billion concerted lending package. For 1988, it is forecasting only $3.3 billion of new private sector loans.

Despite the recent growth in official financing, the most heavily in-debted countries found themselves making large and rapidly growing financial transfers to their creditors. In Latin America, for example, the net resource transfer went from a $10 billion net inflow as recently as 1981 to a net outflow of $18.7 billion in 1982. The transfers rose to a high of nearly $33 billion in 1975, before declining to $22 billion in 1986. Commercial banks accounted for approximately 90 percent of the trans-fers on the total external debt. Bilateral lenders, multilateral lenders, and the IMF were also responsible for a small, but not insignificant, portion of the adverse resource transfers.

The decline in bank exposure between 1984 and 1986 and the mag-nitude of the resulting net resource transfers are especially surprising in view of the numerous "concerted," or "involuntary," lending pack-ages cobbled together during those years. According to the IMF: "About 60 percent of the growth in banks' claims on developing countries in 1984 took the form of concerted lending to Latin America in conjunction with bank debt restructuring and Fund supported programs."[5] For most of this decade, a large portion of the commercial bank loans were part of so-called involuntary lending packages arranged under IMF auspices. Nevertheless, even with IMF prodding and the additional encourage-ment of the Baker Plan, commercial banks still managed to reduce their exposure.

Several factors account for the wide disparity between the large vol-ume of concerted bank lending reported by the IMF and the continued decline in the private sector's exposure. First, while banks were increas-ing their exposure to some countries via concerted lending packages, they were reducing their exposure to other countries, or to those same countries in subsequent years, via asset sales, debt-equity swaps, and write-downs. According to the Bank for International Settlements (BIS): "Most of the decline in banks' claim on the major problem debtor coun-tries in 1986 . . . can be attributed to the conversion of external debt into equity or domestic debt."[6]

Second, the BIS also reports that "another way in which banks' ex-posure has been lowered had been through the transfer of claims to export guarantee agencies and or other similar public sector bodies."[7] Finally, while concerted lending programs were disbursing funds to the public sector, the banks were reducing their exposure to the private sector in many of those same countries. As a result, the banks' total exposure was shrinking, or growing slowly, even while their loans to the public sector were increasing.

Despite the leadership of the U.S. government in managing the Latin American portion of the debt crisis and the leadership role of U.S. banks on many of the country coordinating committees, U.S. banks have been among the first and fastest to reduce their claims on financially troubled debtor nations. As a share of the total debt of the 15 heavily indebted countries, total U.S. bank claims declined steadily from 27 percent in 1978 to 20 percent in 1986. United States bank claims also declined as a share of total bank claims on those 15 countries, falling from approximately one-third in 1978 to only one-fourth today.

It is important to note that these reductions in exposure are not limited to the smaller regional banks. Between the end of 1984 and the end of the first quarter of 1987, cross-border claims of the nine money center banks on Mexico fell by $400 million, on Venezuela by $1.1 billion, and on Colombia by $700 million. Thus, the reduction in U.S. bank exposure has been spread among a wide variety of banks and has affected a wide variety of highly indebted developing nations.

THE SECONDARY MARKET

Are commercial banks acting rationally when they reduce, or resist increasing, their exposure to already overindebted countries? There are good reasons for believing that they are. Specifically, it appears that banks are penalized whenever financially strapped nations increase their outstanding debt. The penalty takes the form of a lower secondary market price for that country's outstanding loans. These market sanctions seem to be based on a belief that making new loans is not a prudent way of either resolving the debt crisis or protecting the value of the banks' existing claims.

Between the end of 1982 and the end of 1985, Latin America's total external debt increased from $318 billion to $368 billion. The proceeds of these new loans were used primarily to pay interest on old loans. Because this allowed banks to avoid, or at least postpone, costly write-downs and charge-offs, it seemed as if new loans were helping to strengthen bank balance sheets.

Unfortunately for the banks, appearances can be deceiving. Table 17.1 lists the October 1986 market price of commercial bank loans to various debtor nations, as well as the external debt for each country in both 1981 and 1985. Finally, the table lists the ratio of each country's outstanding debt in 1981 to its outstanding debt in 1985. A low ratio indicated that the country's debt rose rapidly between 1981 and 1985. As the data suggest, there seems to be a strong inverse correlation between the

Table 17.1
Secondary Market Price of Developing Countries'

	Debt in 1981	Debt in 1985	Ratio 1981/1985	Price Oct.1987	Price May 1987	Actual 1987 Value
ARGENTINA	35.6	50.0	71	67	61	58.8
BRAZIL	79.9	106.7	.75	76	64	124.8
MEXICO-A	78.3	97.4	.80	62	N.A.	
MEXICO-B	78.3	109.7	.71	62	N.A.	
MEXICO-C	78.3	112.1	.70	62	59	132.7
VENEZUELA	28.3	39.0	73	77	74	38.5
ECUADOR	5.6	7.1	.79	66	55	10.2
CHILE	15.7	20.2	.78	69	72	21.8
NIGERIA	12.0	18.3	.66	60	32	37.5
PHILIPPINES	17.4	26.1	67	62	72	24.2

Source: For 1986 prices, *Wall Street Journal*, October 7, 1986, p. 21; for 1987 prices, *The Financial Times*, May 21 1987, p. 4; and for external debt, *World Debt Tables*, 1986–87 edition.

amount of a country's new debt and the market price of its commercial bank loans in late 1986. Specifically, as a country's external debt increased, the market price of its commercial bank loans decreased.

For example, between 1981 and 1985, Argentina's external debt increased from $35.6 billion to $50 billion. The ratio of its debt at the end of 1981 to its debt at the end of 1985 is very close to the October 1986 secondary market price for its commercial bank loans. A similar relationship is apparent for Brazilian, Venezuelan, Ecuadorian, and Chilean debt.

Mexico, on the other hand, does not appear to conform to this general pattern, at least at first glance. But closer inspection suggests that Mexico may be the exception that proves the rule. The ratio of Mexico's 1981 debt to its 1985 debt is significantly greater than the October 1986 secondary market price of its commercial bank loans. One explanation for this apparent anomaly is that the market may not be casting as jaundiced an eye on new loans to Mexico as it casts on new loans to other debtors. However, there is a second and perhaps more plausible explanation.

In 1986, Mexico was the only country to have negotiated a sizable new money package. Even though most of the $12 billion in new loans had not been disbursed of as October 1986, the market appears to have taken these additional claims into account when it determines the value of Mexico's commercial bank loans. Thus, if this $12 billion loan package were added to Mexico's outstanding debt and this new higher total were used to calculate the ratio of its outstanding debt in 1981 to its current outstanding debt, there would be a closer fit between the new ratio and the October 1986 market price.

Admittedly, this discussion might be construed as little more than an exercise in spurious correlation. Nevertheless, there does seem to be a logic behind the market's valuation.

The value of any debt is equal to the present value of its future stream of payments. The fact that the market price of developing nations' debt falls in tandem with the rise in outstanding debt implies that the market does not believe that the country can service the additional claims associated with that additional debt. Sometime in 1981, in other words, the market calculated that the typical debtor had reached the limit of its ability to honor its obligations. Consequently, the *real* value of each country's debt has not increased, despite a significant increase in its nominal, or face, value.

The secondary market price for existing developing nations' debt has fallen further since October 1986, as the fifth column in Table 17.1 indicates. Once again, it is fair to ask whether there is a rational explanation for these recent price declines. The answer for Argentina, at least, seems fairly straightforward. As a result of its mid–1987 new money package, Argentina's external debt is scheduled to grow by approximately $5.4 billion. Once these additional loan commitments are added to Argentina's current outstanding debt, there is a much closer correspondence between the lower secondary market and the revised ratio.

This market assessment might explain why banks have been so reluctant to make new loans and so eager to ensure that their exposure does not increase. By making new loans, banks sense that they are not really enhancing or protecting the market value of their existing developing nation portfolio. Second, although new loans are made with dollars worth 100 cents, those 100-cent dollars are immediately transformed into bank balance-sheet assets that are worth much less. Furthermore, banks must raise additional capital when they make additional loans. Their capital requirements, however, are based on the book value of those new assets, not their market value. Consequently, even though bank claims on developing nations cannot be sold for 100 cents on the dollar, banks have to raise additional capital on the assumption that these assets are, in fact, worth 100 cents. In effect, this regulation raises each bank's cost of capital and forces them to dilute their stockholders' equity—all for the privilege of maintaining the fiction that their old loans are not value impaired.

A related question is whether the market's negative assessment of new loans is rational. Once again, the answer appears to be yes.

From the market's point of view, new loans will increase the value of old loans only if the additional funds are used in ways that increase a country's debt-servicing capacity. On the other hand, if the new loans are being used to pay interest, they add to the future debt-servicing burden without enhancing the future debt-servicing capacity. To see why the market believes that the current strategy for managing the debt crisis is serving primarily to increase the future debt-servicing burden, it is instructive to analyze the new money packages arranged for Mexico in 1986 and Argentina in both 1985 and 1987.

Mexico's 1986 financial rescue package was spearheaded by top officials in the Federal Reserve Board and the Treasury Department. In order to offset an estimated $8 billion annual loss of oil revenues, Mexico is scheduled to receive $12 billion over an 18 to 24 month period. Official creditors pledged to contribute $6 billion, including $1.5 billion from the IMF, $2.0 billion from the World Bank and Inter-American Development Bank, and $2.0 billion of financial assistance from a variety of other official sources. Commercial banks are expected to match these official contributions with $6 billion of new syndicated loans. However, since most of the new money will offset the loss of oil-export revenues and be used to pay interest on Mexico's $98 billion of old debt, only a small portion of the new funds will actually be available to stimulate growth and investment.

The best we can expect is that the Mexican economy at the end of 1987 will be the same size as it was at the beginning of 1986. Yet Mexico's debt will have increased by $12 billion. Thus, after the last loan was disbursed in December 1987, one of the first items on the agenda of the next Mexican president will be the negotiation of yet another "new money package."

The Mexican government is now hinting that it might use some of its newly found reserves to reduce its existing debt. However, this will probably not alter the financial market's bleak assessment of the Mexican economy.[8] Growth rates are depressed. Inflation is threatening to accelerate. Flight capital is returning only because businesses are being strangled by an internal credit crunch. In addition, the government's only hope of maintaining a trade surplus and continuing to service the debt is to keep the economy depressed and import demand stagnant.

Argentina is facing similar prospects. In June 1985, the Argentine government received a new money package consisting of $1.0 billion of fresh loans from the IMF and $4.2 billion from the commercial banks. With this cash infusion, the government eliminated its interest arrears and paid more than one year's additional interest to the commercial banks. In effect, the 1985 new money package transformed Argentina from one of the most recalcitrant debtors into one of the best behaved.

However, that transformation did not take place because Argentina's economy improved, but because its interest payments to commercial banks were being financed by new loans from commercial banks.

As soon as Argentina received the last disbursement on its $5.2 billion new money package, the government announced that it could not continue paying interest-rate concessions. Again, the financial markets responded, prompted this time primarily by fears that Argentina might join Ecuador and Brazil as the third Latin American debtor to declare a payments moratorium in 1987. Under the terms of its 1987 new money package, Argentina will receive $1.9 billion from the commercial banks, $1.35 billion from the IMF, and $2 billion from the World Bank.[9]

Interestingly, while the commercial banks supplied 80 percent of the new money in 1985, their relative contribution this time was less than 40 percent. Once again, the question that the markets are asking is not who is supplying the largest share of new money, but what will happen after the last loan is disbursed?

THE OUTLOOK FOR SOVEREIGN LENDING

The fact that the secondary markets have not warmly embraced new loans and commercial banks have not yet turned on the new money spigot is evidence that new syndicated bank loans will not be available anytime soon. After all, very few of the debtors have taken steps to restore creditworthiness. IMF adjustment programs have not been well adhered to. Privatization has not advanced very far. Structural reforms are only beginning to have an impact on the economic health and vitality of the debtors.

Presumably, if and when the flow of good news outweighs the bad, voluntary syndicated bank loans to developing nation borrowers could resume. However, there is good reason to believe that banks will not be eager to get back into the business anytime soon, irrespective of what credit-enhancing policies the developing countries implement. The 1970s episode of syndicated bank lending to sovereign developing country borrowers may have been more of an anomaly than is generally recognized.[10] Moreover, the range of alternative investments open to the banks is much greater today than it was during the 1970s. Consequently, syndicated loans in general, and syndicated loans on behalf of balance-of-payments financing for developing countries in particular, may no longer be favored by the major international commercial banks.

With higher minimum capital requirements and the low price-earnings ratios of many money center bank stocks, syndicated lending has become a capital intensive, low profit operation. The new buzz words of the commercial banking world, therefore, are securitization, off-balance-sheet assets, and fee-generating financial services. None of these changes in commercial bank business practices argues well for the willingness of the commercial banks to return to the developing nation syndicated loan area.

However, an even more profound change, could have an equally deleterious impact on the developing countries' ability to raise funds in the international financial markets. Specifically, most of the new integration, liberalization, and growth opportunities during the 1980s involve financial market mediation between borrowers and savers in developed countries. Consequently, the two-tier financial markets of the 1970s have been replaced by a one-tier system.

In this new system, developed country borrowers have ready access to both the international bank and securities markets. In addition, precisely because the financial markets are so intently focused on servicing the needs of their developed country customers, they have little need to seek business opportunities in the developing countries. To their dismay, therefore, developing countries are discovering that they are shut out of the international securities markets, as in the 1970s, and barred from the commercial bank loan window as well.

The volume of new international bond issues quintupled between 1981 and 1986, yet almost 90 percent of the new issues were floated by industrial country borrowers. Developing countries were either not able or not willing to enter this market. Similarly, the most rapid growth in the international financial markets occurred in the intermediate range of the maturity spectrum where such Euronote facilities as Eurocommercial paper, revolving underwriting facilities (RUFs), and non-issuance facilities (NIFs) exploded in volume from virtually nothing in 1981 to almost $70 billion in 1986.[11] As with bonds, however, significantly more than 90 percent of all Euronotes were issued by developed country borrowers. The developing nations did not participate in this revolution.

Perhaps the most startling change in the 1980s occurred in the composition of commercial bank lending. In 1981, approximately 60 percent, or $92 billion, of net bank lending was to borrowers in developing countries. In 1986, with virtually the same aggregate volume of net bank lending, $142 billion, or 90 percent was directed to developed country borrowers.

According to the BIS, U.S. residents borrowed $40 billion from the international banking community in 1986.[12] With such large current account deficits, the fact that the United States imported so much external capital should come as no surprise. Yet the BIS also reports that the Japanese were the second largest borrowers from the international banks. In view of the large Japanese current account surplus, this flow of bank capital into Japan seems strange. However, it is easily explained by two factors.

First, borrowing dollars to finance the acquisition of U.S. assets allows

Japanese investors to hedge against a falling dollar. Second, the easing of Japanese capital controls in 1985 gave many Japanese investors their first significant opportunity to acquire overseas investments. Many responded enthusiastically. As a result, the BIS reports that "at $132 billion, net long-term foreign investments by Japanese residents far exceeded the country's current account surplus."[13] The difference between Japanese overseas investments and the Japanese current account surplus was financed primarily by bank borrowing.

Seen in this light, it would appear that large syndicated bank lending to developing countries was more of an aberration than the start of a new long-term trend. For a relatively brief moment, syndicated loans to sovereign borrowers were the best available business opportunity open to the banks. In general, whenever other options were available, the vast majority of commercial banks preferred to pursue them, rather than to do business with developing countries.

As the financial liberalization of the 1980s proceeds apace, the range of new profitable options open to commercial banks can be expected to widen. As it does, the developing countries can expect that the commercial banks will become even less receptive to their need for new cash infusions.

CONCLUSIONS

Elementary logic dictates that there are only two possible solutions to the interest payment dilemma confronting the developing nations and their commercial bank creditors. Either someone must put more money in so that debtor nations can continue paying interest, or less money will be taken out as interest payments.

In the case of a "more-in" solution, the operative question is whether the new money will come from the public or private sector. And in the event of a "less-out" approach, the operative question is whether the relief will be negotiated between creditors and debtors or whether the debtors will be forced to act unilaterally.

My personal hunch is the debt crisis is moving rapidly to a less-out solution. Although they may not admit it publicly, both the public and private sector creditors are waiting for the debtors to act unilaterally. Creditors will then accept those unilateral actions as fait-accomplis. However, under no circumstances will they sit down and negotiate debt relief with even one major debtor. To do so would be seen as countenancing the principle of debt relief. If that precedent were established, it would be extremely difficult to limit the relief to only one or two deserving cases. All debtors would clamor for relief, and if they do not receive it, domestic political pressures will force each of them to seize it unilaterally.

For this reason, creditor nation policymakers see no advantage in acting preemptively. Crisis management is their motto. The goal is to solve today's problem, wait for tomorrow's to arrive, and deal with it only when action is unavoidable. When additional action is no longer possible, then the game will be over.

This approach of "muddling through" and buying time, has not been without merit. It has worked well up to now, at least from the creditors' perspective. The banking system has been given time to build up a financial cushion against the impact of a payments moratorium. Delay has probably not done too much of a disservice to the debtors either. By playing by the creditors' rules, they have gained support for their cause among key political and financial leaders in creditor nations.

This approach was feasible because new money was available to help the debtors pay interest on their old loans. As the statistics in the first section indicated, the system could buy time because the public sector was paying for it. Public creditors, not commercial banks, were putting up most of the new money. Yet if additional rounds of new money are not forthcoming, this strategy will have to run its course.

Thus, the crucial question is whether sufficient new money will be available to keep the old strategy alive for a little while longer. I am not optimistic. The commercial banks have made it abundantly clear that they are not eager to volunteer their funds in aid of a more-in solution, although they are very willing to see public funds commandeered for the task.

Unfortunately, finding the money for foreign aid programs is difficult even in the best of times. Finding the money for what will inevitably be termed a bank bailout is always much more difficult. Virtually every member of Congress has higher priorities than ensuring that debtor nations have enough cash to continue paying interest to commercial banks.

It seems probable that public funds would have a better chance of being made available if they were seen as part of a comprehensive solution and not as a last-ditch effort to revive a moribund strategy. An important component of that comprehensive solution would be the perception that all parties are bearing a fair share of the burden, including the commercial banks. Before the public sector puts more money in, the banks will have to be seen as willing to take less out. Otherwise, any public appropriations via the foreign aid budget could be viewed by a cynical observer as little more than an elaborate laundering mechanism whereby taxpayer funds are funneled to commercial banks via the developing countries' governments.

Yet if the public sector will not make new loans and the commercial banks are not making them either, developing nations will eventually conclude that they have little to gain by making another round of interest payments. That is the most probable outcome.

NOTES

1. Description of the debt relief section of the trade bill can be found in U.S., Congress, *United States Trade Enhancement Act of 1987*, Report of the Committee on Banking, Housing, and Urban Affairs, Report 100–85, 100th Congress, 1st Session, June 23, 1987.

2. Morgan Guaranty, *World Financial Markets*, July–August, 1987, p. 4.

3. Bela Belassa et al., *Toward Renewed Economic Growth in Latin America* (Washington, D.C.: Institute for International Economics, 1986).

4. The Institute for International Finance, Inc., Board of Directors, "Restoring Market Access: New Directions in Bank Lending" (Washington, D.C.: IIF, June 1987), pp. 10–11.

5. Maxwell Watson et al., *International Capital Markets: Development and Prospects*, IMF Occasional Paper 43, February 1986, p. 37.

6. Bank for International Settlements, *Fifty-Seventh Annual Report* (Basel: BIS, 1987), p. 119 (hereafter cited as *Annual Report*).

7. Bank for International Settlements, *Annual Report*, p. 119.

8. For an excellent summary of the current outlook in Mexico, see Jorge Castañeda, "The Unlikely Dilemma of How to Spend It," *Financial Times*, August 26, 1987, p. 15.

9. "Banks Respond Strongly over Argentine Loan," *Financial Times*, June 19, 1987, p. 1.

10. Jane D'Arista, "Private Overseas Lending: Too Far, Too Fast?," in *Debt and the Less Developed Countries*, ed. Jonathan David Aronson, (Westivew Press, 1979), p. 62 (hereafter cited as "Private Overseas Lending"). For a more detailed discussion of this period, see also Jane D'Arista, "U.S. Banks Abroad," *Financial Institutions and the Nation's Economy*, Committee on Banking, Currency, and Housing, House of Representatives, 94th Congress, 2d Session, June 1976 (hereafter cited as "U.S. Banks Abroad"); U.S. Senate, *International Debt, the Banks, and U.S. Foreign Policy*, A staff report prepared for the Subcommittee on Foreign Economic Policy of the Committee on Foreign Relations, 95th Congress, 1st Session, August 1977.

11. For an excellent description of the mechanics of these new financial instruments, as well as the potential dangers they pose to the safety and soundness of the financial system, see Bank for International Settlements, *Recent Innovations in International Banking* (Basel: BIS, April 1986).

12. Bank for International Settlements, *Annual Report*, p. 97.

13. Bank for International Settlements, *Annual Report*, p. 92.

18

TO BORROW OR NOT TO BORROW

Robert Wesson

If general purpose or balance-of-payments lending has come to be unpromising for banks, it may be asked whether it is good for the borrowing countries. The usual, if not universal assumption is that it is eminently desirable, perhaps indispensable for Third World governments to get such financial assistance; the very term "assistance" seems to assure its desirability. Indeed, it seems to be assumed that economic development can hardly proceed without such an external boost, or at best painfully and slowly as a country builds up capital from its own exiguous resources. Again and again, writers argue that the debt problem must be handled in such a way as to maintain the creditworthiness of sovereign borrowers; anything resembling write-offs, indeed any concessions that would cause the banks to lose money, is excluded on the grounds that this would preclude future lending to the beneficiaries.

On the one hand, since loans should have been productive, debtor countries ought to be able to service them, or at least pay interest; on the other hand, they certainly need new loans in order to go ahead building up their economies. It is assumed that loans to governments and state agencies mean productive investments. It is even the common wisdom that additonal lending is the way to generate capacity to handle the debts that presently are so burdensome.

In this general assumption, the lending institutions and the borrowers are wholly in agreement, and outside observers agree with them. Logically, then, all parties want the business of lending to go on as much as possible as in the past; borrowers have been disposed to accept large sacrifices in order to remain in the good graces of the international financial community.

Incontestably, borrowing is good for the people who arrange the loans and handle the funds. Yet if one poses the stark question, "Is general lending to Third World governments the best way to apply the limited amounts of money available for the improvement of their economies?" one might wonder. There are strong arguments for a firm"No"; there are rather feeble arguments for a "Maybe."

To take the latter, what are the reasons for lending to goverments instead of supporting direct investments or lending to private producers? Most obviously, it is easier and simpler. Having a billion dollars to place, we don't care to spend the time and effort to investigate and administer a hundred different loans when we have a willing taker for the whole amount. Executives are busy people and they like to make jumbo loans, just as foundations prefer to make big grants rather than small ones. There was some effort to tie loans to projects when big sovereign lending began after 1973, but it was abandoned in the enthusiasm for transferring capital to the Third World without conditions. It is not only easier and faster; it is the only practical way to get rid of very large amounts of money. One would be hard pressed to find acceptable applications for a billion dollars in Costa Rica or the Dominican Republic, or for some tens of billions in Brazil, whereas the respective governments happily accept such amounts, giving in return a solemn document.

Moreover, there is, or used to be, a good deal of confidence in governments as borrowers. The declaration that "states don't go bankrupt" was not an original idea of the former chairman of Citicorp. Technically, of course, states cannot become bankrupt, although they can and do fail to meet contractual obligations. The government of Brazil will be around for a long time, and it will continue to have a strong interest in international exchanges and is not likely, short of a radical revolution, ever to repudiate its debt entirely. In any case, the lenders have felt easier with an official guarantee, and they have extended this feeling to a strong effort to get governments to guarantee private loans.

In addition, there are ample precedents and allies in the business of lending to governments. The World Bank, IMF, and other agencies lend to governments and were doing so on a large scale long before the commercial banks went heavily into the business, and they have consistently supported commercial lending. Moreover, the U.S. government has encouraged lending to governments, and the banks have reason to expect some kind of backup in regard to their loans to governments, unlike those to private entities. The tradition of merchant banks lending to sovereigns goes back at least to the Middle Ages, and it has often been quite profitable. It was easy to forget that there is also a venerable tradition of default. At various times in the nineteenth century, Latin American republics (and some of the United States) defaulted on bonds. In the 1930s, former allies of the United States defaulted (when their debt service was only about 1 percent or less of exports), as did nearly all Latin American borrowers. But this sad history did not seem relevant to the ebullient 1970s.

From the point of view of the official borrowers, the attractiveness of loans is unequivocal; it is nicer to have them flow through official hands even though the overt purpose may lie in the private sector. It is a blessing to have large amounts of money placed under one's control for whatever purposes; it is politically much more acceptable to undertake a debt than to permit foreign ownership of a considerable part of the economy. In addition, it is infinitely more painless than collecting taxes.

This does not mean, however, that it is good for the nation and its economy. There are weighty reasons to question the desirability of sovereign lending. Simply stated, lending by private institutions to sovereign nations is an invitation to loss for both lenders and borrowers so far as governments are less than completely efficient, responsible, and honest. Corruption, soft or hard, although seldom mentioned in economic analyses, is a major reality in the matter; but any misuse of borrowed money means that it will be difficult to repay. There is no way to make sure than money placed in the hands of nonresponsible persons—and other political powers are never fully responsible to the lenders–will be properly spent.

When loans are negotiated, no one seems to give a thought to the "opportunity costs" in the encouragement of unsound budgetary practices, a mentality of spending, complication of politics, and increase of dependence; little enough thought is given to the means of eventual repayment of the loans. There are differing possible interpretations: one may assert that "nations need loans to develop," or that "politicians like money." Obviously neither is the whole truth, but there is some realism in the latter.

If this is theory, what do the practical results tell us? There was very little commercial bank lending to governments from the Second World War until 1974, yet third world economic development proceeded generally rather well during that period; Latin America particularly prospered. Obviously, the kind of lending we have seen since 1974 was not essential for growth. But is it good for growth? It is certainly hard to claim that the results of the massive lending from 1974 to 1981 were positive. To the contrary, a hundred disastrous earthquakes could not have brought as much devastation to the economies of Latin America as the tremendous foreign borrowing, the intent of which was to bring enormous economic development. The transfer of a great deal of capital from rich to poor countries has left the borrowers much poorer, although as yet they have repaid none of the principal.

The poor effects of a large inflow of money to public powers are confirmed by the disappointing results of petroleum riches in most countries that have enjoyed them. They have led to a boom of sorts but to little sound growth. This has been especially true of Mexico and Venezuela. Both of these in the latter 1970s were well aware of the pitfalls, and they promised themselves to avoid the mistakes and "sow the petroleum," but so much easy money was too much for fallible humans. It led to extravagance, careless spending, and little benefit for the welfare of the majority.

It is not too much to say that the debt calamity represents a tragic turn in world economic history, a grave setback for all efforts to assist the countries commonly called "developing." The gap between rich and poor nations, which seemed to be narrowing, has dramatically widened, and countries that were full of hope a few years ago are full of gloom.

One should hardly have expected anything different. Large sums were placed in the hands of politicians, who were not likely to be efficient economic managers, whose honesty in many cases was qualified and whose priorities were certainly not economic. There was very little effort to control the use of the billions handed out, and it would have been very difficult to do so in any case, because money is fungible. Unless it is restricted to purposes that would not be otherwise undertaken, new funds simply put money into the hands of the rulership. If one gives an alcoholic money for rent, it frees an equivalent sum for booze.

Most loans have been "general," or used to cover deficits, that is, quite uncontrolled; and as soon as money gets into the hands of a government, it easily evades outsiders' tracing. Even if there is some accounting, so that invoices are presented showing, for example, that the money was spent on materials and labor for a highway, this is hardly effective. For one thing, unless the highway would not otherwise be built, foreign financing for it, no matter how well audited, frees money for other uses; for another, expenditures may be arranged in a hundred ways to benefit favored individuals. It can be ensured that capital is used to good advantage (so far as managers can manage) only if those spending it have strong incentives to do so. Executives of a business borrowing against collateral have good reason to apply a loan prudently in order to be able to pay it off and keep their business; politician borrowers have no such incentive.

After the loans became "troubled," the banks sought, of course, to use their leverage of granting new loans to demand, through the IMF, "structural reforms." These may be spelled out in exceptional and rather humiliating detail; for example, Costa Rica's "letter of intent" to the IMF of April 24, 1987, has over ten single-spaced pages of promises covering everything from the growth of the economy to the retirement provisions of certain public employees. Such pedagogic efforts, however, have been generally futile, for obvious reasons. Nations do not make real changes in their way of handling their economies to please outside creditors; and the banks, observing from a distance, are not well qualified to guide foreign governments.

The ostensible purpose of making new loans has often been to support structural changes, but the result is commonly the opposite. Foreign financing relieves a government of the need to make reforms (except for appearances' sake) and creates habits of depending on such support. The more loans one gets, the more one can use. Lenders, governments, international institutions, and borrowers all look to immediate benefits or solutions for immediate needs with little concern about adding to the outstanding principal of the debt. In 1979, a loan was a quick fix for a balance-of-payments deficit arising from the petroleum shortage; in 1987, new loans are still an easy way of getting over the crunch of inadequate revenues to service old debts. Why not? If the creditors aren't even trying to get back principal, does it matter if it grows? Yet borrowing undermines self-reliance, encourages careless attitudes, and increases corruption.

It is like the problem of being overweight; it always feels better to have another rich dessert. More borrowing is ever desirable, because the borrowers are not nations but politicians; in Latin America, as in the Third World generally, the most rewarding career is politics. Recipients may gain not only freedom to spend for popular purposes, but also opportunities to advance personal welfare. The political leadership can probably deal more freely with loan funds not strictly tied by the lenders than they can with monies squeezed out of national taxpayers. There are commissions and charges to be taken from the loan amounts. Loans to government enterprises, which are allowed or encouraged to seek foreign financing, augment benefits for administrators. There are lucrative contracts. Foreign exchange can be made available at much better-than-market rates, amounting to an indirect gift. There is plain corruption, that is, pocketing more or less of the amounts loaned, even perhaps a substantial percentage, as has become notorious in connection with loans to Mexico and the Philippines. The leaders are not responsible owners but temporary custodians of the national finances, who will probably not be in office when loans come due. They must be expected to make use of their position. Democratic politicians are quite as susceptible as dictatorial ones, perhaps more so, because they know their term of office is limited.

Even if governments were entirely virtuous and farseeing, the propriety of commercial institutions providing major funding for them would be questionable. The success or profitability of such business is clearly a political matter, as well as an economic one; and the outcome depends not only on economic but also political events, which are not properly in the province of the financial experts. The deals made are political and have to be considered as such. Of course, high finance is never entirely separable from politics, but the mixture lends itself to abuse. On the side of the borrowers, likewise, there is a mixture of business and politics, in which the political priorities of the governments are sure to deviate and probably sharply from the economic priorities of the lenders.

Since it is so desirable to get loans, governments have been prepared to accept terms favorable, at least nominally and initially, to the banks, with up-front fees, commissions, and higher interest rates than prevalent in domestic business. Consequently, bank officers were rewarded for selling foreign loans. They, like the politicians, probably do not expect to be in charge when the maturities come around; there has been no punisment for having made bad loans when everyone was doing it.

The debt itself makes more borrowing necessary. The indebted country usually suffers not only inflation, but also shortage of needed imports (because of pressure to conserve foreign exchange), bureaucratic controls (to manage foreign exchange), and lack of capital and high interest rates (as capital is drained out by both capital flight and debt service). All these decrease ability to make payments and cause further loss of confidence, more capital flight, and more need to borrow. This induces political as well as economic uncertainty, further reducing investment, both domestic and foreign.

The debt also makes more lending necessary. Recently banks have been continuing to lend on a voluntary basis to Colombia, the sole Latin American debtor that has fully kept up with its obligations without even requiring restructuring. But the Colombian debt continues to grow, perhaps 10 percent yearly, and service becomes more burdensome. The time is sure to come when banks will be called upon to provide more funds to enable and encourage Colombia to keep up its good record. Then they will probably assume that any problems are temporary, and they will find themselves on the slippery slope to a debt problem. On the other hand, if they decide to call a halt, they may well find that the Colombians find it no longer desirable to shortchange their own limitless needs for the sake of nonproductive creditworthiness.

When the loans become problematic, lenders, like borrowers, want to keep the system functioning even at a cost of increasing the outstanding amounts. They have also been encouraged to keep on lending, first by both the conviction that the government would have to come to their rescue to save the financial system and by direct and sometimes energetic official pressures.

The debt crisis beginning in 1982 was brought to a head because of many circumstances that have been amply discussed. But trouble was probably inevitable in any event. Unproductive loans are likely not to be repayable, and easy money brings less sound economic progress than a thirst for more. Much less does it encourage sound policies and careful management. The loans brought some glow of prosperity for a time, but there was little or no relation between lending and investment, and much less investment directed to increasing export capacity. Even if the loans had been well applied, less developed economies could hardly be expected to export large amounts of capital for many years. Sooner or later, debt service had to overtake the buildup of debt, and inability to meet commitments had to follow.

The administrative competence and discipline of Third World borrowers are not high; if they were, the countries would probably rapidly rise from the poverty level. If the U.S. government sometimes spends carelessly and unproductively, what does one expect of Mexico? Brazil is the Latin American country commonly cited as having (under its military government) made good use of borrowed monies for industrial development and sundry projects. It is certainly true that a relatively small proportion of loans to Brazil ("only" about a third) went into capital flight, and private enrichment from public funds has been less of a problem there than in most countries of the hemisphere. This does not mean, however, that the money was applied in the best possible manner. The government inevitably gave priority to grandiose works, such as the immense Itaipú and Tucurui hydroelectric dams, the ecological ills of which are more evident than their near-term economic utility. For a time, the ability of Brazil to pay interest and keep up a statistically high rate of growth seemed to confirm the optimists; Brazil was repeatedly cited, as recently as October 1986, as the outstanding model for other countries to imitate. Yet much of its prosperity was artificial, and the large amounts it paid out in net debt service were at the expense of decapitalizing the economy. After the collapse of the touted Cruzado Plan in November 1986, the purchasing power of the people dropped by half, and inflation roared back to reach an annualized rate well over 1,000 percent in the first half of this year.

The only seriously indebted third world country that seems to have really made good use of its borrowings is South Korea, which has done better than any other to meet its obligations (although even South Korea would have trouble if it were not for a large dollar income from the U.S. military presence). This success is at least partly due to the fact that the Korean government rather borrowed on behalf of private enterprises than for its own uses. In any case, those who quote South Korean debt paper at par are being a bit optimistic in betting that it will remain exempt from the troubles besetting other countries comparably indebted.

One of the ironic contradictions of the debt question is that the banks, with the backing of the IMF, insist above all on the desirability of destatization, privatization of state enterprises and general reduction of official controls and interference with the market economy. Yet they preferentially loaned to governments and to state enterprises, thereby making possible a great expansion of the latter. Placing huge amounts of money in the hands of the state inevitably strengthens it. This is a real effect, against which the programs of "economic reform" demanded by the IMF on the behalf of the banks are trivial in effects.

In sum, the immediate satisfactions of receiving loans are almost certain to be engulfed in due course by the problems of servicing them. Ultimately, of course, the aim must be not merely to handle the debt but to get rid of it. It may be advantageous to lending institutions to have countries permanently indebted, but it is as disadvantageous for countries as it is for individuals to carry a permanent load of debt. Only when they are unburdened can the Third World resume economic development.

Mixing lending with politics seems certain to bring trouble. If, for political reasons, lending to governments may be desirable, it should be done by official entities, with payment terms realistically gauged to the returns to be expected. Inherently risky lending to the third world countries is the proper province of entities that can afford to postpone repayment or modify terms in accordance with needs for political purposes. If emergency help is needed, the case should be considered on its merits and not made subject to the conditions of commercial finance as, for example, in the case of Ecuador's ruptured oil pipeline, repair of which is necessary to permit resumption of exports. If the U.S. government wishes for some reason to promote sovereign lending, it must be assumed that the operation is politically directed. The administration then should explicitly license or conduct the transaction, more or less like sales of armaments and for the same reason: they have strong political implications.

The end of general purpose or balance-of-payments sovereign lending should not hinder but preferably assist sounder types of financing, foreign investment, commercial support, or project loans with built-in means of repayment. The management of capital flows to the Third World is bound up with the basic problem of narrowing the gap between the rich and poor, a problem for which a solution is still missing. In general, equity investment is preferable to loans. Equity investment presupposes an economic calculation, puts risk onto the investor, and calls for repayment only so far as it is productive and in national currency. It bears little risk for the host country. Its impact on the balance of payments may be positive. It brings along with it managerial skills, technology, and entrée to foreign markets. It strengthens the private sector and market forces in the economy. Countries commonly prefer getting loans to attracting investment, but the reasons they do so are not strictly economic. Of course, there is no possibility of investment capital coming to anything like the volume of recent lending, but investment should be able to fill most genuine needs for capital development.

In summary, the policy of large-scale lending to governments proved disastrous, as was to be expected. A great deal of money has been lost, and it is difficult to expect much of the principal, or interest over a long period, to be repaid. A big step toward renewing the world financial flows would be to recognize that international commercial dealing should be, as far as possible, separated from politics.

CONCLUSION

Robert Wesson

The efforts to manage the debt problem since 1982 are fairly understandable if one thinks in terms of the primary, especially short-term, interests
of the parties. The U.S. government has sought chiefly to avoid com-
plications and any danger of collapse of the financial system. With the
Baker Plan of October 1985, it took a somewhat more positive approach
but still left the matter largely in the hands of the creditors; the chief
recent concern of the administration has apparently been to avoid any
crisis in its remaining months.

The creditor banks have acted naturally and normally to protect their
financial interests, trying to secure as much payment as possible with
as little outlay as possible. Their strongest concern, however, has been
to keep their Latin American portfolios on their books at face value. For
a long time they continued to insist that problems were temporary, a
matter of illiquidity and not insolvency; they have been extremely reluctant to make concessions that could be interpreted as admitting that
Latin American obligations are worth less than par. Although the growing secondary market has been saying the contrary more and more
emphatically–it has been a long-term bear market in which prices generally have drifted lower—the banks have continued to pretend that all
was more or less well, or could be well given adequate economic growth
and goodwill on the part of the debtors. Another round of reschedulings
and IMF conditions should set the debtors on the road to recovery and
general happiness. At least, it has seemed essential to keep this picture
alive, even though fewer and fewer believed it; writing off any large
fraction of the debt would be disastrous for the balance sheets.

This procedure of "business as usual" was rather remarkably successful, as for several years, Latin America was paying some $30 billion more than it was receiving, and no major debtor really refused to pay. Yet the containment strategy could really work only if everything went right, and this rarely occurs in our imperfect eden. By 1987 the strategy was fairly well exhausted. The amounts outstanding continued to grow year by year, and it became hard to contend that the bigger debts were more payable than the smaller ones had been. Reform programs made little difference, and no one had any convincing evidence that they would be more successful in the future. The industrial countries had enough trouble with their domestic problems without taking much thought of accommodating the needs of the debtor nations.

The system was staggering when, on February 20, 1987, the largest debtor, Brazil, announced indefinite suspension of interest payments on the bulk of its commercial debt. This should have been no shock, or no surprise, because was well known that Brazil, after the collapse of the Cruzado Plan in November 1986, lacked funds to pay, no matter what its preference. The only new element was the recalcitrant temper of the Brazilian government, which gave no promise of resumption of payments and demanded fundamental concessions. This was the more bitter because Brazil had been the model debtor for several years, paying roughly $10 billion yearly without receiving new loans and at the same time growing economically, at least according to not very reliable statistics. Previously, Mexico and Agentina had been held up as examples of successful debt management (mostly thanks to new financing), but their records were by no means so impressive as the stellar performance of Brazil.

Following the fall of the Brazilian star, in May 1987 Citicorp set aside reserves of about a quarter of the amount of its Third World loans, and other major banks followed its example. The total amount put to reserves, about $23 billion, was only a tiny fraction of the total debt outstanding, but with this move toward realism the situation was obviously changed. The banks continued to insist on the nominal value of their portfolios, but it became harder to keep up the game. Not only did the secondary market (which received increasing attention as its volume grew, despite the efforts of the financial community to avoid publicizing it) say that the Latin American loans were mostly worth only about half of their face value, the banks themselves admitted that their value was questionable. That made it difficult to extend new loans; it is not obvious why a bank should give full value for paper that the market assesses at very much less. Hence new packages for troubled debtors became more and more difficult to cobble, so far as they required handing out money at face value, for paper immediately worth very much less. On the one hand, it was hard to keep in line the smaller banks that very much wanted out of the business; on the other, it was necessary to make additional, although usually minor, concessions to the debtors.

The interest of the borrowers has also been clear. Large payouts in foreign currency have always been difficult; when new loans were no longer coming in abundantly, they implied severe and politically costly sacrifices. Yet Latin American leaders generally felt that they should do their utmost to maintain respectability in the world and keep their countries creditworthy, that is, in a position to get new loans, which are always highly desirable. Consequently, they have tried to be as cooperative as possible at the least possible cost. They also made repeated statements demanding or pleading for more favorable treatment and seemed to threaten to form a debtors' cartel. However, in the showdown they went along with the bankers' basic conditions, swallowing a great deal of bitter medicine sweetened by additional loans.

Five years of those policies have had predictable results. The banks have had time to strengthen themselves financially so that fears of anything like a collapse of the system have largely dissipated, although Latin American portfolios are still larger than the capital of major banks. On the other hand, the borrowing countries have been squeezed, as their debt burden has steadily, although more gradually, grown, while their economies have stagnated or, in a number of cases, gone sharply downhill. No one still contends that there is only a temporary problem of illiquidity or that the debtor nations can expect to outgrow their debts. If they are to continue paying any substantial amount they need new money that the banks are hardly in a position to provide. At the time of this writing, nine Latin American countries (like a host of African states) are in undeclared default, and it would seem that the list can only grow as the incentive to keep creditworthy diminishes with the fading prospect of new financing. The threat that countries failing to comply with their contractual obligations would face dire consequences increasingly seem empty; as long as countries are prepared to make any reasonable gesture toward settlement, or perhaps even if they do not, the creditors refrain from taking legal steps of doubtful utility. They cannot afford to declare defaults because that would require writing down their Latin American assets.

What is to be done? Some conference participants felt that the international agencies should play a larger role, assuming a responsibility of lenders of last resort. However, if they are to increase their role to compensate for the tendency of the commercial banks to pull back, they will require additional support of member governments, that is, of the taxpayers. This is not likely to be given generously, and it is difficult to see that anything they can do is likely to do more than stretch out the period of adjustment.

Shortage of means and lack of political will equally stand in the way of schemes for the World Bank or another agency to take over banks' debt paper in some form at a discount and try to securitize it, presumably as long-term bonds. It may be recalled that the defaulted Latin American bonds left over from the 1930s were ultimately settled at a large discount, mostly at 20 to 30 cents on the dollar. This might seem a precedent, but the present condition is more difficult because the loans in the postwar period were not simply underwritten and sold to investors but kept in the hands of the banks, and hence have been largely insulated from the market. In addition, it is less serious if private investors lose their savings than if banks lose their capital.

Nonetheless, there may be possibilities for an international agency to try to liquidate obligations at realistic prices according to the real ability of debtor nations to pay. Albert Fishlow has proposed such a plan as a start toward reduced debt service in a way acceptable to the banks themselves. However, any such procedure would be seen as a bailout for the banks and would be hard to sell to the American Congress and presumably to democratic authorities of other industrial nations.

Another reason that nothing like this is likely to occur is that the creditors are little inclined to accept an immediate loss for the sake of the long-term gain of clearing away the debt mess. The banks are, as already noted, unwilling to enter any scheme that implies admission of the real value of their nominal assets. One might suppose that it would be better to settle for 20 or 30 cents, but this is not correct. Even if the debtors are paying little or nothing, it is more advantageous for the creditors to keep the loans on their books as nearly at face value as possible, writing them down only 10 percent per year, as legally required. Slow amortization is preferable to a sudden hit and the consequent slashing of their capital, which is, after all, only about 5 percent of their assets. The effect on the unsecuritized remainder of the debt must also be considered. The new obligations would have to have preferential or senior status in order to find investors; the obligations left behind might well become worthless.

This seems to be the expectable outcome of the whole sad affair. The several parties, the debtor countries, the creditors, the IMF, the World Bank, the International Development Bank, and the Paris Club, will doubtless continue their minuet of negotiations, conditions, and accords to keep up appearances without doing anything more than turning in circles. The banks will certainly continue to make deals here and there as best they can, probably even lubricating negotiations with a trickle of new money from time to time, seeking to salvage something, for example, through debt-equity conversions. They will not admit in principle that the obligations are more or less valueless, although it will become increasingly evident that they are. They will engage in only limited lending, perhaps squeezing through yet another package for Brazil or Mexico (through which they hope to get back about as much in interest as they put out in new loans, if not more so far as international agencies can be brought to put in funds). They will certainly shift from balance-of-payments financing to transactional and investment lending, although they will try to keep a little life and interest in the idea of creditworthiness. This may require extending new loans to countries such as Colombia, which has faithfully fulfilled its commitments. Colombia is fairly creditworthy, of course, because it did not get in so deeply in the first place; but its debt and potential problems grow, and the interest rate cannot possibly reflect the real risk. Meanwhile, the U.S. administration does what it can to keep lending going on to postpone a crunch. For example, the agreement for the banks to put up the bulk of a fund to cover arrears of Brazilian interest, reached in November 1987, was essential to keep them from having to show large losses and so depress an already depressed market.

Inflation, which lured the banks into overlending in the first place, may well come back to relieve the situation. It seems to be unlikely, however, that inflation will soon be high enough really to help the debtors. Without rampant inflation, one may guess that the loans will remain on the books, although gradually written down as assets, for very many years. One may recall that the U.S. Treasury to this day keeps the World War I debts on its accounts, with forever accumulating interest; to write them off would increase the nominal deficit, and nobody has at any moment a sufficiently strong urge to clear them away.

The knot of the debt will probably gradually come undone, over a considerable number of years, without anyone's cutting or untying it. Most likely, the crisis will be simply eroded, going out without even a whimper, although with many a groan on the way. The costs continue; without any clear settlement, Latin American countries will doubtless continue to suffer some economic uncertainty and a poor (although perhaps gradually improving) atmosphere for investment for many years. This is regrettable, of course; it would be much better if persons in a position to do so would grapple the problem decisively instead of always looking to short-term solutions. Even if it were decidedly painful—and any solution is going to be painful—it would be much better for both Latin America and the U.S. economy to get rid of the incubus.

In any event, sovereign lending in the old style will be foreclosed, as the banks have often warned. Perhaps after 40 or 50 years it will again be said that countries are immortal and can be counted on to pay their debts, or someone will invent better ways of profiting from the thirst for loans. However, until a new generation comes to the fore without nightmarish memories of "value-impaired" loans to Latin America, in amounts comparable to the total net worth of the institution, bank lending will not again be like what it was in the gilded times of the late 1970s. It will probably be restricted to commercial financing, short-term and more or less self-liquidating, or to specific undertakings, where the lenders can count on collateral or guarantees that compensate for the risks of putting money in the hands of persons over whom the lender has little or no legal leverage.

For good reasons, the banks have held up this outcome as a veritable horror: countries will no longer be able to get the financing they allegedly need for development. Of course, the idea of not being able to get more loans causes consternation in those who have become addicted to them, but one should recall that development proceeded quite well prior to 1974, without the benefit of substantial general financing of third world countries by private capital. Experience since then hardly supports the belief that uncontrolled sovereign lending is a good thing for the sound growth of the borrowers. It would be difficult to put together a convincing argument to rebut the obvious reasons for doubting the suitability of general loans as a means of application of capital to the Third World. To be sure, they are in need of capital, but they are in need of many other things also, and simply injecting large sums of money, however pleasing to a few, is in this world of fallible humans, not the most productive use of resources.

AFTERWORD: UPDATE

Robert Wesson

The road from conference papers to finished book is long, even in the computer age, so it is appropriate for the editor to take advantage of the appearance of page proof and sketch something of developments of the nine months since our experts gathered to hash over the Latin American debt.

Not a great deal has in fact changed, as the creditors and debtors, pursuing the interests discussed in the conference, have continued in about the same routines as they have since 1982, dickering about payments, loans to help keep loans performing, and ineffective IMF conditions. With ups and downs, Latin American economies have deteriorated somewhat, improvement in some countries (such as in Mexico for electoral purposes) being outweighed by worsening in others (such as Argentina and Peru). The region has continued to export capital, both in debt service and as capital flight, although on a somewhat reduced scale. The total debt outstanding has continued to grow gradually but inexorably by virtue of nonpayment of interest. The three biggest debtors, Brazil, Mexico, and Argentina, now owe about $287 billion. Confidence has shrunk a little more, as demonstrated by the weakness of secondary market prices: recent figures for Brazil and Mexico are about $0.50, for Peru $0.07, and so forth. Argentine obligations go for $0.28. Colombia, the faultless payer of only a few months ago, has slumped to $0.65. Banks, however, have continued to add to reserves, and they have (with the exception of the money-center banks that are too deeply committed) made progress toward selling off loans in the secondary market or otherwise shedding them, after writing them off or putting them in the "nonperforming" category. The World Bank itself is squeezed, as countries insist on getting more in new loans than they repay. Both the World Bank and the IMF face serious losses from loans, especially African, that must be recognized as worthless.

Under these circumstances, the commercial banks have become even more reluctant to extend new loans unless they can be sure, perhaps with the assistance of the IMF, to get back in interest at least as much as they handed out. They have, however, done about as well as could be expected. Their bargaining power has continued high, partly because the debtor countries have been completely unable to form any sort of coalition, although their needs and situations are much alike. Each major debtor makes the best deal it can when its turn comes. The leverage of the banks rests mostly on the fact that they can not only hold out the delightful prospect of new loans for thirsty nations but can also do a good deal to make things unpleasant for those who misbehave, raising their costs and financial problems. It is difficult for a country to defy the international financial community without severe penalties, including higher charges for commercial loans and financial services of all kinds. Moreover, noncooperation with creditors causes loss of confidence and capital flight; and a radical policy on the debt seems inevitably to go with radical and probably damaging economic policies. The only country that has seen fit thus far really to defy its creditors has been Peru. And the bankers can point to Peru's sad condition as evidence that it doesn't work, although Peru's troubles come much more from populist domestic policies than difficulties in financing foreign commerce.

The best evidence of the power of the financial community was provided by Brazil. Less than a year after declaring a moratorium on $70 billion of commercial debt, Brazil rather humbly sought its way back into the favor of its creditors and accepted negotiations with the much-disliked IMF. Brazil resumed some interest payments in December 1987, mostly thanks to $3 billion in new money. But it was not easy to reach a longer-term agreement. Brazil wanted $7 billion, but the banks had great difficulty in scraping together $5.2 billion. They were wary of a country with 600 percent inflation, and it was unpleasant that they would probably have to reserve immediately for new loans to Brazil, as they have long since done for other Brazilian paper.

Brazil's climbdown encourages the banks to resist the idea of any form of debt relief. They protest that debt relief or reduction of interest must not be considered because that would make the debtor "uncreditworthy," which seems rather a joke, because bankers of sound mind are not likely to indulge in unsecured sovereign lending to the Third World like that of the 1970s for a generation or so. They continue to insist that they are innocent victims and should not be expected to take losses, probably not because they strongly believe in the justice of this position but because asking for the maximum should help get the maximum.

Old habits thus persist. Nonetheless, there is a gradually growing sense that something different needs to be undertaken in a very unhappy condition that does not go away. The idea that the debtor countries are going to "grow out" of their debts is increasingly unsustainable, contrary as it is to the contention that they need capital inflow in order to grow. Many ideas have been put on the "menu" for debt management, in spite of the obvious fact that no trick can get creditors paid unless someone provides the money, and there is no way the money is going to be extracted from languishing debtor nations.

There has been growing interest in debt-equity swaps or conversions, but no one claims they represent anything like a solution. They have many limitations: from the point of view of the debtor, an external obligation is simply transformed into a possibly larger internal one, and there are many possibilities of abuse of the facility. It would be quite an achievement if conversions could cancel as much as 1 percent of the outstanding debt yearly. The banks, however, look to them as one way in which they can get some real value from the debtors, and they have become a regular part of the package deals.

Most proposals for debt management are suggested by the secondary market, which gives an estimate of what the debt portfolios are "really" worth. One obvious procedure, when a country's debt paper is to be had on the secondary market for a fraction of its nominal value, is for the debtor to use whatever funds are available not for making contractual payments but for buying up part of the principal. This has been done by various countries, usually irregularly and quietly. It seems, however, to have become accepted as legitimate, even to be encouraged. In the case of Bolivia's otherwise hopeless debt problem, a number of European countries loaned money through the IMF explicitly for this purpose. Bolivia was thus able to buy back nearly half its commercial bank debt at $0.11, and it wants to buy the rest.

The secondary market suggests making the debt more manageable by conversion to some kind of negotiable securities, that is, "securitization." In this line, Mexico in February essayed a scheme to reduce its payments, offering bonds backed by U.S. zero-coupon twenty-year bonds. Mexico held an auction, giving new bonds in exchange for outstanding debt paper. As this was going for about $0.50 on the secondary market, Mexico hoped to liquidate obligations at a rate approaching two for one. But the banks did not see much point in taking new paper much below the face value of the old, with no better guarantee except for the eventual payment of principal twenty years down the road. The amount Mexico could reduce its debt this way corresponded roughly to the money it put up to buy U.S. treasuries, and the scheme failed.

Various other suggestions have involved some sort of agency for negotiating debt. For example, Chairman James Robinson of American

Express proposed a scheme for a write-off of $100 billion through an agency linked to the IMF. Remarkably, this did not raise any great outcry. Neither did it arouse much enthusiasm, because it, like similar proposals, required an injection of capital courtesy of the taxpayers, who would in the long run be counted on to make up the difference between what the debtors would pay and what the banks would settle for.

A more effective measure was taken by European nations, which, contrary to the wishes of the United States, decided in June 1988 to forgive part of the debt of destitute African nations. They cancelled one third of bilateral loans to a number of sub-Saharan nations and lowered interest rates on the remainder as much as 50 percent. It was stressed that this would apply to the poorest of the poor and in no way should be a precedent for debt relief for the relatively affluent debtors, such as Mexico and Brazil. Any debt relief, however, is a precedent of sorts; the debt of sundry Latin American nations is about as hopeless as that of the Africans, and they have good reason to demand equal treatment. Their debt, unlike the African, is mostly commercial, but government-to-government loans are not unimportant.

Whether or not the United States assumes responsibility in Latin America corresponding to European responsibility in Africa, there is a growing tendency to recognize the unpayability of much of the debt, which implies doing something to relieve the situation. There is much reluctance, however, to admit a policy of "bailing out the banks," which have profited excellently for many years from foreign lending and who are not without culpability; and remedial measures will probably have to be indirect.

Some bankers seem fairly ready to accept that it is not necessarily good business to press for more than can be obtained. There are sharp differences, however; while a few speak of new initiatives, others remain strongly opposed to any form of debt relief, even if voluntary for creditors. The conservatives are likely to be overruled eventually by political considerations, as chronic stagnation or depression of the economies of Latin America cannot fail to have undesirable political consequences. It is difficult to square nonchalance toward the debt problem with the national political and economic interest in the prosperity and tranquillity of an important group of countries. The industrial nations have, after all, invested a good deal in economic aid to less developed countries; the drain of trying to service loans carelessly extended long ago dwarfs all the economic aid received.

The U.S. government ultimately will have to face the debt problem, if only for national security reasons. It seems clear, however, that the Reagan administration in Washington, having tried to avoid dealing with the debt question during times of more vigor, is not likely to take any bold steps in its waning days. It can hardly do more than encourage the Japanese and others with big trade surpluses to step into the gap. It will be a big problem for the new president.

INDEX

Africa, debt crisis and, 2, 187
Agency for International Development, U.S., 130, 152
Aid. *See* Foreign aid; *specific programs*
Alfonsín, Raul, 34, 35, 95, 97, 98–99, 102, 104, 105, 109, 110
Arab countries, loans and, 40
Arévalo, Juan José, 134
Argentina: Austral Plan and, 95–96, 97, 113; capital flight from, 9, 113; Cuban loans from, 158; debt conversion and, 31, 96, 146, 147; debt crisis and, 29, 91–110, 113–114; debt magnitude, 94, 123, 167; democracy in, 95, 97, 98, 100–101; economic policies, 25, 95; exit bonds and, 30; exports of, 26; fascism in, 106; GDP of, 95, 96–97; industrial reconversion in, 106–110; inflation and, 9, 16, 95, 96, 113; interest payments of, 94; labor and, 97–102; manufacturing in, 92, 106–107; military regime of, 28, 100; new loans for, 165, 169–170; Peronists and, 98, 99–100, 103; political system of, 21, 35, 94; public opinion in, 113, 114; societal characteristics, 103–105; stablization policies and, 102–106; U.S. and, 32, 106

Asian nations: debt of, 2; exports of, 77; Latin American economies and, 11; successful development in, 43; terms of trade in, 11. *See also specific country*
Assmann, Hugo, 85
Austerity programs, 161; government spending and, 53; imports and, 22; industrialized countries and, 77; internal growth and, 27; political cost of, 28, 41; relaxation of, 122–123; social welfare and, 85–86, 87
Austral Plan, 13, 95–96, 97, 113

Baker, James, 12–13
Baker Plan, 42, 161, 163, 164, 165, 185
Balauguer, Joaquín, 117
Balance of payments: debt service and, 20; equity conversion and, 14; exchange rates and, 142; global surplus and, 137; merchandise accounts and, 10; oil and, 8. *See also specific element*
Bank for International Settlements (BIS), 165
Bank of America, 33, 120
Bankruptcy, devaluations and, 142

ABOUT THE EDITOR AND CONTRIBUTORS

CARLOS ALBERTO CARBALLO is an economic consultant in Buenos Aires, bank director, professor at the Catholic University of Argentina, and president of the Argentine Association of Economic History.

FELIX DELGADO QUESADA has a degree in economics from the University of Kansas. He is the deputy general manager of the Banco Central de Costa and assistant in negotiations with foreign banks, the International Monetary Fund, and the World Bank. He has participated in numerous international financial meetings.

ALBERT FISHLOW is professor and chairman of the Department of Economics at the University of California, Berkeley. He served as Deputy Assistant Secretary of State for Inter-American affairs from 1975–76. He has written extensively about Brazilian economic problems and the debt problem.

CHARLES J. L. T. KOVACS, a graduate of the Fletcher School of Law and Diplomacy, has had a long career in the foreign operations of The Chase Manhattan Bank. At present, he is manager for international financial programs, working mainly on new initiatives for rescheduled debt.

JAMES M. LIVINGSTONE, an M.B.A. in International Business, is vice-president and senior economist of the Bank of America. He has recently been engaged in working on the Chilean structural adjustment program.

ROBERT E. LOONEY, a Ph.D. in economics from the University of California, Davis, is professor of national security affairs, Naval Postgraduate School. He has published extensively on third world, and especially Mexican, economic problems.

CARLOS E. MELGAR is president of the Economic Commission of the Peruvian Senate and a prominent member of the Aprista Party.

SUSAN KAUFMAN PURCELL is senior fellow of the Council on Foreign Relations and director of its Latin American program. A former member of the Policy Planning Staff of the Department of State, she has written a book and several articles for *Foreign Affairs* on Mexican politics.

WILLIAM RATLIFF, with a Ph.D. in Latin American history from the University of Washington, is a senior research fellow at the Hoover Institution and scholar/curator of its Latin American collection. He has published many articles on Latin America, especially Cuba and the Caribbean.

CLARK W. REYNOLDS is professor of economics at Stanford University and director of Stanford's U.S.-Mexico Relations Project. He has taught at the Colegio de México and the National University of Mexico and is author of very many books and articles on U.S.-Mexican relations and related topics.

RIORDAN ROETT, with a Ph.D. from Columbia University, is professor and director of the Center of Brazilian Studies at Johns Hopkins School for Advanced International Studies. Formerly president of the Latin American Studies Association, he has published several books and articles on Brazil.

SAÚL TREJO-REYES, a Ph.D. from Yale University, is senior research fellow of the Colegio de México. Formerly advisor to the president of Mexico, he has published several books and many articles on Mexican and Latin American economic problems.

CARLOS H. WAISMAN, an Argentine native, received his doctorate in sociology from Harvard. He has published and lectured extensively on Argentine politics. He is associate professor of sociology at the University of California, San Diego.

ALFRED J. WATKINS serves as economist for the Joint Economic Committee of Congress, in which capacity he has been especially concerned with legislative proposals related to the Latin American debt. Among his books is *Till Debt Do Us Part*.

ROBERT WESSON is senior research fellow at the Hoover Institution with a specialization in Latin American politics. Formerly with the University of California, Santa Barbara, he has published books on various aspects of foreign politics and Latin America.

HOWARD J. WIARDA is professor of political science at the University of Massachusetts, fellow in international affairs at the Foreign Policy Research Institute, and a research scholar at the American Enterprise Institute for Public Policy Research. He has served as a consultant for a number of private and public organizations. He has published some 20 books and hundreds of articles.

GARY W. WYNIA is professor of Latin American politics at Carleton College and the author of many books on Argentine and Latin American affairs, as well as a numerous articles.